Caught Behind

Caught Behind
Race and Politics in Springbok Cricket

Bruce Murray and Christopher Merrett

WITS UNIVERSITY PRESS

UNIVERSITY OF KwaZulu-Natal Press

Jointly published in 2004 by

Wits University Press   and   University of KwaZulu-Natal Press
P O Wits   Private Bag X01
Johannesburg 2050   Scottsville 3209
South Africa   South Africa
http://witspress.wits.ac.za   Email: books@ukzn.ac.za
                                                    www.ukzn.co.za

ISBN 1-86914-059-1

Cover designer: Flying Ant Designs

Main cover photograph per kind permission of Basil D'Oliveira and photograph of B.J. Vorster per kind permission of Die Burger

Typesetter: Patricia Comrie

Printed and bound by Interpak Books, Pietermaritzburg

To Christine Forbes Merrett
and in memory of Dorothy Mary Timmins

The Springbok is and will remain the emblem of sport in South Africa, inalienably white because it has developed that way historically. We believe that the sooner legislation is introduced to elevate the Springbok in fact as the sports emblem of the white Republic, its sport and sportsmen, the sooner the confusion will end. Let there be Proteas, Red Buck, Blue Wildebeest, or what have you, the Springbok is the emblem of white South Africa.

Die Vaderland, 10 January 1972

Contents

Preface and Acknowledgements

Virtually from its inception South Africa's participation in international cricket has been bedevilled by racism and the political intervention of governments. In 1894 the formidable coloured fast bowler, H. 'Krom' Hendricks, was nominated for the first South African team to tour England, but was finally omitted at the behest of Cecil Rhodes, the Cape Prime Minister, on grounds of race. In 1968 B.J. Vorster, the South African Prime Minister, refused to allow Basil D'Oliveira, the South African-born coloured cricketer who played for England, to tour South Africa with the English or Marylebone Cricket Club (MCC) team. This not only resulted in the cancellation of the MCC tour of South Africa but led directly to the cancellation of the South African tours of England in 1970 and Australia in 1971/72, and, with that, to South Africa's exclusion from Test match cricket.

Cricket is the one major sport that has historically been widely played by all the principal race and language groups in South Africa. Until recently, however, the history of South African cricket has generally been written with blacks left out. It has also largely been written with politics left out. As the authors of a recent book on black cricket in Natal have commented, 'It is indicative of the poverty of White cricket writing in South Africa that the game is written exempt from any detailed historical and political context'. This book seeks to provide such a 'historical and political context' for the racially exclusive teams – the Springboks – that represented South Africa in international Test match cricket between 1888/89 and 1969/70. Its central focus thereafter is the D'Oliveira Affair of 1968 and its long-term consequences for South African cricket.

The Springboks played 172 cricket Test matches in 41 series against just three opponents – the 'white' cricket-playing nations, England, Australia and New Zealand. Until the late 1960s the convention was for them to send teams composed only of whites to tour South Africa and, with the exception of a game between the

English tourists and a Malay XVIII in 1892, they played against white teams only. Only one player of colour, the all-rounder, C.B. Llewellyn, represented the Springboks in Tests.

Test matches supposedly constitute 'tests of strength' between the competing countries, and what this book suggests is that the initial weakness of South African cricket created a major opportunity for the selection of racially inclusive rather than exclusive representative teams. The result was not a foregone conclusion, as the controversies over Hendricks and the selection of Llewellyn for fifteen tests between 1895/96 and 1913 indicate. For the 1895/96 Johannesburg Test against England the Transvaal wanted to include Hendricks in the South African team, but his home union, Western Province, would not have it. Instead, C.B. Llewellyn made his debut for South Africa. Incorporating new material, *Caught Behind: Race and Politics in Springbok Cricket* provides the first full account of the experiences of Hendricks and Llewellyn.

After Union and World War I, racism and segregation triumphed, and South Africa even declined the opportunity to become the first Test team to tour India. Segregation in sport became a matter of government policy when the Nationalists took power in 1948, and this book details the impact of apartheid legislation on the playing of cricket.

The political response of anti-apartheid groups at home and abroad resulted in the sports boycott, which called for the expulsion of Springbok teams from international competition, initially on the grounds that they were racially exclusive, representative not of South Africa but of the white population only. In the 1960s the sports boycott secured major victories in the Olympic arena but found cricket a particularly tough nut to crack, as a result of the operation of the 'imperial old-boy network' of England, Australia and New Zealand on the International Cricket Conference.

The crack came with the D'Oliveira Affair of 1968. With the aid of new archival material *Caught Behind* provides the behind-the-scenes story of the event, showing conclusively that Vorster and the South African Cricket Association (SACA) worked assiduously to ensure that D'Oliveira was not included in the MCC team, by endeavouring to engineer either his non-availability or his non-selection. The plan to bribe D'Oliveira to declare himself unavailable was hatched in Vorster's office, and leading officials of the MCC were fully informed of Vorster's attitude. On the very eve of the selection of the MCC team to tour South Africa, a phone call was made from the Prime Minister's office in Pretoria to warn the selectors not to include D'Oliveira. D'Oliveira's initial omission, his belated selection, and Vorster's subsequent ban are examined in this context.

The ban provided the catalyst for South Africa's expulsion from Test cricket. Unlike the case with other sports, South Africa's exclusion from international cricket was more the work of protest action from below than of principled committee decisions from above. Even after the D'Oliveira Affair the 'imperial old-boy network' still sought to protect the country's position in Test cricket, but militant protest action pioneered by Peter Hain's Stop the Seventy Tour campaign in Britain ultimately forced them to exclude the Springboks. Again utilising new archival material, this book provides a definitive account of the decision-making processes that led to the cancellation of the 1970 South African tour of England and the 1971/72 tour of Australia. It explains why the Labour Government in Britain changed policy and finally intervened to effectively force cancellation of the tour of England, whereas the Liberal Government in Australia adopted a position of neutrality, leaving the decision on whether to cancel entirely to the Australian Board of Control under the chairmanship of Sir Donald Bradman. As revealed, Bradman's Board had never been unanimous in its invitation to South Africa to tour.

Confronted by sporting isolation, both the South African Government and SACA belatedly embarked on 'reform', culminating in South Africa's first attempt at unity and integration in cricket – the formation in 1977 of the unified South African Cricket Union (SACU) and the introduction of 'normal' cricket down to club level. *Caught Behind* explores the failure of 'normal' cricket and the intensification of the sports boycott in the wake of the 1976 Soweto uprising, SACU's failure to negotiate a return to Test cricket and its resort in the 1980s to 'rebel' tours to allow the Springboks to play again. When South Africa finally entered the full Test arena in 1992, with its first ever Test against the West Indies in Bridgetown, Barbados, accompanying the dismantling of apartheid, the team was still all white – but for political reasons was no longer the Springboks.

There is a strong documentary base to the making of this book and we are especially grateful to those who assisted us in that regard. Dr Ali Bacher kindly gave permission to examine the surviving records of SACA and the South African Cricket Union; Roger Knight gave permission to consult the minutes of the MCC Committee; Tim Lamb the records of the Cricket Council in England; Tim Murdoch the minutes of the New Zealand Cricket Board; and Alan Kourie and Derrick High provided access to the records of the Transvaal Cricket Union. At Lord's Stephen Green, the MCC Curator of Collections, his successor, Adam Chadwick, and Glenys Williams were exceptionally helpful, as was Janet Fisher of the England and Wales Cricket Board. In Christchurch Greg Ryan kindly perused the NZCB minutes. The Australian Cricket Board, unfortunately, does not allow researchers access to their records.

Special thanks are due to the staff of the South African National Archives, Pretoria; the National Archives, formerly the Public Record Office, London; and the National Archives of Australia, Canberra, for their high levels of professionalism in making records available. Michelle Pickover and Carol Archibald of the Historical Papers division of the Library of the University of the Witwatersrand, Johannesburg, went out of their way to help at all times. Thanks to the concern of Gerald Majola, the CEO of the United Cricket Board of South Africa, the surviving papers of SACA and SACU have now been moved from an untended storeroom at the Wanderers Stadium to the University's library.

For helping in locating material on C.B. Llewellyn, thanks are extended to Anthea Jones of Gloucestershire County Library Service; Chris Coley of Cheltenham; the staff of Hampshire Local Studies Collection at the County Library, Winchester; Neil Jenkinson, Honorary Archivist of Hampshire County Cricket Club; Krish Reddy, cricket statistician of Durban; and the staff of the Pietermaritzburg Archives Repository and the Office of the Master of the Supreme Court. The Inter Library Loan section of the University of KwaZulu-Natal Library in Pietermaritzburg was hugely helpful overall.

Information and insights gained from administrators and players, past and present, have been crucial in supplementing the documentary record. In South Africa, Mark Henning, the late Krish Mackerdhuj and Joe Pamensky; in England, Jack Bailey, Doug Insole and Raman Subba Row; and in Australia, Cam Battersby, Clem Jones and the late Sir Donald Bradman, were particularly helpful.

Jonty Winch was an immense aid overall, generously making some of his own research material available, assisting with the photographs, and providing critical comments on an earlier draft of the manuscript. Peter Oborne also kindly gave some useful leads.

For useful comments and suggestions, and for reading various drafts, we are grateful to Doug Ettlinger, Yusuf Garda, Noel Garson, Clive Glaser, Gideon Haigh,

Hugh Lewin, Tom Lodge, Kenneth O. Morgan, A.J.A. Morris, Graham Neame, Charles van Onselen and Shahed Wadvalla. Karin Shapiro and Ed Balleisen played a central role in providing inspiration for the project and Brian Cleave made useful suggestions regarding the title.

Generous support from the Oppenheimer Fund of the University of Oxford assisted with research in the United Kingdom.

Particular thanks are due to Pat Tucker for her precise editing and creative suggestions, and to Veronica Klipp and Margarethe Mostert of Wits University Press, and Glenn Cowley and Sally Hines of the University of KwaZulu-Natal Press, for making the publication of this book possible. The authors are also very grateful to Frank Merrett for compiling the index.

Abbreviations

AAM	Anti-Apartheid Movement
ABC	Australian Board of Control for International Cricket
ACB	Australian Cricket Board
ANC	African National Congress
CARIS	Campaign Against Racialism in Sport
COSATU	Congress of South African Trade Unions
EPCA	Eastern Province Cricket Association
HART	Halt all Racist Tours
HNP	Herstigte Nasionale Party
ICC	Imperial Cricket Conference
ICC	International Cricket Conference
IOC	International Olympic Committee
IRB	International Rugby Board
MCC	Marylebone Cricket Club
MCU	Maritzburg Cricket Union
MDM	Mass Democratic Movement
NCB	Natal Cricket Board
NSC	National Sports Congress
NZCB	New Zealand Cricket Board
NZCC	New Zealand Cricket Council
NZRFU	New Zealand Rugby Football Union
OAU	Organisation of African Unity
PAC	Pan Africanist Congress
SAABA	South African Amateur Boxing Association
SAACB	South African African Cricket Board

SABCB	South African Bantu Cricket Board
SACA	South African Cricket Association
SACB	South African Cricket Board
SACBOC	South African Cricket Board of Control
SACCB	South African Coloured Cricket Board
SACOS	South African Council on Sport
SACU	South African Cricket Union
SAICU	South African Indian Cricket Union
SANROC	South African Non-Racial Olympic Committee
SAONGA	South African Olympic and National Games Association
SARB	South African Rugby Board
SASA	South African Sports Association
SASF	South African Soccer Federation
STST	Stop the Seventy Tour
TCB	Transvaal Cricket Board
TCC	Transvaal Cricket Council
TCCB	Test and County Cricket Board
TCF	Transvaal Cricket Federation
TCU	Transvaal Cricket Union
TRACOS	Transvaal Council on Sport
UCBSA	United Cricket Board of South Africa
UDF	United Democratic Front
UDI	Unilateral Declaration of Independence
WPCB	Western Province Cricket Board
WPCU	Western Province Cricket Union

PART I

The Making of an Apartheid Game

1

The Roots of Segregation in the Colonial Era

THERE HAS long been a general presumption that the history of South African cricket belongs exclusively to whites. But cricket is a sport that historically involves all the people of South Africa; it is the one major sport that has been widely played by each of the country's major population groups – African, coloured, Indian and white, Afrikaans- as well as English-speaking. Yet until recently it has not served as a point of identification between all communities.

One reason for this is that the tradition within which the game evolved in South Africa was one of racial exclusivity and segregation. Initially this was the result of social choice rather than state intervention, though government policies set the context in which cricket was played. Whites, as in other sports, monopolised the right to represent South Africa in international competition. From 1888/89 until exclusion from Test match cricket in 1971/72, South Africa played 172 Test matches in 41 series against just three opponents – the 'white' nations of England, Australia and New Zealand. During that period only one cricketer of colour played for South Africa.

To begin with, the very weakness of South African cricket opened up the prospect that talented black players might be included in the national team. In 1894 the formidable coloured fast bowler, H. 'Krom' Hendricks, was nominated by the Transvaal for the first South African team to tour England, only to be left behind because of his colour, evidently at the insistence of Cecil John Rhodes, the Cape

Prime Minister. In 1895/96 the Transvaal again pushed for Hendricks's inclusion in the South African team for the Johannesburg Test against Lord Hawke's England, but the Western Province Cricket Union refused to nominate him. Instead another coloured, the Natal all-rounder C.B. Llewellyn, took the field for South Africa, and went on to play fifteen Tests before World War I. Although he and Hendricks were of similar parentage – both had white fathers and coloured mothers from the island of St Helena – Llewellyn's 'colouredness' was evidently more marginal. Officially, he played as a white, and while his colour was a problem for some of his team-mates, it was never made a public issue.

Although South African cricket remained weak immediately after World War I, no attempts were made thereafter to recruit players of colour into the national team. Not until Basil D'Oliveira in the late 1950s and early 1960s was it again even mooted that a 'non-white' should be included in the South African team.

COLONIAL CRICKET

Cricket, an English game, was exported to South Africa with the British occupation of the Cape in 1806. The first recorded game in South Africa was played on Green Point Common in Cape Town in early 1808 between British military officers – who played a key role in the development of the South African game – and locals. The first Western Cape club was established at Wynberg in 1844 and the first 'Home Born' versus 'Colonial' match took place on Rondebosch Camp Ground in 1862. Matches in the 1860s and 1870s had great social significance, but tended to be played between scratch sides rather than clubs, on poor pitches with low scores. Clubs developed in the 1880s, and the game spread into the Boland interior, but it was only in 1893 that a regular league was finally established in Cape Town.

The first South African cricket club was founded in 1843 in Port Elizabeth in the Eastern Cape. On New Year's Day 1844, a match was played between 'Married' and 'Single' at St George's Park. In spite of this early start, the cricket structure of the urban Eastern Cape remained underdeveloped and the game spread slowly into the country districts. In the Border area the first club, in Queenstown, dates from 1865 and King William's Town and Grahamstown were competing against each other by 1874.

A third major coastal centre of South African cricket was Natal, following its annexation by the British in 1843. A club was founded in the colony's capital, Pietermaritzburg, in 1851 and within a year two clubs, West End and East End, were competing on the Market Square. Here, as elsewhere in South Africa in the 1860s, cricket was mostly played between scratch sides rather than formal clubs. The sport also spread into the rural hinterland and by the 1880s even the most obscure country settlements such as Dargle, in the Natal Midlands, had their cricket teams. However, it was not until the 1890s that Pietermaritzburg and Durban were able to establish a regular inter-town club competition.

It would be a mistake to assume that, having established itself along the coastal regions, the spread of cricket inland came only as a result of growing British political influence. In fact the Boer republics – the Orange Free State and the Transvaal – adopted cricket of their own accord, generally among the pockets of English-speaking communities. The Bloemfontein Cricket Club was established in 1855 and teams were to be found in small Free State towns, although their fortunes depended upon the transient presence of travellers to the Transvaal gold fields. Potchefstroom's cricket history dates back to 1861 and its first club to 1863; and the game was introduced to Pretoria in 1870, where it had to compete for space with Boer cultural activities on the Market Square. By 1874 the two towns were competing against each other – on atrocious pitches.

The great boost to the growth of cricket in the interior was the discovery of the diamond fields in the late 1860s, followed by the discovery of gold on the Witwatersrand in 1886. Kimberley, at the centre of the diamond fields annexed by the British as Griqualand West in 1870, became for a while the cricketing capital of the interior, for blacks as well as whites. With the opening of the Witwatersrand gold fields 'droves of players' moved from the diamond fields to the Transvaal.[1] In 1887 an inter-town competition for whites was initiated between Pretoria, Potchefstroom, Barberton and Johannesburg, and in the following year the Wanderers Club was founded in Johannesburg.

The first competition that may be equated in any way with county or state cricket in England or Australia was the Champion Bat series that lasted from 1876 to 1890. It was in origin an inter-town challenge for the Cape Colony, but it contained the roots of a national structure, including, on one occasion, teams from elsewhere; this was the 'extraneous' challenge of 1887 at Kimberley that involved Natal and Bechuanaland.

In 1890 Kimberley staged the first challenge for the Currie Cup, which was to develop into South Africa's domestic inter-provincial competition. The 'Cup' had its origins in the first tour to South Africa – by Major Warton's England side in

1888/89. The tour's sponsor, Sir Donald Currie, the shipping magnate who founded what became the Union Castle Line, donated a cup to be presented to the South African team that 'excels most against the visitors'. Kimberley, later Griqualand West, was awarded the trophy, but in April 1890 Transvaal successfully challenged for it. The Currie Cup was to become white cricket's premier competition and prior to World War I was generally contested as a tournament at a single venue. During seasons that featured a touring side, the Currie Cup competition was suspended, a practice that continued until as late as the 1966/67 Australian tour. Geography, economics and deference to the imperial ethic all hampered the progress of South Africa's domestic structures.

One of the most remarkable historical features of South African cricket was the country's very rapid assimilation into the ranks of Test-playing nations, which, since 1877, had consisted solely of Australia and England.[2] Warton's team of 1888/89, captained by Aubrey Smith, later a Hollywood actor, was a side whose strength reflected the average English county: it played two Tests, at Port Elizabeth and Cape Town, and all its remaining matches against odds*. The tour was clearly intended to promote the concept of Empire and several of the players stayed on in South Africa afterwards.

The South African Cricket Association (SACA) was founded at Kimberley on 9 April 1890, after the inaugural Currie Cup challenge, pre-dating Union by two decades. Limiting its attention from the outset to white cricket, its functions, listed in its rules and objectives, were dominated by the organisation of tours. The second team of tourists, captained by W.W. Read, arrived as early as the 1891/92 season. It was a stronger team, containing the Australians W.L. Murdoch and J.J. Ferris, and was unbeaten, a feat that was all the more remarkable because two other teams representing England were almost simultaneously touring Australia and North America. The tour ran into severe financial problems and at stages its social obligations seemed to outweigh the cricket. In 1894 a South African team (excluding 'Krom' Hendricks) visited England, but the matches it played were not designated first class and the tour was dogged by financial problems, poor weather and an initial difficulty in adjusting to turf pitches. The excluded Hendricks would almost certainly have fared well and have attracted larger crowds.

---

* A cricketing term meaning the normal eleven playing against a greater number, say fifteen or twenty-one.

A team led by Lord Hawke that came to South Africa in 1895/96 inflicted a 3-0 Test whitewash on the hosts and during the tour of 1898/99 the Hawke team lost only one match in nineteen. It was in the course of selecting a team for one of these tours, probably the first, that W.H. Milton, a close associate of Rhodes, urged Lord Hawke not to include in his party the brilliant batsman K.S. Ranjitsinhji, the Indian prince who played for England, on the grounds that 'his appearance would create certain embarrassment in this country'. 'Ranji' consequently never toured South Africa.[3]

These English tours, it was becoming clear, were distinctly imperialist in nature and intended to promote imperial ideology. The first of the two under Hawke's captaincy, coincided with the Jameson Raid. Hawke, Sir Timothy O'Brien, and Charles Wright had a convivial visit with some of those taken captive by the Transvaal Government in Pretoria gaol, including the man who should have been their host, mining magnate Abe Bailey.

South Africa visited England in 1901, in the midst of the Anglo-Boer War, and played its first series against Australia in the 1902/03 season.

In all, between 1889 and 1914, South Africa played in eleven Test series against England and Australia; eight against the former (seven at home and one away) and two against the latter (one each home and away), and the 1912 Triangular Tournament in England against both. The high point was in 1905/06 when the Marylebone Cricket Club (MCC), the governing body of English cricket, undertook its first tour of South Africa, and when South Africa recorded its first Test victory in Johannesburg in January 1906 in its twelfth Test match, and went on to win the series 4-1.

In 1907 the South Africans undertook their first Test tour of England wearing the striped green and gold blazers with the Springbok emblem on pocket and cap that had been introduced by their rugby counterparts for their first tour of the United Kingdom the previous year. It was while making arrangements for the England tour in January 1907 that the SACA committee had voted 16-8 to adopt the Springbok emblem, replacing the lion rampant they had agreed to in 1902.[4] The South Africans lost the three-match Test series 1-0, but their quartet of googly bowlers – Reggie Schwarz, Gordon White, Ernest Vogler and Aubrey Faulkner – captured both wickets and the public imagination.

South Africa's first Test victory over Australia came at Adelaide in the third Test of the 1910/11 series during what Brian Crowley described as an Edwardian 'mini golden age'.[5] Overall, however, the main feature of South African cricket prior to World War I was the regular arrival in the country of under-strength England teams and the very rapid acceptance of South Africa into the international ruling triumvirate of cricket.

The Imperial Cricket Conference (ICC), founded in 1909 to control Test cricket, was largely the result of South African efforts, instigated by Abe Bailey who was himself a former player. The South African-born, English-educated Bailey was among the founders of the Wanderers Club in Johannesburg and captained both the Wanderers and Transvaal at cricket, playing in the Currie Cup tournament in Cape Town in 1893/94. He was also a founder member of the Transvaal Cricket Union in 1891 and served as its president from 1906 to 1936. Bailey took over Cecil Rhodes's Barkly West seat in the Cape Legislative Assembly from 1902 to 1905, allegedly claiming that the 'mantle' of Rhodes had fallen on him. Politically, he never became much of a force, but he did outstrip Rhodes as a financial benefactor of South African cricket, underwriting several overseas tours.

Inspired by South Africa's first Test win over England, Bailey wrote as early as 1907 to the MCC suggesting the triangular tournament that eventually took place in 1912, three years later than he had hoped. The delay was partly the result of a lack of enthusiasm from Australia, which subsequently blocked a repetition. *Wisden* described the Triangular Tournament as the 'first trial of Sir Abe Bailey's ambitious scheme', originally termed the Imperial Cricket Contest, to strengthen 'the bonds of Union within the Empire'. It was an imperial vision that specifically excluded the United States, in the form of the Philadelphians, who had undertaken three successful first-class tours of England between 1897 and 1908.

During meetings held at Lord's on 15 June and 20 July 1909, at which South Africa was represented by H.D.G. Leveson Gower (at both), G.W. Hillyard (June) and Abe Bailey (July), it was decided to confine the term 'Test Match' to contests between the three founder members of the ICC. Other matters agreed upon were player qualifications, hours of play and umpires. The ICC was a consultative body initially viewed with suspicion by Australia. It met infrequently: in 1921, when the eight-ball over was condoned in Australia only; and in 1926, when India, the West Indies and New Zealand were also present. From 1929 'the ICC met annually at Lord's, though their business attracted only the minimum of attention'. Significantly the term 'imperial' was to last for half a century, until the early 1960s, and it was this imperial definition that later came to haunt SACA.[6]

Nineteenth- and early twentieth-century touring teams described as 'England' were ambassadors for Empire as much as for cricket, and might have been more aptly named 'Imperial Wanderers'. As Lionel Tennyson, later captain of England, put it after the 1913/14 MCC tour, 'We were regarded as ambassadors from the old country.' In this spirit, the team enrolled as special constables in Johannesburg to combat a transport strike in support of white miners' demands, a remarkable political act by a sports team, clearly demonstrating its alliance with the Union authorities, the establishment and conservative politicians.

The late Victorian and early Edwardian eras were a great time for privately sponsored touring, and South Africa's strategic importance in the Empire helped ensure that it received its fair share of tours. Writing after the first official MCC tour in 1905/06, the team's captain, Pelham Warner, described 'fighting spirit', 'fair play' and 'hearty good fellowship', all cricketing qualities that he linked implicitly to 'British manhood'. All these virtues were understood to reflect common values and outlooks, and there is every indication that South African cricket was only too pleased to receive touring teams. South Africa was undoubtedly, to use Derek Birley's phrase, a 'favoured nation'.[7]

Although this essentially imperial perspective airbrushed out of the picture the black role in cricket, it is evident that by the late nineteenth century there was huge enthusiasm for cricket in black communities. As Aubrey Smith commented, 'I noticed while driving through the suburbs of Cape Town that every spare patch of ground was used by blacks to pitch wickets – or paraffin cans in some cases – in order to play cricket.' This confirmed for him the opinion of Spencer Todd of the Castle Line, who had told Smith's team on its departure, 'No sport has taken such deep root among the black people of South Africa as cricket.'[8] The Castle Line not only transported touring teams between England and South Africa, but also ferried teams, some of them black, between Cape Town and Port Elizabeth. James Orrock, in his account of his voyage to South Africa on the *Drummond Castle* at the end of 1890, recorded that at Cape Town harbour 'there was on board a team of native cricketers, bound for Port Elizabeth to play a match. They were accompanied to the boat by all their sisters, and cousins, and aunts. Such a scene of kissing and hand shaking I never saw before . . . Cricket is the chief game in the colony.' He added: 'The Steerage passengers are in a great stew about sleeping with the native cricketers. The most of them decided to sleep on the floor rather than occupy the same bunk.'[9]

Cricket had long been well established amongst the coloured community, both Christian and Muslim or Malay, in Cape Town, and in the early 1890s 'multi-racial' cricket was still possible in the Mother City, with at least three Peninsular teams including both coloured and white players. In 1889/90 Newlands provided the venue for the first Malay inter-town tournament, contested between teams from Cape Town, Claremont, Port Elizabeth and Johannesburg.[10] At the second Malay tournament in Kimberley in March/April 1891 the Cape Town bowler E. Ariefden claimed all ten wickets in an innings against Port Elizabeth. After the tournament, a 'Test match' was staged between 'Malays' and 'Europeans', with the white Kimberley XI winning on the first innings. During the 1891/92 tour by W.W. Read's England team, a match was arranged against a black team in Kimberley, but was subsequently cancelled and replaced with a game against an all-white Griqualand West XI.[11] Fortuitously, Read's team played against a Malay XVIII on 22–23 March after the Cape Town Test ended early on the third day with South Africa's defeat by an innings and 189 runs. This was the first match played between black South Africans and a visiting team and the last until 1973. England won by ten wickets, but there were two outstanding performances from the Malays – L. Samoodien scored 55, one of only two fifties scored against England during the entire tour, and, more importantly, 'Krom' Hendricks took four for 50 off 25 overs.

Upper-class Africans were also strongly attracted to the game, believing that cricket presented an opportunity to absorb white culture. In the Cape the vote was attainable, and cricket was a means for blacks in search of the franchise to prove their social acceptability and demonstrate a willingness to adapt to 'civilised' norms, as defined by the imperial establishment. The first African cricket club was founded in Port Elizabeth in 1869 and within fifteen years African cricket, through clubs, leagues and other competitions, was well-established and flourishing in the Eastern Cape. From 1884 there was an inter-town competition in the area and plans were even mooted to send a team to play in England. In 1885, in a match between the winners of the black inter-town league and its white counterparts in King William's Town, the blacks were the winners; and in the same year a black team from Port Elizabeth was similarly victorious over whites at Cradock. André Odendaal, the historian of African cricket in South Africa, points out that black teams regularly beat whites in matches that were often staged on public holidays.[12]

African players frequently hailed from missionary educational institutions such as Zonnebloem, Lovedale and Healdtown, which made a point of inculcating the values of modern Western sport, in particular the controlled use of leisure time. Cricket was taken so seriously at Zonnebloem that budgetary constraints were not applied where equipment was concerned.[13] The names of black cricket clubs such as the Duke of Wellington and the Eccentrics, both of Kimberley, were redolent with British imperialism: 'Cricket . . . was the game that Kimberley's African petty bourgeoisie really made its own.'[14] Matches were prominent on the social calendar, for example during the Christmas holidays, and involved considerable social activity that encouraged incipient class differences within the black community. Positions within the administration of cricket were highly sought after and much prized, and officials came from the ranks of the African elite. John Tengo Jabavu, proprietor and editor of *Imvo Zabantsundu*, South Africa's first independent African newspaper, was a leading figure in King William's Town's black cricket circles and the game was well covered by the newspaper's sports reporter. The Jabavu Cup was the prize for the biennial regional inter-town competition, which flourished in the 1890s. King William's Town and Port Elizabeth were major centres and the organising board was still in existence in 1910.[15] So supportive was Jabavu of imperial games that he endorsed a Cape Bill of 1891 designed to restrict 'tribal' recreation such as initiation dances.

In the 1880s Kimberley developed as a major centre for black as well as white cricket, and by 1890 a team from the town was playing in the African inter-town competition with Grahamstown, King William's Town and Port Elizabeth. Cricket in Kimberley was truly 'non-racial' because the two African clubs that fielded several teams played together with eight other Malay, Indian and coloured clubs in the Griqualand West Coloured Cricket Union. In 1897, Colonel (later Sir) David Harris, a director of De Beers Consolidated Mines, donated in memory of his recently deceased cousin, Barney Barnato, the Barnato Memorial Trophy as the prize for an inter-provincial black tournament segregated from whites. Harris thereby initiated the long association between the mining industry and black cricket.

The trophy was first contested in 1898 in Port Elizabeth and won by a Western Province team composed mainly of Malay players. The Griqualand West team, which came second, was a mixture of Africans and coloureds, and the three Eastern Cape teams – Southern Border, Queenstown and Eastern Province, were African.[16] The tournament was suspended for the duration of the Anglo-Boer War and revived when the South African Coloured Cricket Board (SACCB) was belatedly founded in 1902. It symbolised attempts to bring together cricketers of different communities and was the precursor of 'non-racial' sport later in the twentieth century.

While the popularity of cricket was growing among blacks in the late nineteenth century, the game was simultaneously in the process of being appropriated by a white imperial elite for the purposes of defining and asserting itself. The introduction in 1862 of an annual contest between Home Born versus Colonial in Cape Town was a landmark. Cricket was ceasing to be a purely social sport and was beginning to be played by groups based on inclusivity. The inevitable corollary was the exclusion of others. For some years the Home Born versus Colonial contest was the season's most significant match but it had a more far-reaching significance – it introduced to the game the crucial question of who was a South African, an issue that was to haunt all representative sport until the 1990s.

Sir Abe Bailey described cricket as the 'Empire game'.[17] Towards the end of the nineteenth century it had become a symbol of imperial endeavour, made all the more powerful by its subtlety and mannered conventions, and the difficulty these represented for those not educated in its complexities.[18] According to Lord Harris, one of the giants of early twentieth-century cricket, the game was the most important institution in the Empire, apparently more so than the Crown, and represented 'God's playing field'.[19] The importance of cricket was vested in the system of ethics and morals that governed the style in which it was played: 'ascendancy to a higher plane of awareness of one's individual and *collective* role in life'.[20] It was lauded as a source of character building and self-control. Perhaps most importantly, the game was promoted in terms of the acceptance of the magisterial and impartial authority of umpires, whom we may regard as truly symbolic imperial figures. It followed as a matter of course that the British, or more specifically the English, as cricket was an English game, were possessed of multiple human virtues, above all a sense of fair play, which set them apart, within their imperial boundaries, from everyone else. Wendy Katz describes underlying British imperial psychology as a mixture of insecurity and aggression that found meaning in familiar and comfortable symbols and spaces, which were portrayed by the historian John McKenzie as a 'sediment that settled upon British consciousness'.[21]

Cricket and the imperial project thus became inextricably linked: the game was a key element in the storehouse of British national memory.[22] Its moral metaphor and political symbolism were used to set the British aside from 'lesser breeds', to train them to cope 'under fire, whether from fast bowlers or insurgent tribesmen', and to instil the self-assurance necessary to rule so many potentially hostile indigenous people.[23] This ascendancy, represented by an assumed aptitude both for sport and for governing foreigners, naturally encouraged a sense of otherness. It was in cricket that 'the essence of Englishness, what distinguished us from the effete, inferior foreigner, was encouraged and expressed'.[24] Cricket, writes the historian Eric Midwinter, was a 'badge of Englishness'.[25] The mystique of Empire represented in a game like cricket provided solace and psychological strength in countries such as South Africa in which the writ of white authority could never entirely be taken for granted. Indeed, the sports historians David Black and John Nauright argue that sport, and cricket in particular, was designed simultaneously to impress and intimidate the locals.[26]

Sport, and more especially cricket, thus defined British imperial space in far-flung corners of the world, not only metaphorically but also physically, in circumstances that were generally perceived as hostile. Psychological security required familiarity and the stamp of Britain upon exotic landscapes. Various writers mention 'geographic assurance', 'contagiously English places' and 'England's authentic . . . architecture of belonging'.[27] The club certainly played a role in all of them, as did the culture of private schools in which reverence was paid to the idea of playing life with a straight bat while showing respect for the rules of the game. The playing field engendered security based on comforting symbols and a sense of togetherness, an almost juvenile state of mind from which an aggressive racism emanated. Marina Warner, granddaughter of influential player and administrator Sir Pelham Warner, in a wonderfully evocative description, sums up the fragility of this security: 'The lime demarcation lines in the turf that divided Englishmen from foreigners and natives could be rubbed out in the climate of the [West Indies] all too easily by passing feet.'[28] In India, the journalist Mihir Bose notes, 'The British saw cricket as a way of keeping their own community together with little or no place there for the Indians'; in the phrase of Ramachandra Guha, 'In the beginning cricket was played to get away from the coolie'; and as Jan Morris puts it, 'Settlers all over the Empire fought hard to keep their own little Englands intact'.[29]

Cricket was part of an Englishman's national consciousness. The significance of this becomes apparent when one considers the fact that within the British Empire at the end of the nineteenth century more and more of the non-select were being excluded from places they once frequented. In late Victorian Britain 'social distances were considered an important and integral part of maintaining order'. In South

Africa, this exclusion took on a largely racial form and became part of an official policy of segregation: physical distance was a powerful tool in establishing security. The country was part of an empire that in its obsession with apartness developed 'ineradicable instincts of racial superiority'. Social distance and exclusivity engendered stereotyping and the increasing popularity of a 'cult of gentility' whose sensibilities were heightened by the frontier nature of South African society. The outward manifestation was an aggressive and arrogant white chauvinism based on identification with the 'British Race' that had less to do with sporting fair play than with racial differentiation. The professed spirituality of the Empire had become, with time, simply a crude moral superiority strongly imbued with racism.[30]

In the Cape the liberal tradition waned from the 1880s onwards as Africans were increasingly pushed off the land, out of trading opportunities, off the voters' roll and into segregated institutions. By the end of the nineteenth century sport had become a symbol of racially exclusive white status and national federations were founded on that understanding. In Cape Town itself, ethnic identification and racism took hold in the last quarter of the nineteenth century, encouraging separate sports bodies. In the opinion of the *Cape Argus*, 'The races are best socially apart, each good in their way, but a terribly bad mixture.'[31]

HENDRICKS AND LLEWELLYN

It was in this context of defining and asserting imperial and racial identities that the question of including a black cricketer in the South African national side first arose. The subject of the debate was 'Krom' Hendricks, the coloured fast bowler who had so impressed for the Malay XVIII against the English tourists but who was subsequently omitted from the South African team that toured England in 1894. The thinking behind his omission was probably not far from that of 'Scrutator' who, in the Johannesburg *Star*, wrote that in playing their white English cousins at cricket the white minority in South Africa could not afford the 'victory at any cost' attitude that the inclusion of Hendricks would represent, but should rather learn to 'take a licking like white men'. 'The subject is a distasteful one,' he wrote, 'but, if needs must, I for one should take my stand at any time and in any place, and say that, taking in view the conditions of life in South Africa, it is imperative that the line be drawn sharp, straight, and unbroken between white and coloured.'

While Hendricks had played for the Malay team against the English he protested against being categorised as 'Malay', the term used to describe those coloureds who were Muslims, whether or not they had originally been slaves from Malaya. Hendricks insisted that he was a Christian, whose father was of Dutch descent and whose mother came from the south Atlantic island of St Helena. With the decline of the island's economy following its transfer from the Honourable East India Company to the British Crown in 1833, there had been a steady exodus to the Cape, and later to Natal, of coloured St Helenans, descendants mainly of slaves from the East Indies. In 1873 a group of 442 St Helenans settled in Pietermaritzburg.

Hendricks's career, similar in some respects to that of the Australian Aboriginal player, Jack Marsh, was one of travesty and tragedy.[32] Jonty Winch's research on the life of Monty Bowden, recently published as *England's Youngest Captain*, underscores the nature of the tragedy both for Hendricks and for South African cricket. In Winch's analysis, the supposedly 'liberal' Cape proved to be the bastion of racism in South African cricket.[33]

Regarded as one of the fastest bowlers of his era by South African and English batsmen, Hendricks was widely tipped for selection for South Africa's first tour to England in 1894. Read, the captain of the English tourists, was adamant: 'If you send a team, send Hendricks; he will be a drawcard and is to my mind the Spofforth [the great Australian fast bowler] of South Africa.' The problem, in the South African context, was Hendricks's colour. To negotiate it H.G. Cadwallader, secretary of SACA, suggested that Hendricks be taken as 'baggage-man' for then 'there could be absolutely no objection to Hendricks on account of his being a Malay'. Hendricks at first refused point blank to 'think of going in that capacity' but, evidently in response to prodding from Cadwallader, changed his mind and indicated 'that he would be pleased to go to England if required, on certain low terms for services rendered, and would not for a moment expect to be "classed" with the rest of the team'. On that basis the Transvaal Cricket Union nominated him for selection for the tour. As reported by Johannesburg's *Standard and Diggers News*, the Transvaal committee, chaired by Abe Bailey, was unanimous in his support 'on the understanding that he is willing to go as baggage-man and servant'. The newspaper added, 'Hendricks is acknowledged to be a red-hot trundler, and [wicketkeeper] Halliwell, who will have to "stand up" to him, is the gentleman who particularly insists on the inclusion of this dusky unit.'

But even on the basis of serving as a glorified 'baggage-man' Hendricks was eventually omitted from the touring party, apparently after the application of 'the greatest pressure by those in high authority in the Cape Colony'. According to

Pelham Warner, Hendricks was excluded through the influence of Cecil John Rhodes, the Cape Prime Minister, and Warner somewhat naively expressed surprise at this attitude from a professed empire builder. As recounted by Warner, Rhodes told him at an Oxford breakfast in 1895 that 'they wanted me to send a black fellow called Hendricks to England . . . but I would not have it'.

Rhodes's malign influence was an early instance of the political intervention that came to bedevil South African cricket. Rhodes funded the tour to the tune of £500 and the chairman of the selection committee was W.H. Milton, his private secretary as well as chairman of the Western Province Cricket Union. The committee met for five hours at the unlikely venue of the tiny Karoo village of De Aar on 25 February 1894, with Milton dominating proceedings, to the point of bypassing Cadwallader as tour manager and choosing the colours of the Western Province Cricket Club for the touring side. Despite a good number of South Africa's leading players having declared themselves unavailable for the tour, no place was found for Hendricks in the touring party. According to the brief minute released by Milton, Hendricks was proposed by E.A. Halliwell, representing Transvaal, but there was no seconder. The complaint later registered by Kimberley was that 'the Western Province Cricket Union has, by its high-handed action regarding various matters in connection with the team for England, muddled the whole concern'.

The British press expressed surprise and disappointment at Hendricks's omission, as did the *Standard and Diggers News*. In its opinion, 'It is a case of courting a disaster for the sake of prejudice.' Abe Bailey, in his reaction, captured the sense of lost opportunity in South African cricket: 'I was strongly in favour of sending him, but I have yielded somewhat to the very good argument that, after all, our men are going to England to learn rather than with the hope of achieving any great glory. Under these circumstances, it was argued, it was not absolutely necessary to lift a coloured man up on the account of the moral effect it might have on the whole coloured population.'

That was by no means the end of the Hendricks saga. In October 1894 he and some other coloured players participated in the Cape Town First Cup competition, and Hendricks bowled so well that a campaign was mounted to include him in the Colonial side for the annual match against the Home Born players from the Mother Country. Thomas Lawton, the president of the Western Province Cricket Union, was among those who wanted to include him so as to fulfil 'the boast of cricket that peer and ploughman could meet together in the same field', though he conceded that his committee 'could not be blind to the fact that there was strong opposition to Hendricks in certain quarters'. In the event, Hendricks was not chosen, with the ubiquitous Milton again playing a central role in securing his exclusion.[34]

Hendricks again featured when the Transvaal included him in the squad for the second Test in Johannesburg against Lord Hawke's 1895/96 England team, but his final selection was again blocked by Western Province. The practice at the time was for the host province for a Test to select the home team, usually from nominations submitted by the other provinces. Halliwell, now South African captain, was determined to have Hendricks, and the Transvaal selectors duly included him in their squad, but the Western Province Cricket Union refused to nominate him. Western Province opted instead for J.T. Willougby, who made a reasonably successful debut in the first Test in Port Elizabeth and who was to play again in the third Test in Cape Town. The *Cape Times* complained that the Transvaal, 'noted for its impertinent interference with other centres', sought to upset 'all the rules which govern the picking of a South African eleven by refusing to recognise the right of each union to nominate its own candidates, and including, or professing to be anxious to include, Hendricks in the team'. The *South African Review* was vehement in its dismissal of Hendricks himself:

> Hendricks, the Malay fast bowler, about whom the Transvaal Union is so absurdly solicitous, playing for his club (the United Services) against the second team from the CTCC on Saturday, secured 2 wickets for 34 runs. These are hardly the figures of the bowling 'terror' Rand players had conjured up in fevered imagination. Up there, Hendricks is magnified by the glamour of distance, and they have an idea that he is not fairly treated by the Western Province Union because of his colour. We know better, and submit this performance to our Rand friends as being just what is expected of Hendricks down here. Two wickets for 34 against second rate batsmen is just Hendricks' form. He is no earthly good in a first-class match. Perhaps the Transvaal Union will reconsider their rash and ill-considered invitation to the Malay bowler, and turn their attention to another fast bowler – whose name is Willougby.[35]

In 1897 the Western Province Cricket Union even prevented Hendricks from playing for Woodstock in the club championships. A *Cape Times* editorial justifying the decision stated that coloureds were 'politically equal' but 'socially not so', and that 'both colours should . . . pursue a policy of mutual exclusion'.[36]

One window on the Hendricks saga was opened up by A.B. Tancred, a Pretoria lawyer who played in South Africa's first two Tests and served as a Transvaal selector. In 1894 he had been outraged by Hendricks's 'impudent' initial refusal to make himself available to tour as a 'baggage-man': 'If he wants to go on the same footing as the others I would not have him at any price. As baggage-man they might take him and play him in one or two of the matches when the conditions suited him. To take him as an equal would, from a South African point of view, be impolitic, not to say intolerable, and I would not have him on those terms if he were a better bowler than Lohmann.' When Hendricks backed down and agreed to go on 'low terms', Tancred supported his nomination by Transvaal, but he was never prepared to entertain Hendricks as an equal. In 1897, when the possibility of another South African tour to England was being canvassed, Tancred told *Cricket* magazine: 'Hendricks is a good fast bowler but in the opinion of the great majority of South African cricketers it would not be advisable to send him, on account of the colour question, which in England you no doubt find difficult to understand. What may happen in years to come one cannot say but there are two or three native bowlers coming on well; one of them, a "Cape boy" is as fast as any bowler we have ever had.'[37]

While the Western Province Cricket Union refused to nominate Hendricks for the March 1896 Wanderers Test against Lord Hawke's England team, Natal evidently nominated another coloured player, their all-rounder, Charles Bennett 'Buck' Llewellyn, who had earlier impressed by taking 7 for 150 for the Pietermaritzburg XV against the tourists. Llewellyn duly made his debut for South Africa at the age of nineteen. In all, he was to play fifteen Tests for South Africa between then and World War I, five against England and ten against Australia. By modern standards his Test record is modest: 544 runs at 20.14 with three half centuries and a highest score of 90; and 48 wickets at 29.60 with five wickets in an innings on three occasions, ten in a match on one, and a best innings return of 6-92. He also held seven catches. Throughout his career as a Test cricketer his colour never became a public issue, but a certain ambivalence towards him within South African cricketing circles was consistently evident.

Llewellyn was born, out of wedlock, in Pietermaritzburg on 29 September 1876. His father, Thomas Buck Llewellyn, was born in August 1845 in Pembroke in Wales;

and his mother, Ann Elizabeth Rich, in the same year in Jamestown, St Helena. Llewellyn's father ran a successful house-painting business in Pietermaritzburg, and died in 1914. His mother died in 1920.

A number of Llewellyn's contemporaries commented on his appearance. The famous Yorkshire all-rounder, Wilfred Rhodes, described him as 'like a rather sunburned English player', while J.M. Kilburn, a great admirer of Llewellyn's cricketing achievements, said he was tidy-looking and of sturdy medium height but 'dark-eyed and dark-skinned and South Africans called him coloured'. In spite of this, he played in the Currie Cup for Natal over four seasons, making his debut as a 'dusky eighteen year old' in the 1894/95 season.[38] His patron was Dan Taylor, the Natal captain and father of H.W. 'Herby' Taylor, later South African captain, who employed Llewellyn as a clerk in his Durban business. Llewellyn's reputation as a Natal player essentially related to his bowling skills – he claimed 30 wickets in the 1896/97 Currie Cup tournament and 16 in the 1897/98 tournament and he ranks as the first great slow left-armer in South Africa.

His Test debut at the Wanderers in March 1896 was not auspicious. Although he was South Africa's second highest scorer in the first innings, with 24, as a bowler he went for 71 runs in 14 overs without a wicket as England defeated South Africa by an innings and 197 runs, with the formidable George Lohmann claiming 15 wickets. Llewellyn was not given a chance to redeem himself, being dropped for the third Test in Cape Town. However, his appearances against the tourists enabled him to establish a hugely important relationship for the future with Lieutenant Robert Poore. Poore, a Hampshire batsman serving in the British Army in South Africa, played with Llewellyn for the Pietermaritzburg XV and the South African team, despite having expressed a preference to play for England.

In February 1899 Llewellyn made his next appearance for South Africa in the first Test at the Wanderers in the following series against Lord Hawke's England, a side which included Pelham Warner. Llewellyn took 2-35 and 3-89 in a game in which South Africa might have recorded its first-ever Test win but for a serious umpiring lapse. With the tourists in trouble in the second innings, Llewellyn had Warner 'very smartly stumped', only for umpire A. Soames to give the batsman not out. Warner went on to score a match-winning 132. Soames confessed in later life, 'So far as one can forecast the result of a cricket match, I have little doubt that my bad decision cost South Africa the game, so that I have ever since been self-convicted of losing the Test match.'[39] For the second and final Test in Cape

Town Llewellyn was evidently invited to play, but declared himself unavailable. The *Star* commented: 'Llewellyn, youngster though he is, has proved himself the best all-round player in South Africa, and his absence from the representative team is a misfortune that some of the big wigs at the Cape, one may reasonably think, would have seen to.'[40]

After the series Llewellyn followed Lord Hawke's team back to England, effectively emigrating as a professional for Hampshire (at the instigation of Poore), where he proved an outstanding success. When the South Africans visited in 1901 he pulverised their bowling, scoring 216 in three hours, and was twice thereafter enlisted to help the tourists out. Llewellyn was so highly regarded that he was named in the England squad for the first Test against Australia at Edgbaston in 1902, although he did not play amongst what must have been one of the strongest batting line-ups in history. Qualifying rules were relatively lax at the time: he was eligible through his father but he had already played for South Africa. Warwick Armstrong, the great Australian all-rounder, is said to have queried sarcastically whether the Australians were playing England or South Africa.[41]

Llewellyn did feature that year in Tests against Armstrong and the Australians, but that was for South Africa during the 1902/03 Australian tour of the country. As a Test player Llewellyn was at the height of his powers in that series. In the first Test in Johannesburg he took 9-216 over all and his wickets included Syd Gregory (twice) as well as Victor Trumper and John Darling; he also scored 90 batting at number three in the first innings, putting on 173 with L.J. Tancred for the second wicket. In the second Test, also in Johannesburg, he had match figures of 10-116; and in the third, in Cape Town, his figures were 6-97. Twenty-five wickets at 17.92 were sufficient to place him at the top of the averages. In Cape Town he opened the bowling.

Llewellyn would open the bowling again on the 1910/11 tour of Australia, during which the question of his ancestry evidently became a major torment. According to the cricket historian Rowland Bowen, a noted critic of racism in South African cricket, the 'openly avowed coloured' Llewellyn was 'tormented by his fellow tourists to such an extent that for peace and quiet in the hotels where the team stayed, he had to take refuge in the WCs and lock himself in'. Bowen named J.H. Sinclair, South Africa's star batsman, as his 'chief tormentor'. Herby Taylor, in his recollection of Llewellyn, confirmed that one or two players 'gave Buck a hard time now and again', but underlined that these were occasional occurrences induced by the players concerned having had 'one or two too many'. If Sinclair was indeed the 'chief tormentor', his behaviour was riddled with ambiguity. As SACA minutes make evident, it was at Sinclair's insistence that Hampshire was approached to release Llewellyn for the tour and that Llewellyn was offered a £250 salary plus various expenses. Significantly, opposition to his presence on the tour came from his home province, which argued that he was no longer a South African.[42] In the event, Llewellyn's full expenses were not paid, nor did he receive a bonus. His final tour for South Africa followed in the Triangular Tournament in England where he failed with the ball but scored two half centuries during a dismal series for his side.

The idea that Llewellyn was coloured and had been persecuted while on tour in Australia was vehemently denied by his daughter in an article published in the mid-1970s. She maintained that Llewellyn's mother had been born in Essex and his father in Bootle in Lancashire of Welsh descent. Of her own father she said, 'He was of white stock'.[43] To back up her denial of Llewellyn's harassment by his team-mates she pointed out that in later years when he was employed in the Lancashire Leagues Llewellyn was visited by touring South African players. But she painted a totally erroneous picture of her grandparents. It is entirely in keeping with the times that an elderly woman in 1970s Britain would have attempted to cover up her mixed ancestry.

Llewellyn's first-class career lasted from 1894 until 1912. He scored 11 425 runs at an average of 26.75 and took 1 013 wickets at 23.41 along with over 200 catches. To his eighteen centuries he could add five wickets in an innings 82 times and ten in a match on 20 occasions. There is thus no doubting his status as a great all-rounder: to his left arm orthodox slow medium bowling with a high arm action could be added forcing left-handed batting favouring the cut, and specialised fielding at mid-off. Pelham Warner called him a 'fine all-rounder', and *Wisden* described him as 'in the fullest sense of the words an all-round cricketer'.

There are surprisingly few references to his batting, but *Wisden* commented in 1911 that he was a punishing left-hander, his 'driving power being tremendous'. By way of contrast, his bowling is well documented and widely praised: A.W. 'Dave' Nourse called him 'the best left hand bowler we ever had. He turned the ball so well and kept a wonderful length' even on good wickets. *Wisden* named him one of its cricketers of the year in 1911, describing his 'medium pace bowling' as 'full of life and spin'. His control of length, pace and spin brings to mind a turn-of-the-century Derek Underwood: 'On the slow side of medium . . . if the pitch helped him, his spin was vicious.' Altham names him as the cricketer who 'until the appearance of Fleetwood-Smith, was the only left-hander known to bowl the googly', which he describes elsewhere as the 'chinaman'.

The debate about the origins of the 'chinaman' is ongoing, but Llewellyn was evidently the first to bowl it. He is said to have spent several years practising the googly based on advice given by Reggie Schwarz, who perfected the right-arm googly. The quintessential Hampshire man of letters, broadcaster and cricket writer John Arlott suggests that on plumb wickets where 'natural' spin failed to persuade the ball to turn, Llewellyn bowled wrist spin to induce off breaks and mixed this with the googly. Kilburn, who had the advantage of having watched him frequently, said he was orthodox left arm and reserved judgement on the question of the googly, commenting whimsically that 'perhaps . . . the occasional chinaman was simply an indulgence of Llewellyn's momentary fancy'.[44]

After an outstanding career for Hampshire, Llewellyn left in 1910 to become a professional in Lancashire League cricket, where he played for an extraordinary 27 years. In 1960 he broke his thigh and his health declined progressively until his death on 7 June 1964 at Chertsey, Surrey, aged 87.

His cricket career apart, relatively little is known about Llewellyn. He remains a shadowy figure, a successful journeyman cricketer whose only legacy was a string of statistics and a few biographical fragments. It is highly unlikely that this will change substantially but it is possible to make some deductions about his life. He and his three brothers were undoubtedly, in terms of Natal's social custom, considered to be of mixed blood, although his family was apparently able to pass itself off as white. In late nineteenth-century Pietermaritzburg this would not have been difficult as the coloured community, few in numbers, was relatively well integrated. But race consciousness was deepening for a number of reasons and social custom was beginning to be reflected in law. The coloured population of Natal was small in both absolute and proportionate terms (in 1906 it amounted to 6 700 persons, or 0.6% of the total) so consciousness of his standing in the racial hierarchy is almost certainly likely to have been suppressed most of the time.

The *Natal Almanac* of the last years of the nineteenth century holds a clue to the question of Llewellyn's position in Pietermaritzburg. Population figures for Natal are given under three headings: European, Indians and Natives. But to the first heading is appended, 'including St Helenans, etc'.[45] Charles Llewellyn, in social if not official, terms was deemed 'et cetera', of another category; considered, grudgingly perhaps, a white man, but marked as different because of his mother's origins. The *Almanac* was a well-used reference tool, a compendium of annual information about the province and Pietermaritzburg, and this categorisation of the population would have been widely known.

In some respects, as suggested by Herby Taylor in his recollection, Llewellyn was a forerunner of Basil D'Oliveira, the coloured cricketer who emigrated to England in 1960 and represented England thereafter in 44 Tests. According to Taylor, his father and some of his Natal colleagues raised the money to send Llewellyn to Hampshire: 'In other words, he went to England on the same basis that Basil D'Oliveira did, and like Basil has done, he made a success of it. Mind you, I wouldn't say he was quite as educated or cultured as Basil is.'[46] In an age when it was by no means unknown for South Africans to play in county cricket, Llewellyn was different in that he emigrated, taking out British citizenship. In Brian Crowley's observation, 'Although there is no confirmed record of any strife with his contemporaries due to the colour of his skin, this fine South African player did not return to his homeland after a long professional stint but chose to remain in England.'[47]

Sensitivity about colour might have had something to do with Llewellyn's decision to leave South Africa permanently, but so did career prospects. Cricket was his one major talent, and there was simply no career open to him as a professional cricketer in South Africa. When he left Hampshire in 1910 it was to continue his professional career on more lucrative terms with Accrington in the Lancashire League.

For the 1903/04 season Llewellyn attempted to make a return to domestic first-class cricket in South Africa by playing for Transvaal in the Currie Cup tournament in Port Elizabeth in April, but he was barred by SACA on the grounds that he was a professional. Llewellyn, playing in the English off-season in the Transvaal and working as a clerk at the Wanderers Club, was selected by Transvaal, and taken down to Port Elizabeth, where a special meeting of SACA was hastily summoned to hear an objection against him. The objection was lodged by Western Province, which had historically been ambivalent towards him. Their claim was that Llewellyn had played for Hampshire as a professional in the previous English season and that 'he intends to return to them to continue in their employment as a professional during the coming summer'. Transvaal maintained that in South Africa

Llewellyn was an amateur cricketer, that he had played for South Africa against the Australians in the previous season as a bona fide amateur, that 'he has not and does not receive a penny piece for playing cricket in the Transvaal', and that after his next season with Hampshire he intended to settle in South Africa, the land of his birth. After an 80-minute discussion Western Province carried the day with support from Eastern Province and Griqualand West – Natal abstained – and Llewellyn was barred.[48] Llewellyn never again played first-class cricket in South Africa, nor did he play for South Africa again until the 1910/11 tour of Australia, when he, A.W. Nourse and A.E. Vogler were employed as professionals.

By then, Llewellyn had taken out British citizenship, prompting his former patron, Dan Taylor, and the Natal Cricket Union to protest against the inclusion in the Springbok team of a player who could no longer be regarded as a South African.[49] This was not a protest that Taylor and Natal had entered against Lieutenant Poore of the British Army, Llewellyn's team-mate, when the two had made their Test debuts in 1896. At this remove it is difficult to decipher the hidden agendas at work, but arguably for reasons of race and class as well as rampant provincialism, Llewellyn excited a distinct undercurrent of hostility within the South African cricketing establishment. None the less, at a time of variable fortunes for South Africa's Test team, his considerable skills as a cricketer dominated the thinking of various selection panels, at first for Test series at home, and then, when recalled in the twilight of his first-class career, for Tests abroad.

TURN OF THE CENTURY
Despite Llewellyn's appearances for South Africa a number of accounts suggest that racism was increasingly prevalent in cricket at the turn of the century. British soldiers remarked on the segregation in sport during the Anglo-Boer War, and an army officer who tried to include his black servant in a cricket team was given a lesson in local custom. At the Wanderers in Johannesburg black spectators were banned from the ground in spite of the written protests of Mahatma Gandhi in 1903. The issue flared up again during the 1905/06 England tour when the Transvaal Indian Cricket Union protested. The Wanderers Club tried to defer discussion until after the tour but it was pre-empted by a suggestion from certain members that a strictly segregated portion of the ground be reserved, with separate entrance gates. The proposal that this be tried over a six-month period was defeated and the experiment did not take place.[50]

Coloured players were in demand for practice sessions at white clubs and against visitors. Pelham Warner met the much-respected left-arm fast bowler C.J. Nicholls on the 1905/06 tour and commented on the frequency with which he knocked over his middle stump in the nets. During the tour Nicholls was paid ten sovereigns by England players to bowl on three successive afternoons of practice. He also worked at Diocesan College and was encouraged by Colin Blythe, another England player, to think about a career with Kent, but the consent of his guardian was withheld. He became a general factotum to white cricket, working at Newlands for Murray Bisset, the Western Province Cricket Club captain, coaching on the Western Front and organising service matches during World War I. Having made contact with the Australians, he served as baggage master for the 1919/20 Australian Imperial Forces team visiting South Africa and for subsequent touring sides. Legend has it that he once walked 30 miles to Paarl overnight having lost his train ticket, then opened the Roslyns bowling and took eight for 50. Sadly the wicket keeper had problems with Nicholls's pace and let through 65 byes, which lost the match.[51] If coloured cricketers were stigmatised, coloured spectators were a fixture at Newlands, traditionally supporting the visiting side.

In spite of increasingly unpromising conditions, black cricket existed in Potchefstroom and in Free State towns such as Bloemfontein, Rouxville and Kroonstad. In the Transvaal, the Transvaal Indian Cricket Union was formed in 1896 and two years later the Africans followed suit. By 1904 Transvaal was competing in the Barnato competition and there is evidence that in the first decade of the twentieth century there were matches between black (a politicised elite of land owners) and white (missionaries and ex-British Army settlers) sides in the Thaba Nchu area of the Free State. African opinion held that whites were respected more for having played blacks and sometimes losing, than for refusing to play them at all.[52]

Indian cricket, in Natal and the Transvaal, developed on an organised basis from the 1890s onwards, driven by the educated elite and traders. Some Indian clubs were religiously exclusive, restricted, for example, to Muslim players. The Durban and District Cricket Union was founded in 1896. There is no record of mixing with whites and this may be attributed to the virulent racism directed towards the Indian community, particularly those urbanised, free individuals known as 'Arabs'. In Natal, Indians were perceived both as disease-ridden and as a direct threat to a range of trades and jobs wanted by whites: they were 'taking up work which, in the climate of Natal, could be and should be performed by the white man'.[53] Sir Abe Bailey believed that Indians deserved no rights in South Africa and should be repatriated, encouraging the idea that they were not a permanent part of the population. Indians in general failed to live up to the standards of behaviour and obsequiousness required by Whites, and generally more antipathy was directed towards them than towards Africans.

Africans were treated paternalistically, but also often with contempt. A writer from Hilton College noted a tendency amongst schoolboys to 'be familiar with a Native one minute and kick him the next'.[54] The 1905 South African Native Affairs Commission chaired by Geoffrey Lagden attributed to Africans a number of unattractive characteristics and concluded that segregation was the appropriate solution to the 'Native Question'. Africans were uncivilised, lacked self-control and moral fibre and required a distant and heavy hand. Consequently, they were 'forbidden the sidewalk, footpath and public park'; and 'could not venture into most parks or watch sports contests on athletic grounds frequented by whites'.[55] Segregation was considered to be a liberal policy designed to guide childlike Africans to adult maturity.

The trajectory of both white and black cricket in nineteenth-century South Africa was virtually identical – schools, clubs, leagues, representative inter-town and finally provincial – but it functioned according to different time frames and was ultimately rigidly segregated. Ironically, had it not been for the Anglo-Boer War, South Africa would have played the West Indies at Lord's in 1900 and there were plans for a match with India at the same venue in 1904. On tour, black players were occasionally encountered amongst the opposition. In England, the Indian prince Ranjitsinhji appeared for several teams playing against South Africa from 1894 to 1904. But these matches happened at a reassuring distance from the social customs of South Africa. Historian Alan Cobley puts the situation into an economic and historical context in terms of the 'rise of a racially ordered industrial capitalist system in South Africa'.

Powerful figures in South African cricket in the first decade of the twentieth century such as Henry Nourse, Lionel Phillips and Abe Bailey, saw the game as a catalyst to bring together whites and heal the wounds created by the Anglo-Boer War. For a number of reasons this proved futile: for instance, Archer and Bouillon argue that Afrikaners who had played in significant numbers in the early days of the game were repelled by the founding of the ICC in 1909. But there were also scathing comments made by imperialists: 'The Boers . . . do not play the game according to Lilywhite.' And John Buchan, the novelist, believed that Afrikaners lacked a sense of fair play, the ultimate sin in British eyes.[56]

The significance of this situation is that Briton and Boer did occasionally meet on the cricket field, even during the Anglo-Boer War, whereas games involving black and white players were disappearing from the record from the 1890s onwards. After the battle of Elandslaagte (near Ladysmith) in 1899, Dan Theunnissen and J.H. Piton asked General Joubert if they could organise a 'return match'. The British authorities thought this unwise, but a cricket game was later played at Berea Park in Pretoria with the assistance of Robert Poore, the Hampshire batsman, by then the British Provost Marshall. Fighting was still going on just 50 miles away and the British won this encounter too. In the words of Bernard Wallach, 'Cricket is the great leveller, and hatred, racial differences and bloodshed were forgotten in the common love of the game.'[57] On the other hand, when Sarel Eloff, commanding the Boer forces besieging Mafeking, suggested in April 1900 that some of his men, in a spirit of amity, should participate in Sunday afternoon cricket and evening balls with their opponents, Colonel R.S.S. Baden-Powell, with free use of cricketing metaphor, turned him down.[58]

More emblematic was a match that involved a Boer prisoner-of-war camp at Diyatalawa in Ceylon. Inmates played against Colombo Colts, whose team included several Singhalese players, at the Nondescripts Ground, site of the present Colombo Town Hall. A local newspaper report described this as a match of no significance but it was, in fact, loaded with meaning. At the end of the match (Colombo Colts won by 141 runs) Commandant van Zyl called for three cheers for the Governor and the winners, which, according to press reports, were enthusiastically rendered and accompanied by the waving of hats. They also record the fact that a 'native' crowd, described as over-excited, invaded the field and was dispersed by police with the liberal use of canes. This match was played thousands of miles from South Africa but contains much that was symbolic of its cricket at the end of the nineteenth century including due respect to the imperial power and brisk, punitive treatment of unruly local people. Similar matches involving Boer prisoners-of-war were noted on St Helena and at Amritsar in India.[59]

In 1906, at a farewell function for the touring England team at the Mount Nelson Hotel in Cape Town, the Chief Justice of the Cape proposed a toast to the South African side. Cricket, he believed, had 'done a great deal . . . to bring the two great [white] races of South Africa together'. He was using the game unashamedly to promote the idea of federation, an event that would conspicuously ignore black South Africans, and the notion of white national identity. Sport continued to be significant terrain upon which the very nature of South African nationality was defined. Cricket was used to bind together disparate white communities while simultaneously excluding those of colour. World War I was the occasion for further rhetoric regarding white solidarity, notably from Abe Bailey: 'Sport has played a great part in creating a balance between the two great white races of this Country.'[60] In South Africa cricket was used to unify whites and separate them from everyone else, delineating social as well as geographic space.

2

The Segregation Era, 1910–48

THE PERIOD between the formation of the Union of South Africa in 1910 and the accession of the Nationalists to power in 1948 is often referred to as the segregation era in South African history. In this period a coherent ideology of segregation was developed, and a series of laws enacted to enforce racial segregation on the land, in the workplace, in the towns and in government. Under the Act of Union, passed by the British Parliament in 1909, the franchise was effectively restricted to white adult males in all provinces other than the Cape, and only whites were permitted to sit in Parliament. In 1936 the Representation of Natives Act removed Africans from the common voters' roll in the Cape. Major items of segregationist legislation passed in the interim included the 1911 Mines and Works Act, which imposed the industrial colour bar, the 1913 Natives Land Act, which segregated land ownership by restricting African ownership to the reserves, the 1923 Native (Urban Areas) Act, which enforced urban residential segregation, and the 1920 Native Affairs Act and 1927 Native Administration Act, which provided for the separate administration of Africans.

The period was also characterised by growing industrialisation and urbanisation; much segregationist legislation was indeed a response to the dual processes. The two World Wars, particularly the Second, with the need they created for import substitution, gave an enormous boost to local manufacturing. Industrial growth in turn hastened the movement of peoples, particularly blacks, from the countryside to the towns. Africans provided the greater proportion of the labour required by the expanding industrial sector, and the African drift to the towns has been described as one of the 'major migrations in the subcontinent'.[1] By the end of World War II, Africans constituted a majority of the urban population, accentuating the fear amongst whites that they would be 'swamped'.

White concern about numerical vulnerability – at Union whites numbered only 1.28 million of a total population of nearly six million, including four million Africans – their determination to preserve white supremacy and 'European civilisation' in South Africa, and the demand of the mining sector for cheap migrant labour based on subsistence in the rural reserves coupled with a wider capitalist demand for easily exploitable African labour, provided the broad underpinnings for segregation. It became the dominant ideology, with blacks regarded as children in need of trusteeship and protection from cultural undermining.[2]

Social activity in the country was governed by the 'colour bar', which was more a matter of custom than of law. Its operation served to exclude blacks from 'white' social institutions and activities, notably such things as sports clubs and competitions. But it was not simply a matter that whites and blacks very rarely played with and against one another. Black sport itself fragmented along racial, ethnic and religious lines, and in cricket that process was complete by the end of World War II. Coloureds, Malays, Indians and Africans all had their own separate clubs, unions and competitions. As Hassan Howa recalled of his early playing days in Cape Town: 'When I started playing cricket I found a very sad set up. Moslems played in one league, Christians in another, Indians in another. I couldn't fit in with the Malays, nor with the Indians, and so I fell in with the coloureds of the Wynberg Cricket Union . . . the conditions were highly discriminatory. One had to be a Christian before one could play for Western Province, one had to be a certain lightness and one had to be able to run a pencil through one's hair.'[3] There was similar fragmentation in Natal, at its worst in the later 1920s. In 1926 the Natal Indian Cricket Union, whose delegates were mainly Muslims, expelled Malays, pejoratively dismissed as 'Bushmen Muslims', from its ranks. Initially barred by the coloureds, the Malays formed their own union.[4]

WHITE CRICKET, BLACK MARGINALISATION
Amongst whites involved in cricket in the period after Union there was a desire, and even a missionary zeal in some quarters, to see the game spread widely in

order to bind white society together more firmly. Much was made of the healthy outdoor life led by many whites. Writing in 1927, the cricket administrator and chronicler, M.W. Luckin, advocated the involvement of country districts: 'Perhaps, if this . . . were more highly organised, we might very soon look to our Dutch friends to provide us with the much needed fast bowler.'[5] J.M.M. Commaille, who played twelve Tests for South Africa between 1909 and 1927, was likewise anxious to 'drive our national will in the direction of a great town and country coalition'.[6] There is no evidence that this happened. Indeed, just before World War II it was reported that 'the Boer element in South Africa is not vastly taken up with the game, although some of the papers do print reports of it in Africaans (sic)'.[7] The 1929 club cricket tournament in Johannesburg yielded 100 Smiths but a mere ten Van Tonders.[8] Big centre provincialism and inter-town jealousy, the lack of a consistent provincial competition, and the absence of activity in rural areas where most of the Afrikaans population still resided all conspired to obstruct cricket's development as a national sport. After World War II there was a gradual increase in involvement by the Afrikaans-speaking community; but there was no interest at all in developing potential among blacks. Cricket in South Africa remained an imperial game, anxious to include other white groups but deeply racist where blacks were concerned.

The image of Home still remained strong with some writers, including Luckin, whose motive for replacing matting pitches with grass obviously extended beyond simple playing conditions: 'When the grounds of schools and clubs . . . are to be seen dotted all over the country, and covered with beautiful turf, we shall be reminded of the picturesque playing fields and of the greens of the sweet little villages of England where the great game was cradled. Perhaps then we may catch something more of the spirit of cricket, with its ennobling and unifying influence, than has been possible under the pioneer conditions of the past.'[9] At the same time there was great concern about the size of South Africa and the ability of the organised game to transcend vast distances and involve a small, dispersed white population of about two million.[10]

Eric Louw, the South African High Commissioner to Britain, speaking to the British Empire League in 1929, praised the role of cricket not only in bringing together the whites of South Africa but in forging a national identity in the eyes of the metropolis. Another speaker made a point of the fact that an examination of the fingernails of the South African cricketers would reveal no trace of mixed blood.[11] The powerhouse of South African cricket between the wars comprised Old Boys clubs heavily populated with English-speakers. The clubs provided important connections between business and local government, thanks to which grounds and premises were financed by generous municipal grants. But an all-embracing white cricket nationalism had to wait until the 1960s; in the meantime cricket was nurtured by imperial sentiment.

White English-speaking cricket solidarity was extended to Rhodesians, even though they had decisively rejected incorporation into the Union in a referendum in 1923 by a vote of roughly 60:40.[12] The latter fraction contained the urban and rural establishments most likely to be involved with sport. Rhodesia had taken part in the Currie Cup of 1904/05 but participation then lapsed until 1929/30. Following Rhodesia's return to the Currie Cup, its players were considered for the South African team. In 1935 Denis Tomlinson was included in the Springbok team to tour England, together with Bob Crisp of Western Province, who had grown up in Rhodesia, and Sandy Bell, registered as a Rhodesian player.[13] From then on, South African Test sides frequently included Rhodesians. Commaille argued that 'in cricket matters Rhodesia is effectively an integral part of the Union. Moreover, there is much talent within the borders of this close and cricket-loving neighbour of ours, and no opportunity should be lost of extending the hand of fellowship and encouragement to her'.[14] Identical sentiments could have been expressed about black South African cricketers, but this would never have entered the minds of the inter-war cricket establishment.

In 1939, Lord Nuffield donated £10 000 to the South African Cricket Association (SACA) to be used for national development of the game. It was channelled into the Nuffield Schools Week and the donor expressed the opinion that 'I feel that tournaments of this nature will make the boys of South Africa just one big family, regardless of considerations of race or birth'.[15] The big family was, of course, all white, and the first tournament took place in Durban in January 1940. Subsequent tournaments went to Cape Town (1941) and Durban (1942) and all matches were played on turf. Imperial rhetoric continued to be paraded during tours by visiting Australian and English Test teams. In October 1949, the Mayor of Durban, Leo Boyd, at a function for the Australian team, spoke of 'common friendship in the free association of people called the Commonwealth', doubtless without any reflection upon the fact that South Africans from the African, coloured and Indian communities had no meaningful political rights, nor any hope of playing cricket for their country.[16]

The aim of white cricket between the wars was to be seen as the equal of England and Australia, but while South Africa had the better of England for much of the 1930s its record generally fell short of its ambition. In the 1920s, in which there were seven series, South Africa fared poorly. The national team paid two visits to England (1924 and 1929) and South Africa was visited twice by England (1922/23 and 1927/28) and once by Australia (1921/22). Springbok cricket was perhaps at its lowest ebb in the 1924 tour of England, when an ageing team lacking purpose battled to cope with turf wickets during a wet summer. The Springboks won only eight of 38 matches, losing the Test series 3-0 (two of the Tests being lost by an innings, the other by nine wickets before two rain-assisted draws were achieved), and had to call up G.M. Parker from the Bradford League. During the 1920s South Africa beat England at the Wanderers in December 1922 and again at the same venue and at Kingsmead in January and February 1928, but they could not win a Test in England and lost or drew all their series, including those at home, against representative sides.[17]

It was an inglorious record for a founder member of the ICC, very conscious of its standing amongst the three Test playing countries and aware that New Zealand, West Indies and India were pushing for Test status. The Natal administrator, H.L. Crockett, described South African cricket as 'very near the border line'. Brian Crowley sums up this era by pointing to the enormous gap between South African provincial and Test cricket, occasional individual heroics notwithstanding. The 1924 tour renewed lamentations about a population scattered across vast distances but it did result in a restructuring of administration at national level, with the business of the game between annual meetings of SACA conducted by a Board of Control. The board's first chair, A.C. Webber, portentously compared the Currie Cup to the Sheffield Shield, but admitted to the difficulty of reconciling the need to spread the game to smaller centres while deriving financial benefit from the larger ones.[18]

During the 1930s, South Africa's Test record improved as a wider spread of talent became available and the advantages of playing on turf became more apparent. Some of the controlling bodies, according to the journalist and cricket historian Louis Duffus, became 'not only solvent but in many cases opulent'. There were six tours: England visited South Africa twice (1930/31 and 1938/39) while South Africa visited England in 1935, played away and home series against Australia (1931/32 and 1935/36) and visited New Zealand (1932). During the 1930/31 tour Tests were played on turf (at Kingsmead and Newlands) for the first time and on matting (at Kingsmead and the Wanderers) for the last. South Africa won the series by virtue of taking the first Test at the Wanderers.

Their subsequent tour of Australia was disastrous because of the weather, Don Bradman, and spin bowling. The Test series was lost 5-0, South Africa going down in three matches by an innings. At Melbourne in the final Test the aggregate South African score was only 81 (just 69 off the bat) for the loss of 20 wickets, including eight ducks. Fortunes changed against New Zealand, whose Test history was a mere three years old at this stage, with victories at Christchurch and Wellington.

On the 1935 tour (which made a profit of £8 000) South Africa secured its first Test and series win in England through its victory at Lord's where Xenophon Balaskas took nine for 103 in the match on a damaged pitch. However, the spinners Clarrie Grimmett and Bill O'Reilly were too much for South Africa when Australia visited during the 1935/36 season, winning at Kingsmead (twice), Newlands and the Wanderers. South Africa lost 100 wickets in the series, 71 of them to the spinners (44 to Grimmett and 27 to O'Reilly). England won the 1938/39 series, which included the celebrated Timeless Test* in Durban, following an innings victory at Kingsmead in the third Test. This was the first time England had sent a full-strength team to South Africa. The planned 1940 tour of England was of course cancelled.[19]

Cricket survived in country areas between the wars, but it was dying on the margins in places like Mafeking and Vryburg. In the Orange Free State the only organised cricket was to be found in Bloemfontein, Bethlehem and Kroonstad. However, the key to the game lay in schools, the wealthier of which used English professional coaches. There are many examples: Grey College in Bloemfontein employed George Cox; and Kimberley High School boasted Frank Smith, Charles Hallows and Maurice Tate, although Tate stayed only briefly. In 1947 the United Tobacco Company, amidst concerns about standards, awarded white cricket £4 000 a year to employ coaches.[20]

The defining characteristic of South African cricket between the two World

---

* So-called because it had been agreed to play to a finish regardless of the number of days taken. In the event, after ten days of play (one washed out) over twelve days the game was abandoned as the England players had to catch their train to Cape Town in order not to miss their ship home.

Wars was the development of a racial hierarchy reflected in the organisation of the game that not only distanced black cricketers even further from the centre of power but divided them among themselves. This reflected the growing formalisation through segregation of racism in South African civic, economic, political and cultural life. In future, the only regular role blacks were to play in white cricket was as servants. For the rest, they were deliberately written out of South African sports history.

This relegation is reflected in the literature of cricket. H.W. Taylor of Natal, Transvaal and South Africa, writing in 1927 about the advantages of coaches, went on to extol the merits of ground bowlers for club cricketers: 'They might with° advantage employ coloured bowlers', apparently to provide decent length bowling. 'All the centres have to employ natives to work on the grounds. Why not pay a little more to coloured boys who can bowl, and let them do the ground work as well? I feel sure, apart from saving money, that this method would do infinitely more good in developing our batting.'[21] The scoreboard at Newlands was likewise 'operated by a team of coloured enthusiasts'.[22] Sir Pelham Warner believed that Africans had no inclination to play cricket, but wrote approvingly of the ability of coloured net bowlers and of the presence of spectators from various communities in Test match crowds.

The marginalisation of blacks occasionally slips, as if by accident, into the cricket writing of the era. One such example is provided by Louis Duffus, daydreaming about a match of the 1920s on the Reef:

Out in the centre of the oval Sixpence, the ground boy, is methodically rolling up the mat. As he wheels away the pitch he chants a tune of his kraal-land, a low-toned drawling song that his proud ancestors were wont to sing as night fell over the rolling hills of Zululand.

In another passage relating to schools cricket, Duffus describes 'the native, Jim Fish . . . pulling up the last strip of matting'.[23] These short extracts are very revealing, illustrating the contempt and aloof arrogance directed towards blacks. Neither groundsman is dignified by the use of his own name. Both are clearly lowly servants, working in white man's territory on a temporary basis, hundreds of miles away from home.

Some cricketers' memoirs revealed an amused condescension towards South Africans of colour. The morning after a dinner party at the Imperial Hotel in

Pietermaritzburg on the MCC tour of 1930/31, 'we lined up Tom, James, Harry and the rest of the Indian waiters in the Palm Court ' to receive tips: 'Long John our floor boy, a Bantu, provided us with much cheaper fun; he came forward for his tip, with head bowed and hands stretched forward but clasped as in prayer.'[24]

Jack Fingleton, the great Australian opening batsman of the 1930s and a journalist by profession, wrote with incredulity about the 'grotesque sight' at Kingsmead when it rained, of a long centipede of tarpaulin carried by Indians 'in native white dress'.[25] On 14 March 1939, the last day of the Timeless Test at Durban, 'At 3.15 pm an Indian came out with a tray of cool drinks'; while during the Natal match of that same MCC tour of 1938/39, 'a small army of bare-footed non-Europeans periodically sall[ied] forth, armed with brooms, to sweep away the water from the wicket covers'.[26] A more recent reminiscence of the Timeless Test recalls 'Groundsman Vic Robins and his trusty Indian foreman, the roly-poly Topsy (no one referred to him by his surname)'.[27] In white terms, inter-war cricket possessed a distinct hierarchy: coloured people could be useful net bowlers, scoreboard operators and tour assistants; Indians were at best waiters or assistant groundsmen; and Africans were unfailingly labourers. These relationships were to endure within the sport for several more decades.

For tours by England and Australia to South Africa, the 'unwritten gentleman's agreement', virtually from the outset, was that teams would consist entirely of whites, and evidently on one occasion the South Africans allegedly even insisted on England fielding an all-white team at home. No Aborigines in fact played for Australia – according to Sir Donald Bradman, none was good enough[28] – but two Indian princes, K.S. Duleepsinhji, a nephew of Ranjitsinhji, and the Nawab of Pataudi, played for England between the wars. It was alleged that during the Springbok tour of England in 1929 Duleepsinhji, who played against the Springboks in the first Test, was thereafter kept out of the England team because the South African team management, comprising H.O. Frielinghaus of Port Elizabeth as honorary manager, assisted by A.S. 'Algy' Frames, the SACA secretary and treasurer, objected to him on the grounds that he was Indian born. As related by Alan Ross in his biography of Ranjitsinhji, who closely mentored his nephew:

> One of the Selectors remarked to Duleep that the South Africans objected
> to his presence in the England side but Deane, the South African captain,
> got to hear of this and wrote to Duleep denying it. It was suggested that

the South African government was behind the objection. The rumours left a bitter taste and whatever the truth of the matter Duleep was not picked for the Gentlemen, though easily the leading amateur batsman of the moment. The suspicion grew that had Duleep played a big innings for the Gentlemen it would have been difficult to resist public insistence for his reinstatement.

Duleep was deeply upset. He was being totally supported by Ranji financially and was tempted to return to India and start work. Ranji, disgusted as he was over the situation, persuaded him otherwise.[29]

According to Sir Learie Constantine, the great West Indian player of the inter-war years, Duleepsinhji was told by the English cricket authorities that 'it was not the players but some South African politicians who could not face the risk of a century being scored against their team by a coloured man'.[30]

However, Rex Roberts and Simon Wilde suggest, in their short life of Duleepsinhji, that he was ultimately satisfied that the real objectors to him 'were situated not in South Africa but high in the English game and English society'. In several instances he felt himself discriminated against on racial grounds, though this was the most blatant.[31]

Duleepsinhji's treatment by the English selectors in 1929 remains an altogether murky episode. In the first Test against the Springboks, his debut for England, he scored just 12 and 1, but his scintillating form thereafter for Sussex justified his recall, and certainly his inclusion in the Gentlemen's Eleven. The main formal objection to him was that, by virtue of his Indian birth, he should not be allowed to play for England, although the broad consensus was that he qualified under ICC rules, having played for Cheltenham College, Cambridge University and Sussex, and that the precedent had already been set by his uncle.

When Ranji had first been selected to play for England against the Australians in 1896, the English authorities had taken the precaution of gaining the consent of the visitors, a step not taken in 1929. Whatever the reasons the selectors gave for not recalling Duleepsinhji for the later Tests against the South Africans, these seem to have been sanctioned by the MCC Committee. At any rate, at its meeting at Lord's on 15 July, in the midst of the third Test in Leeds, it considered a letter from H.D.G. Leveson Gower, the convenor of selectors and captain of the MCC in South Africa in 1909/10, regarding the 'selection of K.S. Duleepsinhji for England'. Duleepsinhji's exclusion from the remaining Tests against the Springboks

did not affect his selection for the MCC team to tour New Zealand at the end of
the season. On 18 June, the last day of the first Test against South Africa, the Cricket
and Selection sub-committee agreed that 'definite invitations' for the tour be sent
to fifteen players, including Duleepsinhji.[32] He played in all four tests against New
Zealand, that country's debut in the Test arena.

At the end of the South African series, Duleepsinhji was consoled by Aubrey
Faulkner, the great Springbok all-rounder and his one-time coach: 'I think it is
perfectly scandalous the way you have been treated by the English Selection
Committee. Your omission from the Tests is a blemish on English cricket.' An
anonymous correspondent was less charitable: 'You are not white you are not an
Englishman. So how can you play for England. Play with your black brothers from
India that's your place.'[33]

Duleepsinhji was evidently ruled out of the MCC team to tour South Africa in
1930/31, even though he had starred in the home series that summer against the
Australians, averaging nearly 60 in his seven Test innings. In the frank assessment
of cricket writer Thomas Moult, 'colour prejudice alone was responsible for his
exclusion'. Louis Duffus, who covered the 1929 tour, was equally blunt when he
later wrote in regard to D'Oliveira, 'England knew the law when a much greater
cricketer, K.S. Duleepsinhji, could have been chosen to tour this country. He was
not selected and nothing was ever said about it.'[34]

Two opportunities offered to the Springbok team to tour India were declined.
In 1928, with the formation of the Board of Control for Cricket in India under the
presidency of an Englishman, R.E. Grant-Govan, an approach was made to the
SACA to tour India after the visit to England in the following year. South Africa
might thus have become the first Test team to tour the sub-continent. SACA
temporised over the invitation, explaining that it needed first to select a touring party
then find out if its members were able to extend their leave. In the end the offer
was turned down on grounds of the forthcoming 1931/32 tour by South Africa to
Australia. Another request made by India in 1935 for a tour in the 1937/38 season
was rejected and an invitation from the Cricket Club of India for the South Africans
to be present at the laying of a foundation stone at Bombay was passed over.
Clearly relations with India were not a high priority among the SACA hierarchy.

FRAGMENTATION IN BLACK CRICKET

In 1902 the South African Coloured Cricket Board (SACCB, the 'Barnato

Board') had been formed with a view to unifying black cricket in South Africa; its constitution specified that it 'did not recognise any distinction amongst the various sporting peoples of South Africa, whether by creed, Nationality or otherwise'. The Barnato Cup, donated by David Harris of De Beers, in the hope of advancing the game amongst blacks, was contested only ten times between 1897 and 1930, and was won on every occasion but one by Western Province. The Barnato Board's zenith came just before World War I, after which rumblings of discontent were heard. In 1926 coloureds broke away to form the South African Independent Coloured Cricket Board and played for the Sir David Harris Trophy. This was contested on five occasions prior to World War II, and won by Natal, Western Province (twice), Eastern Province and Griquas.

This breakaway was followed in 1932 by the formation of the South African Bantu Cricket Board (SABCB). Its origins can be traced to Cape Town where five African clubs withdrew from the Metropolitan Coloured Cricket Union in 1928 and formed the Western Province Bantu Cricket Union on the grounds that they were not receiving equitable shares either on the field or in administration, a function of increasing social and physical segregation. The new board had close links with the mining houses of the Transvaal that employed many of the best African players. Their inter-provincial tournament, an annual event from 1932 until the mid-1970s, was contested for the Native Recruiting Company Trophy presented by the Chamber of Mines. Before 1946, Transvaal dominated the tournament, with Border having some success in the mid-1930s. In March 1940 Indian cricketers formed their own national union, the South African Indian Cricket Union (of which Rashid Varachia became the treasurer in 1942) with just two affiliates, from Natal and the Transvaal, competing for the Christopher Trophy for the first time in Durban in 1941.

The racial atomisation of South African cricket was now complete. A similar pattern was evident in British India, where, as Ramachandra Guha wryly concludes, competition between communities provided underlying encouragement for the game.[35] All over India competitive cricket was organised along communal lines, with teams composed according to race, ethnicity, caste or religion. But at least in India there was regular competition on the playing field, most notably in the annual Quadrangular tournament in Bombay that pitted against one another Parsee, Muslim, Hindu and European teams recruited from all round the country. In 1937 the tournament became a Pentangular, with a team of Anglo-Indians, Indian Christians and Jews comprising 'The Rest'.

Indian nationalists, and Mohandas Gandhi in particular, opposed the Quadrangular/Pentangular as an affront to the concept of a shared citizenship and as a symbol of British divide-and-rule tactics. As Hindu-Muslim relations degenerated rapidly in the 1930s, the tournament came to be perceived in certain quarters as a confirmation of the separate status of Muslims as a nation of their own, entitled to their own state when India became free. The fact that the Muslims won the tournament five times between 1934 and 1940 served to heighten the sense of Muslim nationalism. The players, however, generally denied any animosity, regarding themselves as sporting representatives of secularism. Matches drew large and enthusiastic audiences and the tournaments provided opportunities for play for cricketers from a wide spectrum of Indian society. Poor behaviour from crowds included inter-communal abuse, but star players were respected by all communities. As a counter to the communal character of the Quadrangular, the Ranji Trophy was inaugurated in 1934 for competition along inter-provincial lines.[36]

In the West Indies in the inter-war period, cricket was mixed but clubs had an unofficial ranking that reflected social class, although in Barbados lower-class black clubs had a separate competition.[37]

It is worth remembering that inter-war cricket in England, which at that stage in the sport's history was still very influential through the agency of the MCC, was strongly ingrained with privilege, cultural conformity and social differentiation. Issues surrounding class, race and authority remained basically unchanged between the wars and the existing order was accepted with an air of complacent superiority and deference to tradition. Cricket throughout the world was imbued with a sense of English morality and its attitudes: the game was a repository of fair play and conservative faith in the prevailing status quo, to which there was no sustained nor collective opposition. The rhetoric of cricket and its moral authority, together with its hierarchy, went unchallenged. In England the distinction between amateur and professional cricketers created its own version of segregation both at the ground and away from it. Power in cricket was intertwined with that vested elsewhere in society and, in the period between the wars, included a number of characteristics that may be described as feudal.[38]

In South Africa this translated into racial prejudice and discrimination. Sterling feats accomplished by black cricketers were ignored by the mainstream white press and thus written out of South African history, some of them possibly never to be retrieved. The African player Frank Roro, described as the 'W.G. Grace of African cricket' and considered to have been the premier batsman of the era, scored a century of centuries in senior club cricket that included an innings of 304 for Crown Mines versus Main Reef (a record in African cricket) and ten centuries in inter-provincial tournaments – 3 000 runs in all, an amazing achievement on matting wickets. At the age of 43 he made 228 against a Transvaal coloured team. Taliep Salie, a Malay spinner from the Cape Town club Roslyns, was considered to be the best inter-war black all-rounder. He turned down opportunities to play in England out of fear that he would not find mosques close to cricket grounds. In a Malay XI versus European XI match he took ten wickets in one innings, including those of 'Dave' Nourse, Xenophon Balaskas and A.W. Palm, all Springboks. His contact with foreign players was simply as a net bowler and Clarrie Grimmett, who encountered him on the 1935/36 Australian tour, believed he was good enough for Test cricket. He once hit 224 for Western Province versus Natal and was a good slip fielder.[39]

SEGREGATION AND UNEQUAL FACILITIES

For whites, growing urbanisation in the decades after Union brought with it enormous improvements in recreational facilities. White towns were favoured in the aftermath of World War I by arrangements that might well be described as municipal socialism. The difference between this development and similar trends in, say, Britain was that public funds were put at the exclusive, usually private, disposal of whites. As the historian C.W. de Kiewiet described it, 'the towns were expanded and beautified, and the amenities of modern life were introduced'.[40]

Whites benefited from the public fiscus in a number of ways: provision of land, development funding, granting of loans for the erection of buildings and land improvement, and annual grants-in-aid. In addition, municipalities built and maintained public swimming baths and parks. There was very little differentiation between the funding of private and public facilities, with most of the money in the latter category also going to whites, because none but a handful of 'liberals' would have included voteless and rightless blacks in the definition of the 'public'.

Under these favourable circumstances white cricket took a number of strides forward between the World Wars, which put an even greater distance between it and the game played by other communities. Perhaps the most significant was the introduction of turf pitches, which allowed white South African cricketers to come to terms with the game as it was played in other countries; although belatedly, as a result of a 'lack of administrative vision' together with a genuine fear that in South African conditions grass would struggle to stand up to the wear and tear. Matting wickets, while they produced exciting cricket, tended to encourage a lack of diversity: a reliance on spin bowling and back foot batting at the expense of the drive, described by Commaille as 'retrograde' and accounting for 'South Africa's crablike progression among those stagnant pools of cricket into which gravel and the mat have driven her'. H.W. Taylor ascribed the survival of matting wickets in part to Transvaal influence while Commaille blamed nostalgia for the era of South Africa's googly bowlers of the first decade of the century. The main proponents of turf were the administrators J.J. Kotze in Cape Town and H.L. Crockett in Durban.

Between 1926 and 1939 grass wickets spread from Test to club level amongst whites, making them competitive at international level. Grass wickets in South Africa required considerable investment in view of climatic difficulties: before the first Currie Cup match was played on grass at Kingsmead in Durban between Natal and Border on 16 December 1926, there had been four years of development entailing the then enormous sum of £800. During the 1927/28 season Natal played the MCC on grass in Durban and the first Tests played on turf were at Newlands and Kingsmead against England during the 1930/31 tour, although the other three took place on matting. The first Currie Cup match played on grass in Johannesburg was between Transvaal and Orange Free State in March 1935 and the home side scored a then record 609 runs in their first innings. When the England side of 1938/39 toured southern Africa, the only occasion it encountered matting was in Rhodesia. During this same season, Port Elizabeth was able to provide every first league match with a turf pitch and even Uitenhage, Grahamstown and Kowie had one each. Kimberley offered turf pitches in spite of the shortage of suitable land, persistent drought and high water costs.

At the time of Union in 1910, all the provinces had regulations providing for the creation and control of native locations, but it was the Native (Urban Areas) Act of 1923 that empowered local authorities to compel Africans to live in them. This legislation established a national norm and cemented the concept of the town as a white preserve. There was amongst whites a major concern about health and a fear of contagion from Africans and Indians that made segregation imperative. As the historian Maynard Swanson put it, 'urban segregation had become necessary to save both Africans and the cities from each other'.[41] Proclaimed urban areas were to be self-financing, operating self-balancing Native Revenue Accounts.

Amongst the statutory sources of revenue were profits raised on the sale of sorghum beer. The beer account later became chargeable only with specified expenditure, which included recreational amenities. This created the bizarre situation in which sports facilities were financed out of the profits of heavy drinking, and often drunkenness.

Policy on urban segregation followed the Rhodesian example of setting up 'native villages'. These were seen as providing security, the opportunity to control immorality and the context in which to inculcate a work ethic. Policy towards urban locations was governed by European perceptions. They were thus regarded not just as a means of controlling the African population but as a place of temporary abode, as all those living in them were assumed to have a permanent home in a rural reserve. There was, therefore, a predisposition not to develop and equip locations with the amenities increasingly enjoyed by whites. The argument that to make the locations too comfortable would encourage unwarranted assumptions about permanence was widely held and obstructed the development of facilities.

Thus South Africa's urban areas took on their characteristic duality in which a modern town was juxtaposed with a poorly equipped location, the buffer strip between them sometimes consisting of sports fields. Location recreation facilities frequently consisted only of streets, yards and waste ground. The desire of the residents of the townships to improve this situation was part of their struggle for 'recognition and acceptance'.

In the period between 1920 and 1960, in the city of Pietermaritzburg, over 85 per cent of all municipal grants-in-aid to sports bodies benefited the white community, and only 2 per cent of direct municipal expenditure in the same period was directed at the African township of Sobantu. As early as 1908, members of the Tuberculosis Commission, commenting on facilities in the townships, observed that the African urban dweller was there 'for the use and benefit of the town, and personally he derives very little, if any, advantage from any municipal improvements. Parks, baths, entertainments and such amenities do not benefit him in the least'.[42]

The popular white view of blacks in urban areas was of a transient population of agitators, liquor sellers, prostitutes and vagrants. But from the late 1920s municipal Native Affairs Departments began to accept the notion that the provision of sports facilities and promotion of organised physical recreation for Africans could be beneficial, controlling (sometimes described as 'moralising') leisure time, distracting attention from political involvement, instilling discipline and compliance and improving physical fitness. The Phelps Stokes Commission on Africa of the same era argued that blacks should be 'taught to play healthfully'.[43] The strategy appears to have worked: in the early 1930s Eddie Roux, the Professor of Botany at the University of the Witwatersrand and one-time member of the Communist Party of South Africa, complained that participation in sport lowered attendances at party meetings. Also in the 1930s, author Sarah Gertrude Millin crudely commented that 'even Kaffirs have their tennis and cricket and football clubs'.[44]

The pioneers in providing urban space for African sport were the Durban and Johannesburg municipalities. In the aftermath of riots and protests in Durban in 1929 and 1930, sports facilities for Africans were developed at Somtseu Road, and included a 'fully equipped cricket pitch', although a household survey showed that the game ranked third in the interests of the inhabitants after soccer and tennis. In Johannesburg the Bantu Sports Club, located on twelve acres of wasteland at the south-eastern end of town, was opened in 1931. By 1939 Johannesburg had an official African population of 230 000, fielding 60 cricket teams, but recreational space provided was only 8 per cent of that suggested by international standards.

In the Transvaal, the mines provided a high proportion of black sports facilities, with the mining companies positively promoting cricket among African clerks – the Chamber of Mines donating a trophy to this end in 1915. Cricket was more than just a game, it was employed as a diversion from potential political involvement, as a pastime likely to elicit loyalty to the mine, and as a mechanism for setting clerks apart socially from the rest of the black workforce.[45] In the 1920s, Philip Vundla obtained a job at Crown Mines as a clerk:

> It was a good post. Philip always claimed that he only got it because he was a good cricketer . . . he was expected to play cricket for the mine that engaged him. This was no hardship . . . his passion for cricket . . . took up most of his weekends. He was a good bowler and much in demand. On Saturdays and Sundays he would leave the house at eight in the morning and return about six or seven in the evening. His family came a very poor third.[46]

The locus of African cricket consequently shifted to the Transvaal: André Odendaal notes that on a Sunday in November 1932 there were 24 Transvaal Bantu Cricket Union league fixtures, most of them played at mines, but he also points out that Eastern Province players and administrators remained key figures.[47]

For the migrant workers who worked underground on the mines, 'war dances', athletics and soccer were encouraged as a means of promoting a fit and compliant labour force.[48] Although soccer was a relative latecomer amongst Africans, with origins in late nineteenth-century Natal stimulated by missionaries and the British Army, by the 1930s it had far outstripped cricket in popularity. The rapid proletarianisation of African society made this inevitable, and soccer established itself in the townships as a mass sport for spectators and players. In 1939 the Native Affairs Department was aware of 230 teams, and fixtures controlled by the Johannesburg Bantu Football Association could attract up to 20 000 spectators. The game was cheap and easy to play almost anywhere, so much so that teams migrated back en bloc to Natal from the Reef in the annual holidays.

Cricket, with its relatively more complex and expensive facilities, was less easy to transplant and the position of African cricket was further disadvantaged by its detachment from the 'non-racial' Barnato Board and its broader base in the black community. In the Transvaal it became identified with a narrow African chauvinism and with Chamber of Mines patronage. African cricketers were marginalised as a middle-class, socially conservative group, perceived to be relatively privileged. In the words of André Odendaal, 'cricket was welded into the lifestyle of the black elite of the mid-20th century'. Nevertheless, although in relative decline, African cricket had a national organisation and a provincial tournament, strong roots in both the urban and rural Eastern Cape, and clubs in Cape Town, Bloemfontein and Kimberley as well as in the Transvaal. Its presence in Natal was minimal, although the province was runner up in the 1938 NRC tournament. Cricket was also significant as a symbol of African aspirations; in the late 1930s the SABCB was optimistic about recognition by SACA and the MCC.[49]

Cricket among the Indian and coloured populations was likewise constrained by segregation, municipal regulation of land usage and financial niggardliness, as well as pervasive ill health. In Pietermaritzburg, for example, facilities amounted to little more than patches of waste constantly under threat from planned road or industrial development. In 1930, loans and grants-in-aid to these two communities for recreational purposes totalled just 0.05 per cent of municipal expenditure. Burrows's survey of health issues amongst Indian families at the beginning of World War II showed that nutritional standards were low, in part because of the high price of rice. Both malnutrition rates and the percentage of income spent on food were high; some people simply could not afford sufficient food and, as a result, 'children are often weak, under-nourished, and under-weight'.[50] However, middle-class Indians amassed enough capital to establish schools and develop social amenities, with the trader and educated elite prominent in cricket administration. In Durban, the City Council agreed to lease 23 acres at the foot of the Botanic Gardens to the Durban United Indian Sports Association on the understanding that the 'onus of laying out and equipping the grounds be upon the Indian Sports Bodies', and in 1932 the new sports area was opened as Curries Fountain. Thereafter Indian cricket in Natal positively flourished. As G.H.M. Docrat recalled: 'The best cricket was played in the 1930s and 1940s. There was a fantastic atmosphere. Everybody was interested.'[51]

RESISTANCE AND REHABILITATION

Disintegrative tendencies within black cricket between the wars may be attributed to growing racial segregation, political powerlessness, economic disability and social problems such as poor health, housing and diet. Black cricketers resisted their total subordination and marginalisation in three main ways. First, a limited amount of mixed cricket took place under the auspices of inter-race boards or at a social level. Second, black unions pestered SACA for fixtures against touring MCC teams. And, third, at the end of World War II moves were underway that would eventually lead to the reunification of black cricket.

Black cricket was not entirely atomised. From 1936 onwards, inter-race boards were active in the Transvaal, Eastern and Western Province and the Northern Cape, organising matches across racial boundaries. In the Transvaal a white team was involved. These mixed-race matches were forerunners of a national, non-racial federation for cricket.

As late as 1931, the African elite was still identifying cricket as a sport to play for social reasons. In that year the Bantu Sports Club opened in Johannesburg and a cricket match between Africans and Europeans watched by 15 000 spectators was held to mark the occasion.[52] Such events were rare, informal, symbolic, and formed no regular part of ordinary life. Higher education provided some inter-racial contact: cricket matches between Rhodes University College and Fort Hare, the university college for blacks in the Eastern Cape, were staged regularly during the inter-war years.

Other, specially arranged, matches took place from time to time. For instance, there is a record of a match between a Malay XI and a White XI including Dave

Nourse and Xenophon Balaskas in which the Malay spinner Salie took all ten wickets in an innings. In Natal, a similar match took place in 1930 at the Albert Park Oval in Durban where W.G. Brown's White XI beat a Moslem XI by five runs. Foster Bowley, later President of the SACA, recalled pre-war matches between white and Indian sides on the polo fields at Willowbridge in Pietermaritzburg, which also involved mixing for lunch.

On 1 January 1944, a South African Indian XI played a Transvaal Cricket Union XI in aid of the Bengal Famine Relief Fund at Old Wanderers. These were troubled times for Indian South Africans in view of the mounting pressure of segregationist legislation. Furthermore, they were not familiar with grass wickets. The High Commissioner for India, Sir Shafa'at Ahmed Khan, addressed the two teams at the Langham Hotel before the match and put forward an idealised view of the sports field as a place of equal opportunity. The drawn match featured the Test players Xenophon Balaskas, Sid Curnow and Len Brown for Transvaal. The Indian XI was captained by Essop Saloojee from Krugersdorp with Goolam Mahomed, the Natal all-rounder, as vice-captain; and included Mohammad Yusuf, who had scored 412 in 170 minutes for Schools CC versus Star CC in a Bulawayo league match in 1936/37, and A.I. Timol, one of the country's best wicket keepers. The *Rand Daily Mail* called the contest the match of the season, and held that the reputation of the Indians as good cricketers and fine sportsmen would ensure a big attendance of Europeans anxious to see the 'foreigners' in action.[53] The TCU XI made 284-7 (Frank Warne 65 not out; Ahmed Dababhay 3-52) and the SAICU XI 159-3 (Dawood Hassen 71) by the close. The amount raised was £1 000.

Author Tom Reddick recalled that in the late 1940s and possibly the early 1950s, 'before the tightening of laws I had been able to arrange the occasional cricket match against coloured players in the Cape'. The late Donald Woods, former liberal editor of the East London *Daily Dispatch*, reminiscing about De La Salle College, recalled: '. . . seeing our senior team playing against a local Indian cricket club invited by the Brothers for a friendly match. That was in 1945, and although it was considered unusual it was not against the law.' A tradition also developed of mixed benefit matches to assist black cricketers en route overseas, the most famous of whom was to be Basil D'Oliveira. Archer and Bouillon speculate that such residual contacts survived because a certain 'social distance' could be maintained.[54]

SACA's attitude towards cricket within the coloured and Indian communities was consistently patronising and dismissive. In 1931 the SACCB, the Barnato

Board, requested a fixture against the MCC team that was touring the country. The matter was discussed at a meeting of SACA on 23 February when the tourists were already in the middle of the fifth and final Test at Kingsmead. It was agreed that the 'request be not acceded to'. Four years later, the West Indies Cricket Board suggested a tour by a South African coloured team, to which SACA responded piously that it 'had no jurisdiction over coloured cricket in this country'. Legally speaking this was true, but SACA clearly exerted influence. In 1946, a request by the South African Indian Cricket Union (SAICU) for fixtures was turned down on the grounds that Currie Cup commitments and the forthcoming 1947 tour of England made them impossible. That year, a request from the Peninsula and Western Province Districts Cricket Board elicited a slightly more sympathetic response to 'the coloured and native fraternity' and the Board was advised to approach the Western Province Cricket Union, which was, in turn, urged to be helpful. However, in 1948, SAICU requests for matches against the MCC were again rejected.[55]

By 1944 the historically multi-ethnic Barnato Board had been revived, and from January 1945 moves towards the reunification of black South African cricket began. They were initiated by the Indian body under its president, veteran activist and cricket administrator the Reverend B.L.E. Sigamoney, who had been a strong supporter of the inter-race boards. The idea of an over-arching South African Cricket Board of Control (originally known as the South African Inter-Race Cricket Board) for all black cricket bodies began to gain support. As the era of apartheid dawned, black cricket was beginning to close ranks.

William Milton

Abe Bailey

The First South African Team in England, 1894

Standing: W.V. Simkins (manager), C.O.H. Sewell, G.S. Kempis, D.C. Davey, F. Hearne, C.H. Mills,
J. Middleton, A.W. Secull
Seated: T.W. Routledge, G. Cripps, H.H. Castens (captain), C.L. Johnson, E.A. Halliwell
Front: G.A. Rowe, D.C. Parkin, G.K. Glover

C.B. Fry and C.B. Llewellyn go out to bat for Hampshire, 1909.

South Africa vs England, Wanderers, February 1899

Standing: G.H. Shepstone, J.H. Sinclair, W.R. Solomon
Seated: J. Middleton, V.M. Tancred, M. Bisset (captain), H.H. Francis, R.R. Dower
Front: C.B. Llewellyn, G.A. Rowe, R. Graham

Boer Prisoners of War vs Colombo Colts

Back Row: Oosthuizen, C. Kotze, J. Coetzer, W. de Fransz, P. du Plessis, C.E. Perera, Tennant (umpire) A.C. Solomonsz (umpire)

Middle Row: J. Ludovici, C. Otto, S.P. Joseph, A. Smuts, T. Kelaart, Dunn, E.A. Joseph, A.T. Pollocks, J. Forsythe, Hilder

Seated: J. Heyzer, J. Kelaart, C. van Zyl, A. Raffel (Colombo captain), P.H. de Villiers (Boer captain), G. Sennett, L. Thomasz, J. Scheepers

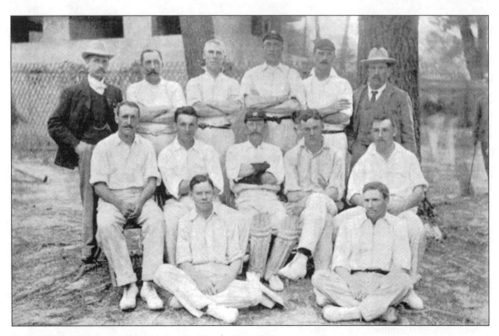

South Africa vs Australia, Newlands, November 1902

Standing: F. Hearne (umpire), J. Middleton, W.A. Shalders, C.M.H. Hathorn, A.W. Nourse, W.H. Creese (umpire)

Seated: L.J. Tancred, C.B. Llewellyn, E.A. Halliwell (captain), J.H. Sinclair, J.J. Kotze

Front: C.J.E. Smith, P.S.T. Jones

The First Cricket Springboks, England, 1907

Standing: A.J. Atfield (umpire), W.A. Shalders, J.J. Kotze, J.H. Sinclair, E.H.D. Sewell, G. Allsop, Rev. C.D. Robinson, A.W. Nourse

Seated: H.E. Smith, L.J. Tancred, C.M.H. Hathorn, A.E. Vogler, P.W. Sherwell (captain), J. Bamford, S.D. Snooke, G.C. White, G.A. Faulkner

Front: R.O. Schwarz

South African Team in Australia, 1910/11

Insets: T. Campbell, A.E. Vogler

Back Row: W. Bardsley, S.J. Pegler, C. Kelleway, C.B. Llewellyn, V.S. Ransford, C.O.C. Pearse

Second Row: W.W. Armstrong, A.W. Nourse, H.V. Hordern, L.A. Stricker, D.R.A. Gehrs, A. Cotter

Seated: J.H. Sinclair, V. Trumper, P.W. Sherwell (captain), C. Hill, R.O. Schwarz, W.J. Whitty, G.A. Faulkner

Front: S.J. Snooke, C.G. Macartney, M. Commaille, H. Carter, J.W. Zulch

K.S. Duleepsinhji

4th Inter-provincial Tournament, Barnato Trophy, Kimberley, March–April 1913

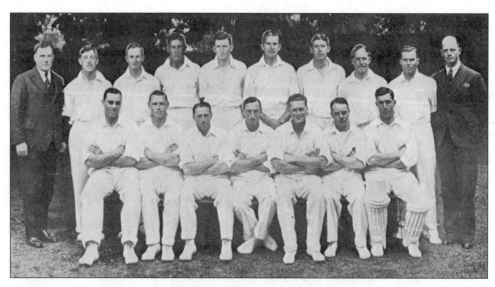

South African Team in England, 1929

Back Row: H.O. Frielinghaus (manager), H.G. Owen-Smith, B. Mitchell, D.P.B. Morkel, A.J. Bell, J.A.J. Christy, N.A. Quinn, Q. McMillan, E.L. Dalton, A.S. Frames (secretary)

Seated: I.J. Siedle, A.L. Ochse, H.W. Taylor, H.G. Deane (captain), R.H. Catterall, E.A. van der Merwe, H.B. Cameron

South African Indian XI vs Transvaal Cricket Union XI, Wanderers, January 1944

Standing: Hoosen Jabjhay (SAI manager), Hamied Khan, H. Maile (umpire), C. Jenkins, S.H. Curnow, G.M. Larkin, Goolam Mohamed, S. Marsh, S. Nicol, G.H.M. Docrat, M.Yusuf, J.L. Heaney, L.S. Brown, F. Burton (umpire)

Middle Row: C.H.K. Jones, X.L. Balaskas, F. Warne, Ahmed Dadabhay, Essop Saloojee, A. Gardee

Front: E.E. Dinath, M. Anthony, A.L. Timol, D.J. Chellan, Saley Asvat, Dawood Hassen, R.E. Somers-Vine.

3

Apartheid Cricket

IN MAY 1948, in perhaps the greatest upset in South African electoral history, Dr D.F. Malan's National Party and its allies defeated General Jan Smuts's United Party in the first general election after World War II. For only the second time since the formation of the Union of South Africa in 1910 an election had forced a change of government: the National Party, 'the hegemonic mass organisation of Afrikaner nationalism', was thereafter to win every general election and remain in control of government for the next 46 years, until South Africa's first democratic elections in April 1994.[1]

The fundamental policy of the Nationalist regime was that of apartheid, a comprehensive programme of racial and social engineering designed to entrench white control, supremacy and privilege and promote, by way of government intervention, the fuller segregation of the races. The general laws that underpinned the apartheid edifice were rapidly enacted. The Prohibition of Mixed Marriages Act of 1949 and the Immorality Act of 1950 made marriage and sex between whites and other race groups illegal; the Population Registration Act of 1950 allocated everyone to one of four racial groups, white, coloured, Indian and African ('Native' and later 'Bantu' in the terminology of the times); the Group Areas Act of 1950, which enforced residential and a significant amount of commercial segregation; and the Reservation of Separate Amenities Act of 1953, which enforced social segregation in all public amenities.

Apartheid reached into every corner of South African life, including sport. By 1948 South African sport was already thoroughly segregated. It was not only that whites and blacks did not play with or against one another on any regular basis, but also that most black sport was itself divided along racial lines. Once in power, the Nationalists made sporting segregation a matter of government policy, though they preferred not to enact specific laws to prohibit sporting engagements between whites and blacks; mixed sport itself was never made illegal in apartheid South Africa, except for boxing and wrestling, governed by the Boxing and Wrestling Control Act of 1954.

This reticence was partly the result of concern that an outright legal ban might compel international retribution. Instead, the Nationalist Government relied on the general laws on which apartheid was built to enforce sports segregation, notably the Group Areas and the Reservation of Separate Amenities Acts. At the height of apartheid, Proclamation R26 of 1965 issued in terms of the Group Areas Act would go so far as to prohibit blacks from watching sport in 'white' areas, except with the issue of special permits for particular events, and provided that separate seating, entrances and toilets were available. Otherwise government depended on the active co-operation of white sports bodies in maintaining their own traditions of segregation on the sports field, even if they had at times to be bullied into preserving this tradition. Segregation included selecting whites-only teams to represent South Africa in international competition and ensuring that visiting international teams were composed entirely of whites, and only played white teams.

For the South African Cricket Association (SACA), past practice regarding segregation moved seamlessly into an age governed by apartheid legislation. From SACA's standpoint there was a clear understanding that their traditional opponents, England, Australia and New Zealand, would select all-white teams to tour South Africa. For their part, the overseas cricketers who toured South Africa in the post-war era generally – although not universally – ignored both the racialism in South African sport, and apartheid itself. South Africa was still by no means unique. Though change was underway elsewhere – in 1947 Jackie Robinson became the first black to play major league baseball in the United States – racialism remained manifest in sport across the world.

What struck visiting cricketers was not so much apartheid or the racialism of South African cricket as the keenness of the competition, and the wonderful hospitality. In cricket circles, certainly, a tour to South Africa was particularly highly regarded. 'Perhaps I am biased about South Africa,' Denis Compton, the great English batsman who married a South African, recalled in his cricket autobiography, 'but I enjoyed myself there on tours more than anywhere else.' Bobby Simpson, the Australian batsman who first toured South Africa in 1957/58, concurred: 'A tour of South Africa probably can be as enjoyable as any cricket trip anywhere. The hospitality is tremendous.'[2] His team, however, was not at all impressed by what they saw of the facilities available for black cricket.

The fundamental change in the post-war era was in the organisation and playing of black cricket. Despite apartheid, the trend was to break down racial divisions, with the South African Cricket Board of Control (SACBOC), a federal body of the different ethnic organisations that had been founded in July 1947, developing into a 'non-racial' union.

However, SACA showed no interest in developing black cricket and, as it had before World War II, it maintained its policy of turning down requests from black cricket organisations for games against touring teams, declining the application for a game against the touring MCC in 1956/57, even though the representative side of SACBOC had just beaten the touring Kenyan Asians 2-0.[3]

CRICKET IN POST-WAR SOUTH AFRICA

The history of black South African cricket in the immediate aftermath of World War II must be contrasted with that of the inter-war years. The latter was an era in which the centrifugal forces of segregation, based largely on custom but increasingly on municipal regulations and statute law forced black cricket apart and destroyed its non-racial turn-of-the-century origins.

After 1945 these same centrifugal forces were augmented by apartheid law and National Party policy, a formidable barrier to integration. Yet new centripetal tendencies within national black politics, engendered to an extent by the war itself, had a profound and lasting effect on cricket and other sports codes.

For white South African cricket the late 1940s and the decade of the 1950s was a time of growing success, fulfilling forecasts made at the end of World War II that the sport would thrive. Before the war it had been a game representative of the English-speaking fraction of the white community and it still carried with it much imperial baggage. After 1945 this began to diminish, although at a reception for the touring Australians in October 1949 the Mayor of Durban made enthusiastic references to empire building and British heritage.[4] Commaille complained, revealingly, that the national team was unrepresentative and recommended a concerted effort to use the game for reconciliatory purposes between Afrikaans-

and English-speakers, even going so far as to advocate government subsidies.[5] Kaplan noticed a growing number of Afrikaans-speaking players at school and club level immediately after the war, and during the 1950s the number of Afrikaans clubs grew significantly, although it was only from the 1960s that cricket became a truly national white game.[6] In the meantime, Rhodesia continued to participate in South African domestic cricket and, by the 1960s, no fewer than eight of their players had won Springbok caps.

On the international scene, the Springboks struggled in the immediate post-war years. They lost the 1947 series in England 3-0, the 1948/49 home series against England 2-0, and received a thorough 4-0 drubbing from Lindsay Hassett's touring Australians in 1949/50. As Luke Alfred has detailed, the 1950s were central to the transformation of the Springboks from the whipping boys of Test cricket into a major force.[7] The first glimmer of something new was the 1951 tour of England when the Springboks, captained by Dudley Nourse, won the first Test at Trent Bridge, their first Test victory since the war and their first in England for sixteen years, before losing the series 3-1. The turning point was the 1952/53 series in Australia in which the Springboks twice came from behind to draw the series 2-2. The South Africans then went on to beat New Zealand easily in a two-match series. This was a particularly significant victory given that the team, captained by Jack Cheetham, had been considered by some to be too young and inexperienced even to leave South Africa. In 1953/54 New Zealand toured South Africa for the first time, with Cheetham's Springboks winning the series 4-0, greatly assisted by the fast bowling of Neil Adcock and the spin of Hugh Tayfield.

In the mid-fifties, two very closely contested series between South Africa and England – victors over Australia in the Ashes series of 1954/55 and 1956 – seemed to confirm that the Springboks were now a force to be reckoned with in international cricket. In the 1955 tour of England, the Springboks, captained for the last time by Cheetham, came from 2-0 behind to level the series, before losing the final Test at the Oval to the spin of Jim Laker and Tony Lock. During the 1956/57 MCC tour of South Africa, the Springboks, led by Clive van Ryneveld, again came from 2-0 behind, winning the last two Tests to tie the series. Although the Springboks succumbed 3-0 at home to the Australians in 1957/58, there was a new air of expectancy about their cricket.

In black sport the trend in the post-war era was to bring together in national competition race-based unions, leading ultimately to the formation of 'non-racial' units based on provinces or geographic regions. Cricket led the way. The first significant step was the revival in 1944, at the instigation of Transvaal, Western Province and Griqualand West, of the South African Coloured Cricket (Barnato) Board, which had promoted 'non-racial' cricket at the turn of the twentieth century. The South African Indian Cricket Union, under the presidency of the Reverend B.L.E. Sigamoney, took the initiative from 1945 onwards in setting up a proposed South African Inter-Race Cricket Board.[8] In July 1947 this emerged as SACBOC. In drawing together different strands of black cricket, SACBOC mirrored national developments in black politics symbolised by the Joint Declaration of Co-operation between the African National Congress, the South African Indian Congress and the Communist Party of South Africa. SACBOC embraced Indian, coloured and African cricket but, ironically, the Barnato Board distanced itself. It was eventually admitted as the South African Malay Cricket Board in 1953. To begin with, the administrators and cricketers of the South African Bantu Cricket Board were strong supporters of SACBOC, and there was great enthusiasm for 'Tests' between the different race-based unions. In the early 1950s there was still the occasional informal match between white and coloured teams in the Western Cape and whites and Indians in Natal.[9]

Under the auspices of SACBOC, which followed SACA in adopting the springbok as its badge, the 1950s proved to be something of a golden age for black cricket in South Africa. SACBOC's biennial tournament for the Dadabhay Trophy, initially similar to the old Quadrangular in India, was played on a racial basis in 1951, 1953, 1955 and 1958. A series of two-day matches took place at a centralised venue – in the case of the first three tournaments this was Natalspruit, near Johannesburg, a nominally Indian ground that hosted a great deal of inter-racial sport and a number of anti-government political meetings. The four tournaments played between 1951 and 1958 were shared 2-2 between the Indian and coloured sides.

'I loved playing for the coloureds against the Malays, the Indians and the Bantus in national tournaments,' Basil D'Oliveira later recalled.[10] The first match for the Dadabhay Trophy at Easter 1951 was between the teams of the Bantu and Indian boards and almost resulted in a win for the former, for whom Frank Roro, then aged 53, scored 116, the only century of the series. Quadrangular tournaments were also played at provincial level, and under the Eastern Province Cricket Board of Control a league was organised for the best clubs from the different racial groups.

Brian Crowley records that in the 1950s a number of South African doctors training in India played in the Ranji Trophy competition. Dr E.J. Bhorat of Stanger scored a century for Western India and Dr Aziz Kazee and Dr K.S. Naidoo of Pieter-maritzburg also played first class cricket in the sub-continent. In South Africa, Bhorat had played in the Christopher Trophy competition and for the South African Indian team.[11]

SACBOC unsuccessfully sought contact with India, Pakistan and the West Indies, but links were made with East Africa, leading to home and away tours. It is important to put these into context. To a significant extent they signalled compliance with Nationalist Government thinking at the time: black South Africans playing against other black nations, although policy was about to change. But they also symbolised a new sense of confidence and accomplishment in black cricket, emphasised by a picture of D'Oliveira on the cover of a cricket periodical above a caption reading 'South African cricket captain'.[12] And of course they took place just as the first intimations of a sports boycott became evident.

In 1956/57 a Kenyan Asian team visited South Africa in the first ever tour organised by a local black cricketing body (SACBOC). They played three repres-entative matches against multi-racial teams representing all four South African black communities, although Malay and coloured players predominated. Mixed trials and an integrated selection committee were set up. Amongst the touring party was Shakoor Ahmed, who had played for Pakistan, and a number of others who had participated in the Ranji Trophy in India.

The first 'Test' in Cape Town put onto the field for the first time a South African team representative of all its black cricketers, proudly described by D'Oliveira as 'the first multi-racial Springbok side'.[13] It was played at Hartleyvale, a soccer venue, on a matting wicket laid on top of gravel as neither Newlands nor any other white ground was available. Ahmed scored a century for Kenya in the first innings but could not prevent a South African win by six wickets. The second match was played at Natalspruit, where Salmodien Raziet registered the first century by a black South African for a national side. Ahmed made another for Kenya, but again South Africa won by 39 runs. The Durban match was played at Kingsmead, a white ground, and was marred by two days of rain that produced a draw. Under the captaincy of Basil D'Oliveira the 'non-white' South Africans had won their first representative series 2-0. Over the three matches Ben Malamba, with his off cutters, took 16 wickets at 15.25 a piece.

The Quadrangular tournament of 1957/58 was the last played: the coloureds beat the Malays in a match fittingly decided off the last ball of the final over. In 1958/59 a 'non-white' South African team, again under D'Oliveira's captaincy, visited East Africa. He described it as the 'proudest [team] ever to leave the shores of South Africa'.[14] Ten of the players were from Western Province, three from Natal and two from Transvaal and several of them, such as John Neethling at Colne and Owen Williams at Radcliffe, were later to achieve success in English league cricket. After losing the opening match against Kenya Asians by five wickets, South Africa won thirteen matches and drew three. The representative matches were all won – by 135 runs, seven wickets and 215 runs. One of the matches in Kenya was against a white side.

Following the fourth and last national inter-racial SACBOC tournament in Cape Town in January 1958, delegates met in the library of the City Hall to discuss full unification. After lengthy discussion, and encouraged by increasing flexibility amongst players (for instance Ben Malamba had left Langa to play for a coloured club that offered a higher standard of cricket) they accepted the motion of the Reverend Sigamoney, seconded by the rising star Hassan Howa, to abolish racialism in black cricket. The selection of a black South African team to play the Kenyan Indians had evidently helped to blur boundaries that had previously appeared rigid.[15] Fittingly, the first match under the new dispensation, in February 1961, was to be played by Western and Eastern Province in Cape Town at Green Point. Provincial and geographic boundaries thus replaced race, but the decision was not unanimous: the Malay Board abstained and the South African Bantu Cricket Board, although voting in favour, soon broke away. Fearing that SACBOC would not accommodate the needs of African cricketers, it retained its ethnic character, changed its name to the South African African Cricket Board (SAACB), and moved increasingly towards a relationship with white cricket. Otherwise, the Cape Town vote brought the organisation of black cricket into line with the non-racial ideals of the Congress Alliance. In 1961 SACBOC was reconstituted as a national controlling body of non-racial boards, although many clubs remained ethnically distinct.[16]

APARTHEID LEGISLATION

A major obstacle to integrated black cricket was found in the Group Areas Act of 1950. Its purpose was to control, in urban areas on the basis of race, the ownership of immoveable property as well as the occupation of land and premises.[17] It had a profound effect on residential patterns, and thus on cricket, in an era in which clubs were often based on defined suburban areas, or even specific streets. It also had a major impact on the right of individuals to play sport in particular areas. The government's demand for social segregation was directly at odds with the move, particularly amongst Indian and coloured South Africans, for integrated sport. The Group Areas Act built upon existing discriminatory legislation aimed at Indians, but it was the first major piece of legislation disadvantaging the coloured community. Social distance and territoriality were seen as the basis of self-sufficient, racially defined socio-economic units, although apartheid ideologues never did solve the conundrum that economic prosperity depended ultimately on some level of integration. As late as 1950 a government report mentioned the possibility of repatriation of the Indian community.[18]

Black South Africans were allotted to population groups in terms of their appearance, habits and way of life, descent and general social acceptance, and this determined the context in which cricket was played. In his study of Cape Town, John Western argued that 'one is one's address. In this way . . . group areas aid[ed] in racial definition.'[19] In a 1958 court case, the successful petition of an individual to be classified white was supported by eleven factors, one of which was admittance to the white section of sports grounds.[20]

The Act was not simply intended to preserve the status quo, it had the truly radical purpose of altering the occupation and use of urban land.[21] In legal test cases that arose out of the Act much hinged on interpretations of what constituted occupation of land for substantial periods of time; vagueness in wording was a condition that inhibited much social activity, including sport, in apartheid South Africa. A 1957 amendment to the Act concerned itself with occupation for a 'substantial period of time', although it was never ascertained whether this included a transitory event such as a cricket match. With tongue in cheek, John Didcott, one of the lawyers who grappled with this issue in the 1970s, advised that the legislation prejudiced batsmen who might score a century but favoured those out for a duck: 'The successful litigation strategy,' he advised, 'would be to bowl brilliantly, bat badly – and not to stay for tea.'[22] The amendment did, however, make it clear that consumption of refreshments fell within the ambit of occupation. An important consequence of the vague and convoluted nature of the Act was that it fixed in the minds of most South Africans, whites in particular, the idea that mixed sport was either entirely illegal or subject to official permission.

The Group Areas Act was first applied rigorously in the Durban area. The North Coast Cricket Association was dissolved in 1962 when Riverside and Prospect Hall became white group areas. Long standing clubs in Durban disappeared altogether, although some survived elsewhere: Clares of Mayville moved to Asherville when the former area was affected by forced relocation. Players tried unsuccessfully to maintain ties with old clubs from new suburbs like Chatsworth, but 'the task of rebuilding cricket cultures was a long and arduous one'.[23]

The municipalities decreed that each group area should be sufficiently provided with recreational space, but such new facilities were often shunned by communities contesting their right to continue to use grounds traditionally occupied by them. The Reservation of Separate Amenities Act, which regulated the use of specific public facilities and was enforced on the basis of individuals' appearance, also had an impact, especially where different black communities were playing cricket together.

During the post-war period a major problem created by apartheid legislation, especially group areas determinations, was uncertainty about the future: as Muriel Horrell put it, a sword of Damocles hung over whole communities.[24] Plans for group areas removal were drawn up years before they were implemented and this situation stymied development of all kinds, including the improvement of sports facilities. Black cricketers were frequently little more than squatters on their playing fields, and where facilities had been developed they were sometimes lost, often to industrial development, as racial demarcation of urban land gathered pace. Furthermore, South African apartheid law criminalised behaviour that in free societies would be regarded as totally normal. Laws regarding gatherings that might be construed as political demonstrations and concerning land use encouraged the interference of political police and state bureaucrats in activities as innocuous as cricket matches. Enforcement of the laws was not, however, without its problems. It was easy enough to establish a racial housing pattern, but more difficult to police the use of a sports field and open spaces. Ultimately the government never did find a definitive answer to this problem.

CRICKET AND THE BLACK COMMUNITY

Black cricket was also bedevilled by poverty and poor nutrition. A survey conducted amongst Natal Indians in the early 1950s revealed that only 27 per cent of them existed above the Poverty Datum Line and that unemployment was high.[25] A post-war survey of the Edendale Valley, west of Pietermaritzburg, noted a single cricket club in the Indian area of Mount Partridge, but commented drily that the game required 'relatively expensive equipment and properly kept grounds'.[26] As another survey laconically observed in the early 1950s, 'International sporting events have their Indian following but their interest, so far, is merely that of spectators.'[27] Nonetheless, educational, social and recreational facilities were established by the community, and administrative positions within sports unions were highly sought after, possibly by way of compensation for the lack of political rights. Leading administrators, who often remained in office for years, were generally conservative individuals, with radical politics where sport was concerned. Meetings were formal and long. Committees were called 'Cabinets' and positions on them often fell largely within the grace of the president.

André Odendaal's pioneering work on African cricket has demonstrated how it was strongly rooted in certain communities. He has documented a history in New Brighton near Port Elizabeth in the Eastern Cape stretching back to the beginning of the twentieth century and competitions that were at their height in the 1950s. Community roots included the heavy involvement of women, who, although they had their own club attire, were there largely to respond to the needs of male players, catering, sewing, washing and supporting. In the villages of the Eastern Cape, well-supported Christmas tournaments were held involving migrant workers back home from the Reef and other industrial centres. There was some disapproval of the Christmas tournaments on the grounds that they undermined the game played at a higher level – for example, the inter-provincial tournament dominated by Eastern Province in the late 1950s – and were sometimes so disorganised that financial irregularities occurred. Nevertheless, the social cohesion they represented was in strong contrast to the divisiveness in the Transvaal where a Mine Workers' Cricket Union was set up in 1953 at East Rand Proprietary Mine in an attempt to separate miners from their compatriots in the locations. While standards were maintained in the townships those on the mines began to deteriorate.[28]

In spite of many disadvantages, black players of stature emerged, although they were largely unknown to the white South African public. Apart from Raziet, Malamba, D'Oliveira, Neethling and Williams, other prominent names were Cecil Abrahams (who played for fifteen seasons in the Lancashire League for Milnrow, Radcliffe and Oldham and whose son, John, captained Lancashire in the 1980s) and the Abed brothers (Babu, Goolam, Dik, Lobo and Tiny) of Roslyns. Their success was all the more remarkable in the face of the poor conditions under which black cricket was generally played. In 1949, the Australian, Ray Robinson, wrote about unfenced playing areas, players changing on the field and wickets that 'no first class player would normally have set foot on, even if his life insurance was doubled'.[29] André Odendaal described black cricket's playing conditions as 'ignoble', and D'Oliveira recalled the Cape Town City Council ground with its 25 pitches with overlapping boundaries and one wooden hut for the gear.[30] When members of Ian Craig's touring Australian team of 1957/58 saw the facilities in Port Elizabeth (including a tram car converted into a pavilion) they were shocked. Significantly, SACA complained about this extra-mural visit and the Australian players were reprimanded by Jack Norton, their manager.[31]

Marshall Lee was one of few white journalists to show an interest in black cricket and although he wrote in the 1960s his descriptions would not have been out of place in the 1950s. At Queens Ground, Vrededorp, he described matting wickets and overlapping, glass-strewn outfields; lack of changing facilities and the problem of pedestrians crossing the field. Lenasia, he noted, had pitches called Gravel 1 and Gravel 2.[32] Colin Cowdrey, who described a South African tour as a 'safari by Rolls Royce' with 'overwhelming hospitality', recalled the pressure brought to bear to dissuade him from joining a township match.[33]

In the main, when black cricket was noticed by whites it was parodied as divided, fractious, of a low standard and governed by incompetent administrators. Players were stigmatised as political troublemakers. Dennis Brutus, a coloured schoolteacher and poet in Port Elizabeth, one of the strongholds of black sport, described this attitude on the part of whites as 'menacing'.[34] Leading black South African boxers and weightlifters tended to go into exile where some of them played a part in the anti-apartheid sports movement. Cricketers tended to spend a few years in the English leagues or trying to establish themselves in county cricket, and then returned home.

Black, particularly non-racial, cricket was ignored by the influential white press and thus effectively written out of history. At Test grounds black spectators could not be ignored in quite the same way, but they were confined by wire netting to a segregated section of the new Wanderers ground in Johannesburg and at Newlands by a six-foot high fence. As Alex la Guma noted, 'at the [Newlands] test match you were admitted at gate 5 which is the gate that admits coloured and Indian people'.[35]

The lowly position of blacks within the hierarchy of South African cricket, and of course within South African society as whole, was challenged in various ways, but one of the most public was vocal support for visiting teams up against white South Africa, a phenomenon as old as South African Test cricket itself. At its most voluble and passionate it involved shouting at the home players. On 26 December 1957, at the Wanderers Test of the 1957/58 Australian tour, black spectators booed and jeered the Springbok team. The Transvaal Cricket Union announced that it might raise prices in order to exclude an undesirable and unruly element.[36] This sort of behaviour was encountered more frequently at rugby matches and, in a satirical piece written in 1961, Alex la Guma describes a bottle 'flung from the Malay stand'.[37]

Demonstrations of this sort were not unique to South Africa and minor unrest occurred during Tests in Trinidad and Guyana from the mid-1960s to the late 1980s, when members of the local Asian community demonstrated their displeasure by supporting visiting Indian and Pakistani teams. This coincided in part with an Africanist phase in West Indian cricket as a whole.[38] Opposition to the white South African cricket team even extended to white political detainees held under the 1960 State of Emergency who lost their hidden wireless to the authorities when Joe Slovo, while listening to a Test match commentary, responded over exuberantly to the fall of a South African wicket.[39]

By the end of the 1950s the disintegrative influences on and tendencies within black cricket had largely been overcome, although African cricket had cut itself adrift, seeing its best interests served by a subservient relationship with whites. The reinstatement of non-racialism within black cricket was achieved just as apartheid legislation began to take serious effect. These diametrically opposed developments were not lost on the outside world; the eventual outcome was the growth of an international sports boycott of South Africa.

PART II

Exclusion from Test Cricket

4

Cricket and the Sports Boycott

FOR THE FIRST decade of Nationalist rule, international awareness of apartheid was limited, and criticism sporadic. The Sharpeville massacre of 21 March 1960 – when police opened fire on Africans protesting the pass laws, killing 69 people and wounding another 180 – changed matters. It was a watershed event. Internally, the apartheid state responded by clamping down on black dissent, proclaiming a state of emergency and then banning both the African National Congress (ANC) and the Pan Africanist Congress (PAC). Apartheid entered what some historians call its 'second phase', marked by intensified state repression and controls and the development of the 'homelands' system.[1] Externally, the apartheid state was subjected to an unprecedented barrage of criticism. Sharpeville generated a continuing international critique of the injustices and brutality of apartheid, and helped produce a sustained campaign to impose sanctions – economic, diplomatic, military and sporting – on South Africa. The government was henceforth under constant and growing pressure from abroad.

Two things ensured that the Sharpeville massacre would prove particularly damaging to the apartheid regime's position in the world. The first was the fact that it coincided with the success of the independence movement elsewhere in Africa. In international organisations, notably the United Nations, the newly-independent African countries took the lead in making apartheid a major issue of concern and campaigning for South Africa's isolation. In 1966 the newly-formed Organisation of African Unity (OAU) established the Supreme Council for Sport in Africa which lobbied internationally for the expulsion of

South Africa from the Olympic Games and international sporting federations. The second was the flow of exiles initiated by the security clampdown in the wake of Sharpeville.

Leaders of both the ANC and the PAC went into exile, as did many others who worked assiduously to secure South Africa's isolation and the ultimate destruction of apartheid. Among them were Dennis Brutus, who departed South Africa in 1966 after serving a term on Robben Island for breaking his banning order, and the young Peter Hain, whose family left for political reasons in the same year. They became lynch-pins in the sports boycott movement which aimed to have South Africa expelled from international sport on the grounds that Springbok teams were not representative of South Africa, but only of white South Africa. The sports boycott was to develop into the most extensive, sustained and effective movement of its kind in the twentieth century and in the end it succeeded in isolating South African teams from official international competition. Both abroad and within South Africa it reached or affected constituencies largely untouched by other anti-apartheid campaigns and by effectively 'denying the deniers', as Dennis Brutus phrased it, it forced the South African Government to make its first major concessions in its overall policy of racial discrimination and black exclusion.

Sport became the soft underbelly of the apartheid regime, which had politicised it by making sports segregation a matter of government policy, and in so doing opened itself up to the possibility of political counter-attack through sport.[2] The whole relationship between sport and politics in South Africa subsequently became replete with contradiction. The Nationalists, the arch-enforcers of segregation, insisted that segregation on the sports fields of the country was not a matter of law but of custom and tradition; that all they were doing was upholding the 'normal' state of play. When the then Prime Minister, Dr H.F. Verwoerd, prohibited Maoris from touring South Africa with the New Zealand rugby team in 1966, his Minister of the Interior, Senator Jan de Klerk, explained that this did not amount to 'political interference in a purely sporting matter': 'The Government was elected to oppose the various forms of integration, including social integration. It had to see that national policy was respected in the field of sport as in all other spheres.' It was consequently the anti-apartheid groups, with their 'ulterior' motives, who intruded politics into sport by challenging sporting segregation and promoting a sports boycott of South Africa.

Proponents of 'non-racial' sport in South Africa concurred that there was no law against it, and challenged white administrators to abandon segregation in their sports or face the prospect of international isolation. The response of white sports administrators with no taste for 'non-racial' sport, but mindful of their international vulnerability, was that they were simply observing government policy, and it was beyond their brief to venture into a 'political' confrontation with the government. For anti-apartheid activists sporting apartheid was inherently political, and the sports boycott constituted a political answer to the political intrusion into sport of the apartheid regime and the political decision of white sports bodies to hide behind government policy.

From about the mid-1950s onwards, the notion developed among certain anti-apartheid activists that by successfully striking against racialism in sport they could initiate 'a reversal of the whole political and social trend in the Union'.[3] Father Trevor Huddleston, the anti-apartheid Anglican cleric, was an early advocate of an international boycott of South African sport in the belief that it would begin unravelling the apartheid system. In *Naught For Your Comfort*, published in 1956, he contended: 'Just because the Union is so good at sport, such isolation would shake its self-assurance very severely . . . It might even make the English-speaking South African awake to the fact that you can't play with a straight bat if you have no opponents.'[4] Those who led the sports boycott thereafter shared Huddleston's sense that they were striking directly at the white South African psyche. In the opinion of Peter Hain:

> In the early 1960s, sport might have appeared an unusual choice for political protest, at best peripheral, at worst eccentric. But this was misunderstanding the whole white South African psyche. Whites were sports mad. Afrikaners were especially fanatical about rugby. Whether it was participation in the Olympics or a rugby or a cricket tour, international sport gripped the white nation as nothing else did – and more importantly granted them the international respectability and legitimacy they increasingly craved as the evil reality of apartheid began to be exposed by horrors such as Sharpeville. Moreover it was easier to achieve success through practical protest against sports links than it was to take on the might of either international capital or military alliances.[5]

As critics, cynics and hardliners saw it, it likewise became 'easier' for governments to demonstrate opposition to apartheid by lending support to the sports boycott rather than by embarking on costly trade sanctions.

To a remarkable extent, South Africa's sporting isolation in the decade after Sharpeville was the achievement of South Africans themselves. South African exiles, the Mauritian-born Chris de Broglio, and Reg Hlongwane, both weightlifters, together with Dennis Brutus at the head of the South African Non-Racial Olympic Committee (SANROC) in London, and later Peter Hain, chairman of the Stop the Seventy Tour (STST) Committee in Britain, spearheaded and co-ordinated the boycott. Their most useful ally was the apartheid government itself, which, through its stubborn and even provocative behaviour, hastened rather than hindered South Africa's progress towards sporting isolation. During Verwoerd's tenure as Prime Minister (1958–66), a rigid adherence to sports apartheid ensured isolation virtually of its own accord. The statement by Senator Jan de Klerk, in June 1964 that 'in no circumstances will the Government allow mixed sports teams to represent South Africa in international competitions' summed up the Verwoerd Government's unyielding attitude on sports apartheid and put the seal on South Africa's exclusion from the Tokyo Olympics later that year.

In 1966 the New Zealand Rugby Football Union (NZRFU) called off the tour of South Africa scheduled for the following year after Verwoerd, in his notorious 'Loskop Dam' speech, intimated that Maori players would not be welcome.[6] S.C. 'Billy' Griffith, the Secretary of the Marylebone Cricket Club (MCC), the governing body of English cricket, indicated that if the MCC ever found itself in the same position as the NZRFU, it would likewise cancel.[7] In an effort to avert a self-inflicted sporting isolation the assassinated Verwoerd's successor as Prime Minister, Balthazar Johannes 'John' Vorster, who, before his appointment in 1966 had established his reputation as a tough Minister of Justice, announced a new sports policy which would in future allow South Africa's traditional sporting rivals to send mixed race teams to tour the Republic. But his refusal thereafter to accept Basil D'Oliveira as a member of the MCC team to visit South Africa in 1968/69, led directly to South Africa's exclusion from Test match cricket.

Until the D'Oliveira Affair, South African cricket seemed to be weathering the sports boycott, and might have continued as part of international cricket for a good deal longer had it not been for Vorster's blatantly political intervention. 'SANROC', the *Rand Daily Mail* commented, 'could never have achieved results more to its liking'.[8]

ORIGINS OF THE SPORTS BOYCOTT

Within South Africa, the onset of apartheid after 1948 generated an upsurge in popular protest, and with it the beginnings of ANC mass action in the Defiance Campaign of 1952–53, which sought to mobilise mass defiance against unjust laws. It also generated new opposition political formations. In the aftermath of the defeat of the Defiance Campaign, the ANC came together with the South African Indian Congress, the South African Coloured People's Organisation and the radical white Congress of Democrats in the Congress Alliance, which, in 1955, adopted the Freedom Charter, embracing the principles of democracy and non-racialism. In 1953 the mainly white-led Liberal Party was founded on the platform of a qualified adult franchise and the fundamental principle of non-racialism.

The sports boycott had its origins in this internal challenge to racialism and white domination. More specifically, it had its origins in the movement of black sports organisations towards non-racialism and the black challenge – assisted from time to time by white liberals – to white domination of the country's international sporting recognition and representation. The central point made was that teams described as 'South African' were representative only of white South Africans, who comprised about a quarter of the total population; that they were not in the least bit representative of the country as a whole. The Nationalist Government agreed; South Africa's traditional international sporting relations were white sporting relations.

In the post-war era previously racially fragmented black sports bodies had begun to come together in national ethnically based federations and ultimately in 'non-racial' unions. Cricket was a pioneer in this process with the formation of the South African Cricket Board of Control (SACBOC) in 1947. In soccer the South African Soccer Federation (SASF), formed in 1951, brought together the majority of the racial associations – the South African African, Coloured and Indian Football Associations – in a single federation, with the notable exception of the South African Bantu Football Association. Between 1958 and 1962 the SASF was reorganised along 'non-racial' lines.[9]

Apart from the 'non-white' South African Table Tennis Board, which was given international recognition in 1956 in preference to the white South African Table Tennis Union, the new black national federations could not obtain international status. International federations recognised only one affiliate in each country, and recognition in the case of South Africa generally already belonged to white controlling bodies. In 1955 SASF applied to FIFA, the international football federation, for recognition, on the basis that it had far more members than the white Football Association of South Africa (FASA). Following the visit of a four-man delegation to South Africa, and FASA's deletion of the colour-bar clause from its constitution, the FIFA congress voted in 1958 to turn down the application. In 1955 SACBOC likewise unsuccessfully approached the Imperial Cricket Conference (ICC) for admission; the ICC response was that its constitution ruled out affiliation of two bodies from the same country.[10]

In response to this flurry of applications by 'non-white' sporting organisations for international recognition the Nationalist Government made its first major formal pronouncement on apartheid sports policy. On 27 June 1956 the Minister of the Interior, Dr Eben Dönges, announced that no mixed sport would be allowed within the borders of South Africa, that no mixed teams would compete abroad; that international teams competing in South Africa against white South African teams must themselves be all white, and that 'non-white' organisations seeking international recognition must do so through the recognised white organisation in a particular sport. If they wanted international contacts they would have to become subordinate affiliates of the national white controlling bodies that represented South Africa on international federations. 'The government', he added, 'will not issue passports for subversive non-white activity abroad, designed to change South Africa's traditional racial divisions by any process of eliminating white South Africans from international competition.'[11]

In promoting the idea of affiliation, the government's transparent desire was that black sportspersons would meekly accept a subordinate role within white umbrella bodies. At the time, affiliation was a subtle and convenient policy, which helps explain its longevity. For international consumption, affiliation encouraged a fiction that integration was taking place, while in truth it was designed to maintain the status quo and promoted a future based on white terms. When questions were asked about the continued existence of all-white teams, it was explained that blacks had not yet attained the necessary standard. As Reg Honey, the South African member of the International Olympic Committee (IOC), told an IOC meeting in 1960: 'There's no racial discrimination in South African sport; it's all lies; it's just that there are no blacks fit to take part in the Olympics. If there were they would be selected like everybody else. But they are running around wild.'[12]

The domestic purpose of affiliation was to sustain the myth of white superiority and maintain a social system in which blacks were treated as inferiors in receipt of privileges. Magubane makes the important point that it was crucial for whites to see blacks as an amorphous group. The danger of uncontrolled, non-racial sport was that 'from an undifferentiated mass of non-Whites [the black sportsperson] becomes known as individual'.[13] The affiliation policy was directed to ensuring that 'legitimate' black sporting endeavour could only take place within the parameters of apartheid.

The lure extended to black sportspersons included financial aid, coaching, training and the promise of international competition in separate teams. In 1961 the South African Non-European Amateur Boxing Association agreed to affiliate to the white South African Amateur Boxing Association (SAABA) on terms which guaranteed the white body's pre-eminence and respected the policy of 'separate development'; under the auspices of SAABA two boxing teams, composed of white and black boxers respectively, subsequently toured Rhodesia and the United States. In the event, no major 'non-racial' sporting organisation accepted affiliation.[14]

In October 1958 the emerging black challenge to white hegemony and racialism in South African sport took a major step forward when various black sports organisations set up the South African Sports Association (SASA) at a meeting in East London. The SASA agenda was wide-ranging. It aimed in the longer term to open up South African sport at all levels to non-racialism, but more immediately it sought to promote greater co-ordination and the principle of non-racialism among black sports bodies, to secure domestic and international recognition for them, and to ensure the rights of black sportsmen to represent South Africa. Dennis Brutus was installed as secretary and Alan Paton, the white author and liberal, was a patron and one of several vice-presidents. In January 1959 SASA held its inaugural conference in Durban.[15]

The charismatic Brutus was the driving force behind SASA. Born in Salisbury, Rhodesia, in November 1924, he grew up in the Port Elizabeth suburb of Dowerville in middle class circumstances; both his parents were teachers. In 1947 he graduated from Fort Hare, the university college primarily for Africans, with a degree in English and Psychology, and like his parents, became a teacher.

In 1961 he was dismissed from his post and placed under a highly restrictive banning order in terms of the Suppression of Communism Act for his involvement in anti-apartheid politics; in July he had helped organise the Malmesbury Convention, which sought unity between coloureds and Africans. Brutus moved to Johannesburg just before he was banned, enrolling, with ministerial permission, as a law student at the University of the Witwatersrand. In 1963 he broke his banning order by meeting a foreign journalist, was arrested and released on bail. Soon afterwards he was arrested on the Swazi-Mozambique border en route to an IOC meeting in Germany. Illegally handed over to the South African police – he was travelling on a Federation of Rhodesia and Nyasaland passport with a Mozambican visa – and fearful of disappearing without trace, he attempted to escape from custody in a Johannesburg street, but was shot through the back and left lying in the open for 30 minutes. The first ambulance to reach him was for whites only, and he had to wait until another one for 'non-whites' was summoned.

The *Rand Daily Mail* stated prophetically that the bullet that entered Brutus's back would ultimately damage white South African sport more severely than it had damaged Brutus. Eighteen months in prison ensued, including a spell on Robben Island. Placed under house arrest on his release, he left the country in 1966 on an exit permit to Britain. Both before and during exile his role as a poet was particularly potent, giving vivid and powerful expression to the frustration and deprivation experienced by black South African sportspersons.

Brutus was a shrewd politician, with a keen eye for issues and a dogged determination to pursue them and it was he who had the insight to see that sports apartheid was potentially acutely vulnerable to international pressure. The key, as he perceived it, was the Olympic Charter, with its prohibition of racial discrimination. While a student at Fort Hare he had encountered two outstanding athletes who had bettered South African records but who could never hope to represent South Africa at the Olympics because they were black. This so incensed him that he thereafter became determined to rid South African sport of discrimination, or else secure the country's expulsion from the Olympics. In 1956 he played a key role in attaining international recognition for the South African Table Tennis Board. Politically, as well as temperamentally, he was an independent, though his roots were in the Non-European Unity Movement and he actively associated with the non-racial Liberal Party.[16] The campaign against sports apartheid suited him because it was effectively under his control – a niche he carved out for himself.

Virtually simultaneously with the creation of SASA – Brutus described it as a 'happy coincidence' – the Campaign Against Race Discrimination in Sport was set up in Britain, and the two organisations rapidly became allies. Formed by Trevor Huddleston, Fenner Brockway, the veteran Labour politician, and others in 1958, the Campaign challenged the participation of all-white South African and Rhodesian teams in the Empire and Commonwealth Games in Cardiff that July. According to Antony Steel, the Campaign's secretary, in a letter to SACA, its purpose was not to get white South African sportsmen barred from international competition but rather to secure fair and equal treatment for all sportsmen regardless of race.[17]

The same spirit initially informed SASA, though with the caveat that if white South Africans failed to 'conform to the principles of international sport' they would ultimately be 'doomed to dispirited games of *jukskei* in their own backyards'.[18] The ultimate goal was non-racial sport in South Africa, and truly representative national teams, but as a means to that end it might first become necessary to exclude white South Africa from international sport.

For strategic reasons SASA's primary target was the Olympic Games; the Olympic Charter prohibited racial, religious and political discrimination against any country or person; the Olympics were already thoroughly political in nature, and they incorporated a large range of sports codes. A breakthrough at that level would be the trigger to breakthroughs elsewhere. Consequently SASA wrote to the IOC charging the South African Olympic and Commonwealth Games Association with practising racial discrimination and urging that South Africa be asked to cease violating Olympic Games principles.

In the wake of Sharpeville, the move to challenge racialism in South African sport rapidly escalated into a full-blooded campaign to impose a sports boycott on South Africa. In 1961 FIFA suspended FASA because of racial discrimination in South African soccer. In the next year SANROC was set up, effectively superseding SASA, to direct the campaign to expel the South African Olympic and National Games Association (SAONGA) from the IOC. Although SAONGA undertook to select a single team comprising both whites and blacks, and affirmed its acceptance of the principle of non-discrimination at the Games, it was barred from the Tokyo Olympics in 1964 for declining to renounce publicly apartheid in sport.

In the Olympic arena and in soccer, the support of the African, Asian and Communist countries was pivotal to building up the momentum of the sports boycott. While the IOC and FIFA were still dominated by (mainly) elderly white administrators and delegates from Western countries, many of whom, like Avery Brundage, the American president of the IOC, and Lord Exeter, the vice-president, were basically sympathetic towards white South African sportsmen and intent on keeping 'politics' out of sport, in the end they could not ignore the co-ordinated pressure of the Afro-Asian and Communist countries. That lesson was firmly underlined in 1968 when these countries acted to prevent South Africa attending the Olympic Games in Mexico City. The threatened boycott of the Games by nearly 50 countries prompted the IOC to reverse its decision to invite South Africa to Mexico City after the Vorster Government had conceded that a single team composed of both whites and blacks might represent the country.

Unlike the Olympics and soccer, which were genuinely world-wide in their reach, cricket and rugby were team sports with a more limited appeal, and the political dynamics within them were consequently different. Both were generally classified as 'imperial games', the preserve largely of countries that in the nineteenth century had been incorporated into the British Empire. Played and transmitted by the soldiers, civil servants, missionaries and settlers of the Empire, they had taken strong root in what in the early twentieth century became the white Dominions of the southern hemisphere – Australia, New Zealand, and South Africa. Outside of southern Africa they had made limited inroads in Africa, although cricket gained a firm foothold in East Africa largely through its white and Asian populations. At Test match level rugby developed as an overwhelmingly white imperial game; the International Rugby Board (IRB) comprised the four 'home' countries, England, Ireland, Scotland and Wales, together with Australia, New Zealand and South Africa. The one major Test-playing country without an imperial association was France, another white nation.

The truly imperial game in terms of both reach and identity was cricket, as was reflected in the name of the body that until 1965 controlled international cricket and conferred Test match status, the Imperial Cricket Conference (ICC), with is headquarters at Lord's and its administration provided by the MCC.[19] Unlike the case with the all white IRB, there were three black cricket-playing nations represented on the ICC; in the West Indies and on the Indian subcontinent the game introduced by white colonial elites had developed into 'the people's' game. Structurally, what further complicated the situation for SACA was that it automatically lost its membership of the ICC when South Africa became a republic outside the Commonwealth in 1961. None the less, in cricket, as in rugby, South Africa still had powerful friends abroad. What Christopher Merrett and John Nauright have called 'the imperial old-boy network', headed by the MCC, operated thereafter to protect the interests of white South African cricket within the ICC, described by Derek Birley as 'really MCC's Colonial Branch'.[20] As Dennis Brutus complained to the MCC at the time of the D'Oliveira Affair, it had consistently declined to give consideration to the grievances of 'non-white' South African cricketers, and had 'in fact been the staunchest in maintaining the rights of a racial body to participate in international cricket'.[21] In his estimation, the operation of the imperial old-boy network made cricket one of the toughest nuts to crack.

CRICKET

Although not an Olympic sport, cricket was soon high on the SASA agenda as, with soccer, it was one of the two major sports played by all racial groups in South Africa. Ironically, it was SACBOC's proposal for a 'Test' series against the West Indies that triggered SASA's intervention in the affairs of cricket.

The plan, conceived by SACBOC and approved by the government was for an all black West Indies team, captained by Frank Worrell, to tour South Africa at the end of 1959 to play all black sides. The government's stipulation was that seating at grounds had to be segregated as did any other facilities for spectators of different race groups. SACBOC applied to hold matches at Kingsmead, Newlands and the Wanderers as it had no turf wickets of its own. Conditions for the use of Kingsmead included specially erected corrugated iron dressing rooms and toilets, and there were also plans to erect temporary structures at Newlands.

The purpose of the tour, championed chiefly by SACBOC's Transvaal officials, Rachid Varachia, A.M. 'Checker' Jassat and 'Bree' Bulbulia, was to promote black South African cricket; show that it had players of Test quality; and demonstrate to the ICC that SACBOC was capable of organising major international tours. The team that was to tour was a formidable one, including such stars as Everton Weekes, Gary Sobers, Conrad Hunte, Alf Valentine and Sonny Ramadhin, and Worrell was convinced that the tour would prove of 'inestimable benefit to the Coloured people'. From the standpoint of C.L.R. James, the West Indies Marxist intellectual and cricket enthusiast, such a tour represented 'a brilliant political step'. In his opinion it would simultaneously have dealt a blow to racialism in the West Indies, where only whites were appointed as captains of the national cricket team, and to South Africa, by promoting black pride and embarrassing the apartheid regime. 'From the beginning,' he wrote in his celebrated book, *Beyond a Boundary*, 'I was certain that, whatever the South African Government might say, it did not want this tour. Racialists do not want the eyes of the world on their crimes.'[22]

From the standpoint of SASA, however, such a tour represented a capitulation to apartheid in that it would take place 'on the basis of racial discrimination' and would regularise apartheid in Test match cricket. White South African teams would continue to play Tests against white nations, and black South Africans would be confined to 'Tests' against black nations. In a letter to Varachia in February 1959 Brutus accused SACBOC of a lack of interest in real international status for black South African cricketers, an 'unwholesome provincialism and racism', and contempt for opposition to apartheid. In appealing to the West Indies Cricket Board of Control to intervene to stop the tour, Brutus urged that racially based matches compromised the aspirations of black South African cricketers, and that 'the tour by Mr Frank Worrell will be a grave setback to our hopes, and may defer them indefinitely'.[23] To the chagrin of Basil D'Oliveira and many other black cricketers, SASA played a central role in persuading SACBOC to call off the tour by engineering a threat that the ANC Youth League would disrupt games.[24] ANC leaders, among them Walter Sisulu and Nelson Mandela, also put pressure on SACBOC to cancel.

With D'Oliveira very much in mind as a prospect, SASA next turned its attention to SACA over the tour to England in 1960, inquiring whether 'non-white cricketers' would be considered for the trials. From Britain the Campaign Against Race Discrimination in Sport wrote in support, advising SACA that it knew 'of at least two Non-European cricketers in the Union who are first rate' and urging that they be included in the team so that it might be 'truly representative'.[25] When, in the event, only white players were invited to the trials, SASA wrote to all the players asking them to withdraw as 'non-whites' had been excluded.

Whereas SACBOC had conceded, SACA was totally dismissive. When Dennis Brutus spoke to the leading office-holders in SACA – Arthur Coy, as president, and the redoubtable A.S. 'Algy' Frames as secretary, he found them positively unhelpful. To Brutus's threat that he might persuade the MCC to take action against South Africa, Coy retorted 'Go ahead and try'. In a meeting at the Wanderers Club, where he long served as secretary, Frames told Brutus in his best avuncular style: 'My boy, if we were to include any blacks in our team to England there would be a riot.' When pressed about his sources, Frames responded 'Have you ever heard of MI5?' At the time, Frames was the longest serving senior administrator in international cricket, having been secretary and treasurer of SACA since 1927.

The tour of England by D.J. 'Jackie' McGlew's Springboks in 1960, in the immediate wake of Sharpeville, marked the birth of the campaign that would ultimately lead to South Africa's exclusion from Test match cricket. Altogether the tour was a miserable affair from the viewpoint of the Springboks, who might well have done with D'Oliveira's all-round skills. The weather was abysmal, the Springboks were lacklustre as they slid to a 3-1 series defeat, and Geoff Griffin, their fast bowler, was no-balled out of the series for 'throwing'. Of longer term significance was that the tourists were beset by the first bout of organised agitation in Britain against a visiting South African cricket team, a very different reception from those given the Springbok tourists of 1947, 1951 and 1955. The Reverend David Sheppard, the Sussex and England player and a member of the MCC Committee, refused to play against them, making his reasons public. 'I am sorry to say,' Ronald Aird, the MCC secretary, reported to Frames on 11 April 1960, 'that David Sheppard, who feels very strongly on racial matters, has today announced that he will not accept any invitations to play against the South African team, and he is giving his reasons why, which of course are not personal ones against any of the South African cricketers. He feels that by doing this he can express his sympathy with the coloured people in South Africa.'[26]

The demonstrations, and the call for a public boycott of the tour, were organised jointly by the Anti-Apartheid Movement and the Campaign against Race Discrimination in Sport, both founded in London in the previous year. The target of the Anti-Apartheid Movement was apartheid itself; racialism in South African sport was the more immediate target of the Campaign against Race Discrimination in Sport. While the demonstration that greeted the tourists at London Airport was dismissed by Aird as 'a very feeble affair' and *The Times* welcomed the Springboks as 'old friends', the cricket establishment was for the first time forced to confront the dual issues of apartheid and racialism in South African cricket. At the annual general meeting of the MCC Major Rowland Bowen, the editor of the *Cricket Quarterly* and cricket historian, 'regretted' that the South African tour of England had not been cancelled as a consequence of Sharpeville.

SASA played a central role in ensuring that the tour put the question of racialism in South African cricket onto the international cricketing agenda, persistently maintaining that the Springbok team could not be considered representative, and thereby qualified to play internationals, as it was selected on the basis of racial discrimination. Brutus carried out his threat by writing to the ICC to this effect, and urging it to turn its attention to racial discrimination in the national cricket body in South Africa. The ICC's response was, however, less than helpful. At its meeting at Lord's in July 1960 it referred the matter back to SACA as a 'domestic' issue between it and SASA.[27]

Central to SASA's challenge was that SACA practised racial discrimination of its own accord; that it was all white from choice; and that the exclusion of 'non-whites' from the national team was not imposed on it by law. Stung by a suggestion from A.W. Steward, the Director of Information at South Africa House in London, that this might indeed be the case as 'the selection of sporting teams was not a governmental matter', SACA wrote to the government for a directive. It was not only the national team that was at issue. Central, in turn, to SACA's standpoint was that selections could not be made in a vacuum. For black players to be considered for the national team they must first prove their ability in competition with whites at the provincial level, and black selection for provincial teams would necessitate 'the playing of Club cricket games between European and Non-European Teams'. On 16 June 1960 Dr Dönges, the Minister of Interior, who was himself a keen cricketer, responded:

> The Government does not favour inter-racial team competitions within the borders of the Union and will discourage such competitions taking place as being contrary to the traditional policy of the Union – as accepted by all races in the Union. The policy of separate development is in accordance with the traditional South African custom that Whites and non-Whites should organise their sporting activities separately. The inclusion of different races in the same team would therefore be contrary to established and accepted custom.[28]

To settle the 'domestic' issue between itself and SASA, the SACA Board of Control resolved at its meeting on 24/25 September 1960 to inform SASA of the government's decision. This was finally done in a letter dated 11 November, which declared that 'this correspondence should now cease'. But SASA stubbornly declined to accept the matter as closed as it failed to see 'why the normal administration of sport should be subject to Ministerial rulings or Government pressure'. In February 1961 SASA again approached the ICC, this time with the radical proposal that South Africa should be deprived of both its membership and its Test match status until such time as South African teams were truly representative.[29]

At this juncture South Africa left the Commonwealth and, with the country's loss of Commonwealth membership, SACA automatically forfeited its membership of the ICC. In July 1961 R.E. Foster Bowley, the SACA president from Natal, was invited to the annual ICC meeting at Lord's as an observer to oversee SACA's request for a change of rules to enable South Africa to remain a full member of the Conference. The request divided the ICC along racial lines, with the MCC, Australia and New Zealand supporting South Africa, and Pakistan, India and the West Indies in opposition. For the next three decades the issue of South Africa and racialism in South African cricket would continue to divide the ICC, with the cricket world threatening at different times to split in two between white and black.

Muzafar Hussain, representing the Pakistan Board of Control, insisted that any request from South Africa to be associated with the ICC should only be considered if SACA gave a clear undertaking that it would drop its attitude of 'exclusiveness' and would 'engage in international contests with all other Conference countries irrespective of colour'. The wider question of apartheid in South African teams, he suggested, might be postponed for later consideration. M.A. Chidambaram of India supported the general position of Pakistan, but J.B. Stollmeyer, the former West Indies captain of Portuguese descent, intimated that the West Indies Board of Control would first require SACA to give an assurance that it would promote 'multi-racial' cricket in South Africa. He challenged the Conference to declare itself opposed to apartheid in cricket.

In response, Foster Bowley offered nothing to assist SACA's cause. He advised that SACA had decided against challenging government policy by arranging inter-racial games as this would only invite the government to make them illegal, thereby preventing the occasional unofficial game, and while SACA would gladly send teams to tour Pakistan, India and the West Indies, it could not reciprocate by inviting them to South Africa. In sum, his message was that SACA could give no undertakings 'to take effective steps to remedy the existing situation' as this would involve it in 'politics', with potentially 'disastrous results'. The ICC subsequently deferred the question of South Africa's membership until its next meeting and, in the meantime, matches between South Africa and other member countries would rank as 'unofficial Tests'.[30]

At the next ICC meeting, in July 1962, the deadlock continued, with Pakistan opposing New Zealand's proposal that Test matches against South Africa be regarded as official until the membership issue was resolved. On the membership issue the cricket correspondent of *The Times* reported:

This is, to all intents and purposes, a straight political issue between on the one hand England, Australia and New Zealand and, on the other, West Indies, India and Pakistan. The President of the MCC could, in his discretion, exercise a casting vote. Yesterday however the status quo was retained with never a suggestion that the constitution of the conference might be altered to allow South Africa in.

What the white cricket-playing nations successfully insisted upon was their right to continue playing South Africa. Colonel Sir William Worsley, the MCC president, put it on record that it remained open for any member of the conference 'to visit or receive visits from any other country they liked'.[31]

This policy was confirmed at the 1963 meeting of the ICC.[32] A stalemate had been reached. The ICC's constitution would not be changed for the purpose of permitting South Africa's membership, but South Africa would continue to play against its traditional white rivals, England, Australia and New Zealand. The ICC's position was that these would rank as 'unofficial Tests'. For the 1961/62 New Zealand tour of South Africa 'Tests' were reduced to four days, the series being tied 2-2. However, when South Africa toured Australia in 1963/64 the Australian Board of Control for International Cricket made it clear that it regarded the series as 'official', with Tests being contested over the traditional five days.

As Foster Bowley acknowledged, South Africa received 'preferential treatment' from the ICC 'at the expense of member countries', remaining part of the official ICC roster of tours and thereby provoking some shows of displeasure from the West Indies and India. At the ICC meeting in July 1963 Frank Worrell of the West Indies, then engaged in a hugely successful tour of England and anxious for another, suggested that South Africa's scheduled short tour of England in 1965 might be deferred, as it was likely to prove embarrassing 'in view of the existing political situation'. When at the July 1966 meeting G.O. 'Gubby' Allen proposed the MCC draft programme of tours for 1969–72, which included a full tour of England by South Africa in 1970, both the West Indies and Indian delegates protested that this 'might be construed as an insult to full member countries'. Allen's retort was that South Africa was one of the oldest cricketing opponents of England, and that if cricket in South Africa was not encouraged by those 'allowed to play against them', the high standard there would deteriorate very quickly, with 'disastrous' consequences for cricket throughout Africa.[33]

The attitude of cricket administrators in England, Australia and New Zealand in the 1960s to playing with South Africa was aptly summed up by Jack Bailey, then assistant secretary at Lord's:

> The cricket world was strongly inclined to getting on with the game with South Africa – or anybody else – leaving politics to the politicians. It was, and always will be, an attitude of substance if your brief is the administration of your sport and the well-being of your sport and your penchant is loyalty to good, time-honoured and loyal friends, and if you believe contact is more productive than isolation.[34]

As Derek Birley observed, South Africa 'occupied a special place in the affections of the cricket establishment'.[35] Within that establishment there was a shared identity with South Africa, or, more particularly, with the 'British' population in South Africa, deriving from South Africa's role in the foundation of the ICC, the hugely enjoyable tours to South Africa, and the historic rivalries on the cricket field between the white cricket-playing nations; rivalries that were perceived as cementing bonds both between the white Dominions of the southern hemisphere and between them and the Mother Country. In MCC circles it was never forgotten that South Africa fought alongside Britain in the two World Wars, and that two Springbok cricketers, A.B.C. Langton and A.W. Briscoe, made the supreme sacrifice in World War II. Since the advent of the Nationalist regime, there had developed a special identity with white South African cricketers. Because they were mainly English speaking they were considered to be the pro-British, 'English', side of South African society which, itself, was being marginalised by Afrikaner nationalists who had demonstrated their anti-British and pro-Nazi proclivities when they opposed South Africa's participation in World War II.[36] The 'Englishness' of South African cricket was confirmed by B.J. Vorster himself when told that '*die Engelse*' had lost three wickets for 42 runs in a Test between South Africa and England. He responded: '*Hulle Engelse of ons Engelse?*' ('Their English or our English?'). Richard Thompson, the New Zealand sports historian and anti-apartheid activist was struck by the 'social, political and business relationships' that existed between the white segment of the international cricket establishment and South Africa.[37] These relationships were exemplified by C.J. Lyttleton, the tenth Viscount Cobham, captain of Worcestershire in the four years before World War II, president of the MCC in 1954 and Governor

General of New Zealand from 1957 to 1962. His mother was South African, and he had extensive banking interests in the country.

Politically, the cricket establishment in the white cricket-playing countries generally, and England more particularly, tended to the conservative. In the memorable 1950s observation of Sir Walter Monckton, a member of Harold Macmillan's Conservative Government, the right-wing opinions of the MCC Committee made the Cabinet appear like 'a band of pinkos'.[38] The MCC's official position was that it was intent on keeping the game 'above politics', which, translated, meant preventing political considerations from upsetting the status quo in world cricket. The dominant mentality in the white cricket establishment was that politics had no rightful place in sport. In this respect South African cricket was perceived as a victim of the political intervention of the apartheid regime, which prevented whites from playing against blacks; from this standpoint, to penalise cricket for the sins of the government was to compound the injury. As Gubby Allen put it to the ICC, to exclude South Africa from the ICC and international cricket was to 'support those in favour of apartheid, and to add to the difficulties of those who were anxious to help'. The official position of the MCC became that cricket ties with South Africa should be fostered as a form of 'bridge-building', that through cricket 'multi-racial' sport might be promoted, whereas isolation was purely negative.

In practice, little or nothing was attempted to counter the application of apartheid policy to cricket. With its position in international cricket protected by the operation of the imperial old-boy network, SACA felt no compelling need or desire to confront the issue. In the main, its affairs were in the hands of men who were at best timid and at worst reactionary, in dealing with matters of politics and race. Their mindset was that sport and politics did not mix, and that certainly SACA could not be expected to tackle or even undermine the government's policy in sport.

In 1968, when Donald Woods, the liberal editor of the East London *Daily Dispatch*, told a public banquet attended by some Springbok cricketers that the cricketers themselves should speak up in favour of non-racial cricket, there was an uproar in the audience. He was denounced for dragging politics into sport, and one of the Springboks walked out.[39] Into the 1960s the large majority of white cricketers simply had no interest in playing with their black counterparts on a regular basis, and many, indeed, were positively opposed to the prospect.[40] Blacks were still generally regarded as inferior, as was black cricket. The underlying fear, perhaps, was that black cricketers would dent the myth of white superiority.

Soon after SACA's departure from the ICC, there was a flurry of activity with a view to securing readmission, but anything that smacked of a challenge to government was rapidly abandoned. The tactic adopted by Foster Bowley was to attempt to satisfy Pakistan's demand that South Africa should signal its willingness to play against all member countries of the ICC. As he impressed on the members of the SACA Board of Control, the time for 'trying to sit on the fence' was over and 'we should state our position in relation to playing the non-White countries as soon as possible, and in precise and definite terms'. He consequently wrote to Pretoria for a ruling, and was advised by the new Minister of the Interior, Senator Jan de Klerk, that the government would 'certainly frown upon cricket competitions between White and non-White teams within the Republic, irrespective thereof that one of the teams was from abroad'. There was, however, no objection if 'a White team from this country competes against a non-White team in another country'. Thus armed, Foster Bowley urged that SACA 'tell MCC that within the bounds of that ruling, we are prepared to play any of the non-White Countries'. His naive conviction was that such a gesture would 'pave the way for our re-admission in the Imperial Cricket Conference'.[41]

The main initiative in terms of domestic cricket came from Eric Rowan, the former Springbok batsman, who proposed that 'Non-European' clubs should affiliate to the existing provincial unions. In submitting his proposal to the Transvaal Cricket Union (TCU) in October 1961 he warned: 'The time has come to safeguard ourselves against the future'. What he envisaged was that 'Non-European' clubs would continue to run their own leagues, but under the jurisdiction of the TCU, and that matches would be arranged for them against visiting overseas teams. In March 1962 the TCU Board, after 'considerable discussion' and the expression of 'diverse views', referred the matter to SACA as 'this question involved the whole country'.[42]

At this point the Minister of the Interior intervened. On 30 March, in the midst of IOC deliberations on South Africa's participation in the Tokyo Olympics, he issued a statement reiterating the government's opposition to mixed sport within the country, and mixed teams either touring South Africa or representing South Africa. With regard to administration, he affirmed it was government policy 'that non-White associations exist and develop alongside the corresponding White associations'. The notion of black clubs affiliating directly to a white provincial union did not correspond with government policy, even if the leagues remained separate.

For the SACA Board of Control that was the end of the matter of 'Non-European' affiliation, and the TCU was advised that 'there was no point in pursuing the matter further'. However, Dawie Marquard, the long-standing Free State delegate with impeccable liberal credentials, believed the Minister's statement constituted a clear signal that, unless altered, government policy was sentencing South African sport to exclusion from international competition. 'It is clear to me,' he impressed on his colleagues in a letter dated 26 April, 'that all sports will have to fight to keep their place in international sport, and that the SACA should take the lead in organising this fight.' What he proposed was a meeting of representatives of all the major white sporting bodies in South Africa to thrash out the whole question of the relationship between whites and 'non-whites' in sport and to decide on what steps to take, including an approach to government. It was too bold a move for his colleagues to countenance. At its May meeting the SACA Board of Control responded that 'it was not for this Association to take the initiative in this matter', although it did authorise Bryan 'Boon' Wallace, the Western Province delegate, to have 'an informal talk' with the president of the South African Rugby Board, Danie Craven, to ascertain the views of the board. Their discussion later in the month did not progress beyond the Rugby Board's own primary concern with the racial composition of visiting touring teams.[43]

SACA's loss of ICC membership did not make it any more receptive to SACBOC, now organised on 'non-racial' lines, and SASA. To SACA's dismay it received, in January 1962, a letter from A.M. Jassat, the honorary secretary of SACBOC, proposing that representatives of the two bodies meet to discuss the possibility of a merger. A copy of the letter had been sent to the MCC and the move was perceived by Foster Bowley as a ploy on the part of SACBOC to replace SACA on the ICC 'in the hope that we would turn down their proposal'. Given government policy, he could not see how they could possibly consider a merger, and urged that SACA should stall for time by requesting more precise information. To SACA's evident relief, SACBOC did not respond to the request for more information.[44] SASA's challenge in 1963 to the racial composition of teams during the Nuffield week, the annual inter-provincial schoolboy tournament, received short shrift; government policy simply did not allow for whites and 'non-whites' to play together.[45]

These challenges clearly highlighted once more that it simply was not true that SACA was the helpless victim of the political intervention of the apartheid regime.

SACA was at least a willing collaborator with the government in enforcing segregation on the cricket field, and white cricket generally showed no interest in promoting black cricket or in pursuing the notion of non-racial cricket. The point was further underlined when, as a follow up to Eric Rowan's suggestion that the TCU move to affiliate 'Non-European' clubs, the 'non-racial', effectively Indian, Pageview Cricket Club applied at the beginning of the 1963/64 season to affiliate to the TCU and play in its senior league.

The chairman of the Pageview Club, S.A. Haque, was well-acquainted with Springbok player John Waite. He purchased his cricket equipment from the sports store run by Waite and, in 1961, Waite led a 'White' team, including four Springboks and six provincial players, against Haque's combined 'Non-White' team in a match that Haque's team had won by 20 runs. In 1963 the success of Haque's team was not a consideration; all that counted in the eyes of the TCU was government policy. After sending a deputation to the Secretary of the Interior in Pretoria, the TCU advised the Pageview Club that 'in view of the Government policy the application for affiliation could not be accepted'. Haque responded by writing to the MCC and other international cricketing bodies to complain that the TCU '*voluntarily* carries out the Government's policy of apartheid in spite of the fact that racially mixed cricket is *not* illegal', and called on them to suspend South Africa from all international cricket should the TCU and SACA 'refuse to change'. The response of Billy Griffith was to advise the Pageview Club that he was referring the matter to SACA, as the TCU was under its jurisdiction. 'Sorry to worry you with this,' he wrote to Algy Frames on 6 November, 'but I always find these letters extremely difficult to deal with as one does not want to appear completely unaware of the problem.'[46]

In the international arena, regular tours to and from South Africa continued after SACA's departure from the ICC, and they did so with limited controversy and disturbance. Before the 1961/62 New Zealand tour of South Africa the New Zealand Cricket Council (NZCC) simply ignored SASA's appeal not to send a team to South Africa on the grounds that it 'would be playing against teams which represented only the White section of the population', and refused even to receive a deputation from the Canterbury Association for Racial Equality to discuss racialism in South African cricket.[47] During the tour Gordon Leggat, the New Zealand manager, did agree to meet Dennis Brutus to discuss apartheid and cricket, but his main complaint concerned the financial consequences for the New Zealand team of the campaign, 'Operation Sonreis', mounted by Brutus and SASA to persuade black sportsmen and spectators 'not to support any form of racial sport'. 'I can tell you we are losing on the tour,' Leggat informed Brutus, 'and this is one thing which will not endear you to people in New Zealand.' He dismissed the notion that New Zealand should have declined to send a team to South Africa: 'You would only be depriving a group of players of the game and you would not be doing yourself any good. You would be punishing players who are not *allowed* through *no* fault of their own to play with Non-Whites.'[48]

For the 1963/64 South African tour of Australia and New Zealand, not only SASA but also a former Springbok captain, Clive van Ryneveld, proposed that the team be selected purely on merit. In Van Ryneveld's view, any worthy 'non-white' should be selected, even if the government prevented him from touring by denying him a passport. Rather than adopt such a confrontational approach, the Springbok captain for the tour, Trevor Goddard, requested and was granted a meeting with Prime Minister Verwoerd on how to handle questions about sport and apartheid; as a bonus he also received a briefing on Verwoerd's fifteen year plan for the country.[49] The tourists encountered some protests, chiefly picketing, and the pitch at Wellington was damaged before the Test there. However, the Australian Prime Minister, Sir Robert Menzies, an ardent cricket follower and a great friend of white South Africa, told Goddard he hoped for a Springbok victory so as to 'clear away all this nonsense about your Test matches being regarded unofficial'.[50] The Springboks tied the series with Australia 1-1, gaining a famous ten-wicket victory at Adelaide largely as a consequence of the outstanding batting of Eddie Barlow and Graeme Pollock. All the Tests against New Zealand were drawn.

The 1964/65 MCC tour of South Africa passed without incident, England taking the series 1-0. Some members of the touring team met SACBOC representatives in Kimberley and, in response to a query about the chances of their being considered for associate membership of the ICC, the team manager, Donald Carr, 'suggested that they should always work in conjunction with and under the auspices of the South African Cricket Association'. He reported back to the MCC that this suggestion had been accepted.[51] The return tour of the Springboks to England in 1965 again generated protest action, co-ordinated by the Anti-Apartheid Movement. The protests were largely overshadowed by the brilliant cricket played by Peter van der Merwe's South Africans, who captured the imagination of the

British cricket-watching public in the process of winning the three-match series 1-0. The Anti-Apartheid Movement complained that 'the press was generally unsympathetic to our campaign although local newspapers gave widespread coverage to action taken in their areas'.[52]

The Australian tour of South Africa in 1966/67 produced a rumpus over umpiring, but not over the inclusion in the touring party of the dark-complexioned Graham Thomas, who claimed to have Cherokee blood in him but who was evidently the descendant of a runaway slave from the American South. As no Maoris or Aborigines had previously played cricket for their countries, the question of their selection for teams to tour South Africa had, unlike the position with All Black rugby, never arisen as an effective issue, and Thomas was not regarded as Aboriginal. Prior to the selection of the Australian team for South Africa, Sir Donald Bradman, then chairman of the Australian Board of Control for International Cricket, sounded out Thomas about how he would feel if he did not go. Thomas, a hard-hitting batsman who had made his Test debut in 1965, was adamant that he wanted to go, and was duly included. Before the team was announced, however, Prime Minister Menzies checked on his acceptability to Pretoria by showing some photographs of Thomas to the South African ambassador to Australia. As Menzies recalled to his close friend, Jack Fingleton, the journalist and former Australian batsman:

> I told him it was understood that Thomas had some Red Indian blood, though anybody who looked less like a hawk-faced Red Indian I could hardly imagine. The ambassador told me . . . that he thought there would be no difficulty whatever, the objection on the part of his people being to people who presented what he called a 'negroid' appearance.[53]

Thomas did not feature in any of the Test matches in South Africa. The Springboks won the series 3-1, their first ever series victory over Australia, and were coming to be regarded as one of the two foremost teams in the world, the other being the West Indies.

In playing terms, white South African cricket had entered its golden era. Since World War II, the number of those playing the game had more than doubled, and increasingly the newcomers to 'white' cricket were Afrikaners. Cricket ceased to be the game largely of 'die Engelse', and was becoming a truly national sport. The acceleration in the rate of Afrikaner urbanisation and their massive advance into the middle classes exposed them more and more to 'English' influences, and the very success of the Springboks in the field generated a nationalist enthusiasm for the game. In 1965 the first Afrikaans version of the 'Laws of Cricket' was published.[54] Cricketing siblings Peter and Graeme Pollock commented at the end of the Sixties in their book, *Bouncers and Boundaries*, that cricket in South Africa was 'booming', and 'perhaps the most pleasing feature is the manner in which the Afrikaner has adopted this game'.[55]

Black cricket, for its part, went into a shallow decline in the 1960s. The Dadabhay Trophy was contested five times during the 1960s, still on a centralised basis with two-day matches, but now inter-provincial and non-racial. The first inter-provincial tournament was held in Johannesburg in 1961 and won by Transvaal. Seen as a success, it involved eight centuries, of which Ivan D'Oliveira was responsible for the highest. Subsequent tournaments were held in Port Elizabeth, Durban, Cape Town and Kimberley, and the title was won by Western Province three times and shared on another occasion with Transvaal. Increasingly, black South African cricketers, like their counterparts in boxing and weightlifting, had to go overseas in order to succeed at a high level. In addition to Basil D'Oliveira, a number of SACBOC cricketers played in the Lancashire and other leagues in England and a few had matches for county second XIs.

On the international scene, the West Indies alone stood between the Springboks and world cricketing supremacy, and in the euphoria that followed the South African triumph over Australia Rothmans Cigarettes proposed to the MCC that Rothmans underwrite a two-Test series between South Africa and the West Indies in England in 1968. In advancing the proposal Rothmans, in the person of M.J. 'Tienie' Oosthuizen, the UK managing director of the Carreras Tobacco Company, of which Rothmans was a subsidiary, failed to take into account the implacable hostility of the West Indies to apartheid. While the MCC thought that 'from a cricket point of view' the proposal had merit, the West Indies Board of Control was 'unanimously opposed'.[56] Nor was the South African Government impressed by the fact that the proposal was made by Rothmans, part of the tobacco empire of Anton Rupert, the Afrikaner tycoon and supposedly a loyal member of the Afrikaner Broederbond, the all-male secret society of Afrikaner intellectuals and professionals. The new South African Prime Minister, B.J. Vorster, expressed his annoyance at the fact that 'tobacco companies and other interferers' were meddling with the functions of the National Party and creating trouble 'where trouble never existed'. Frank Waring, the former Springbok rugby player and United Party MP, who Verwoerd had installed as the country's first Minister of Sport and Recreation, added for good measure in a statement that reverberated around the world: 'If whites and non-whites start competing against each other, there will be such viciousness as has never been seen before.'[57]

In the midst of the euphoria over the Australian tour SACA officials were fully conscious that the next scheduled tour of South Africa, by the MCC in 1968/69, might not proceed as smoothly, or even proceed at all, given government policy. White South African cricket had, thus far, both willingly conformed to the government's apartheid policy and comfortably survived all attempts to secure its international isolation. But there was one major potential point of vulnerability, government policy on the racial composition of visiting teams. Politically it was becoming virtually impossible for South Africa's traditional rivals to continue to select all-white teams to tour the Republic. This was underlined in 1966 when the New Zealand Rugby Football Union found itself obliged to cancel the tour of South Africa for the following year after Verwoerd indicated that, as in the past, Maoris would not be welcome.[58] The major challenge to South Africa's discriminatory policy was to come in the form of Basil D'Oliveira, the South African-born coloured who was now playing for England.

In SACA's view, the '80-year-old unwritten agreement' between itself and the MCC that the MCC would select whites-only teams for tours to South Africa still existed.[59] The three Asian princes who played for England prior to World War II – the great Ranjitsinhji, his nephew K.S. Duleepsinhji, and the Nawab of Pataudi – had evidently all been overlooked for tours of South Africa.

According to Vorster, in the post-war era, the Anglo-Indian Raman Subba Row who had played four Tests against South Africa in England in 1960, had deliberately been left out of teams to tour South Africa.[60] This was not in fact the case. Subba Row's Test career fell between the MCC tours of South Africa in 1956/57 and 1964/65. D'Oliveira's Test career for England began in June 1966.

Basil D'Oliveira learnt the game of cricket in the narrow streets of Bo-Kaap on the slopes of Signal Hill and on the uneven grounds of Greenpoint Common in Cape Town and, determined to 'make his name' in cricket, had gone to England in 1960. Frustrated by the apartheid restrictions that consigned him to the margins of cricket in South Africa, and bitterly disappointed at the cancellation of the West

Indies tour in 1959, he seized the opportunity arranged by John Arlott, the strongly anti-apartheid BBC cricket commentator, to play for Middleton in the Lancashire League. In 1964 he was signed by Worcestershire, qualifying thereafter both as a Worcester player in the county championship and as a British citizen. In order not to prejudice his chances as a professional cricketer in England, D'Oliveira lied somewhat about his age, later confessing that he was already 35 when he first appeared for England in the Lord's Test against, appropriately enough, the West Indies; he was fighting age as well as race.[61] A dynamic all-rounder he enjoyed an excellent series, shining in the middle-order as a batsman and as a medium-paced bowler. He was an obvious candidate for the tour to South Africa.

Billy Griffith had already warned that the MCC would follow the example of the NZRFU and cancel the tour rather than accept restrictions on team selections. To help clarify the situation, and to brief him about their own situation, SACA invited him over for part of the Australian series. On his return to Britain, Griffith reported to the MCC Committee that he had been warmly received, had watched some 'magnificent' cricket, and had some 'interesting' discussions with SACA, which was anxious to be readmitted to the ICC now that it had changed its constitution to become the International Cricket Conference with associate members outside the Commonwealth. He apparently warned SACA that if any preconditions were laid on the selection of the MCC team the tour would not take place, but also gained the impression from unofficial talks with 'a leading Government official', Dr Dönges, that by the time the team was selected 'the attitude towards multi-racial sport might have changed for the better'. When asked by Crawford White of the *Daily Express* whether an MCC team with D'Oliveira in it would be accepted in South Africa, Griffith replied, 'this is a matter that must be left until the situation arises'.[62]

The situation did indeed arise and when it did, in 1968, it spiralled out of the control of all the major parties concerned.

5

The D'Oliveira Affair

THE 'D'Oliveira Affair' of 1968 marked the turning point in South Africa's relations with the international cricket world. In the view of many at the time – and since – Basil D'Oliveira (who, in the ensuing months would become widely referred to by headline writers and newspaper readers as 'Dolly') warranted inclusion in the MCC team to tour South Africa in 1968/69 when it was first selected on 27 August 1968. The fact that he was not included caused an uproar in Britain; the allegation was that the selectors had not chosen the team purely on merit, but had instead capitulated to South Africa's apartheid government, which would have refused to admit an MCC team with D'Oliveira in it. The situation was further complicated by the fact that when, on 16 September, Tom Cartwright, a medium-paced bowler, dropped out of the team through injury, D'Oliveira, initially regarded by the selectors purely as a batsman, was immediately selected in his place.

B.J. Vorster, the South African Prime Minister, represented this decision as a capitulation by the MCC to political pressure from the anti-apartheid movement, and he refused to accept a team which, he alleged, was no longer that of the MCC, but had become the team of 'the anti-apartheid movement, the team of SANROC, and the team of Bishop Reeves [the anti-apartheid former Anglican bishop of Johannesburg]'. 'Whereas we are and always have been prepared to play host to the MCC,' Vorster announced at the National Party congress in Bloemfontein on 17 September, 'we are not prepared to receive a team thrust on us by people whose interests are not the game but to gain political objectives which they do not even attempt to hide.'

The consequence was that the tour was cancelled by the MCC and a huge impetus was given to the movement to exclude South Africa from Test match cricket. As the *Rand Daily Mail* predicted, '[Mr Vorster's] decision to bar not only Basil D'Oliveira but the MCC team as a whole means, without a shadow of a doubt, South Africa's exclusion from the world of Test cricket.'[1] Within three years that exclusion was effectively complete. Following the tour by Australia in 1970, South Africa did not play Test cricket again for 22 years.

Despite the vast amount of literature on the D'Oliveira Affair, two questions have for long remained unanswered and matters of speculation.[2] The first is, would Vorster have accepted D'Oliveira as part of the MCC touring team had he been selected in the first place? The second is, if not, was this made known to cricket administrators in South Africa and England, including the MCC selectors, and did it influence the decision not to include him?

The opening of relevant government records in the South African National Archives, Pretoria, and The National Archive, London, have made it possible to answer the first question with certainty, and to come closer to an answer to the second. As is evident from the Cabinet minutes and other documents of the Vorster Government, D'Oliveira would never have been accepted as part of an MCC team, and this information was conveyed to officials of SACA and, through them, to officials at Lord's, the headquarters of the MCC. Precisely how this information was handled at Lord's remains something of a mystery. Following the announcement of the MCC team, without D'Oliveira in it, Vorster phoned Arthur Coy of SACA to congratulate him on the satisfactory resolution of 'our respective problems'. Coy wrote back: 'The inside story of the two final meetings held by M.C.C. I hope to have the privilege of telling you when the opportunity presents itself.'[3] Although the full 'inside' story of the selectors' meeting on 27 August, and of the MCC Committee meeting the next day to ratify the team, still awaits a public telling, the essentials can now be conveyed.

D'OLIVEIRA AND VORSTER

After a debate in the House of Assembly on the D'Oliveira Affair on 21 April 1969, in which Vorster simply evaded all questions, John Wiley, the opposition United Party MP for Simon's Town, dropped a note to Frank Waring, the Minister of Sport and Recreation, asking 'if the MCC had selected him in the first place, would he have been allowed to come to S.A.?' As a postscript Wiley added: 'My own view, for what it is worth, is that you would have accepted him.'[4]

Wiley's view was wrong. At its meeting on 27 August 1968, the day the MCC selectors met to decide on the team to tour South Africa, the Cabinet resolved, '*M.C.C. kriekettoer 1968/69. As D'Oliveira gekies word is die toer af*' ('If D'Oliveira is chosen the tour is off').[5] The hand-written minute book, effectively a record of Cabinet decisions, contains no details of the discussion, though according to Ben Schoeman, the Minister of Transport, not all ministers agreed.[6]

The question that must now be asked is why, contrary to Wiley's assumption, Vorster and his government were not prepared to allow D'Oliveira to tour with the MCC? Wiley had good reasons for assuming that D'Oliveira would have been accepted if he had been selected in the first instance. Vorster was in the process of 'liberalising' Nationalist Government sports policy in the effort to retain South Africa's traditional sporting links with the outside world, and the acceptance of D'Oliveira would have been entirely consistent with such 'liberalisation', while rejection would have been a self-defeating exercise. Why, then, was it impossible for Vorster and his government to accept D'Oliveira?

Traditional Nationalist Government policy certainly required a ban on D'Oliveira, as was made clear at the outset by P.M.K. le Roux, the Minister of the Interior, when asked by a Johannesburg newspaper to respond to Billy Griffith's evasive comment to the *Daily Express* on what would happen if D'Oliveira was included in the MCC team to tour South Africa. Le Roux, who owed his position in the Cabinet to his loyal support of Dr Verwoerd, was reported in the South African *Sunday Express* of 22 January 1967 as saying: 'Our policy is clear. We will not allow mixed teams to play against our white teams here. That is our policy. It is well known here and overseas.' Later, after reportedly being reprimanded by the Prime Minister, and taunted in the House of Assembly by the United Party MP, Marais Steyn, for doing 'something which no politician should ever do, he answered a hypothetical question', Le Roux denied making the statement. However, he made it clear that 'We simply do not want other countries to force us here to depart from our traditional point of view and policy.'[7]

Le Roux's reported statement caused a furore in Britain which included the tabling of a motion in the House of Commons, signed by 200 MPs of all parties, calling on the MCC to cancel the tour. After consultation with the General-Purposes Sub-Committee of the MCC, Denis Howell, the minister responsible for sport in the Labour Government and a former football referee, assured the House: 'The MCC informed the Government that the team to tour South Africa will be chosen on merit and in this respect any preconditions that the host country lays down will be totally disregarded. The Government are confident that if, when the time comes, any player chosen for the touring side were rejected by the host country, then there would be no question but that the MCC would find such a condition wholly unacceptable and the projected tour would be abandoned.'[8] At its meeting of 1 February 1967, the MCC Committee, presided over by Sir Alec Douglas-Home, the former Conservative Prime Minister, accepted that Howell's statement 'conformed to MCC's views'. The Treasurer, Gubby Allen, contended, however, that the minister 'should not have been so definite or so strong' without the MCC Committee having first considered the matter. Allen added that if it appeared likely that D'Oliveira would be selected for the South African tour it would be essential to make a definite decision before the 1968 season.

It was at this juncture that Vorster decided to intervene. It was during Vorster's premiership that the first cracks began to show in the apartheid wall constructed by his predecessors, and that the attempt to 'reform' apartheid was initiated. A new pragmatism entered Nationalist decision-making and, at the outset of his tenure, his primary thrust was towards arresting South Africa's slide towards international isolation through his so-called 'outward policy', which involved establishing diplomatic relations with independent African states, accepting black representatives of foreign governments, and staving off sporting isolation by relaxing apartheid restrictions on visiting teams. A keen sportsman himself, Vorster was much more anxious than his predecessor to maintain international sporting contacts.[9] He was also intent on making the National Party the home for a broader white South African nationalism rather than a narrow ethnic Afrikaner nationalism.

With the cancellation of the New Zealand rugby tour of 1967 behind him, the possible cancellation of the MCC cricket tour looming before him, and anxious to secure South Africa's return to the Olympic Games, Vorster thrashed out a new sports policy in the Nationalist party caucus. He did so in the face of fierce opposition from a group of ultra-conservatives, including P.M.K. le Roux, who were later labelled *verkramptes*, and who resisted all attempts to 'reform' discriminatory policies as marking the beginning of the end for apartheid.[10]

On 11 April 1967 Vorster announced his new sports policy to the House of Assembly, speaking, according to Sir John Nicholls, the then British ambassador, with 'an uncharacteristic cautiousness and deliberation'. Vorster insisted that no mixed sport would be permitted between white and non-white South Africans within

South Africa – an insistence which made it impossible for the Indian golfer, Sewsunker 'Papwa' Sewgolum, to continue to play in 'white' tournaments in the country – but matches involving inter-state relations, as distinct from purely personal relations, were in a different category.

South Africa would, for instance, be prepared in the future to send a single multi-racial team to the Olympic Games, most immediately the 1968 Games in Mexico City, as it was a requirement that each country be represented by only one team. Mixed trials, however, would not be permitted. South Africa was also prepared to host the Canada Cup golf tournament and ties in the Davis Cup tennis competition, even though 'coloured' countries participated. In the case of rugby and cricket, South Africa's relations were not with the whole world – in cricket there were no relations with the West Indies, India or Pakistan – but the white rugby and cricket boards had traditional sporting ties with the British Isles, Australia and New Zealand, and, in the case of rugby, with France and Argentina as well. To preserve existing ties these countries would in future be permitted to send mixed race teams to tour South Africa. The government, Vorster stated, would not prescribe to any country with which traditional sporting ties existed how to select their own teams and would instead rely on 'the sound judgment of the sport administrators in the country which is invited to South Africa'.

The Prime Minister warned, however, that his new policy was subject to the condition that relations with other countries were not impaired, that sport was not exploited for political purposes, and that relations between the people of South Africa were not harmed. He also made it clear that Springbok rugby and cricket teams touring abroad would remain all white and that any ultimatum 'that our Springbok team would not be welcome unless it included all race groups' would be rejected as an invasion of South Africa's rights: 'If that demand is made of us and is attached as a condition for the continuation of sporting relations, then I say: I am not prepared to comply with that condition, because that is exclusively our own affair.'[11]

At the time, Vorster's speech was perceived as clearing the way for D'Oliveira to tour South Africa. The general sense was summed up by Nicholls, who reported to the Foreign and Commonwealth Office that Vorster 'made it quite clear that Maoris might be admitted as members of an All Black rugby team; and, although he did not say so specifically, it is a reasonable assumption from what he said – and one that everyone has made – that Mr Basil D'Oliveira may come here as a member of an MCC Team'.[12] However, as commentators later realised, Vorster's statement was 'cloudy and cryptic', and his provisos related directly to D'Oliveira.

Politically, Vorster's speech was a masterpiece of its kind; it forced no hands, generally refrained from interfering in the affairs of other countries, and kept possibilities open for touring teams.

Thereafter, however, he and his government refused to be drawn in public on the D'Oliveira issue. He had specifically warned in his April speech that he did not consider it to be in 'the interests of sport in South Africa' for people to name an individual long before a tour was due to take place and ask 'will you or will you not receive him?'. It was only on 27 August 1968, the very day that the MCC selectors met to choose the team for South Africa, that the Cabinet formally decided not to admit an MCC team with D'Oliveira in it. Vorster's strategy until then had been to avoid staking out a formal position on an issue that was potentially as explosive as it was hypothetical, and to avoid giving any public appearance of dictating to another country how it should select its team. Unlike Verwoerd, about whom R.J. Holyoake, the New Zealand Prime Minister, had complained that he wanted to dictate to New Zealand the composition of its teams, central to Vorster's whole public stance was that he was not a selection committee. 'In a sense,' the South African *Sunday Times* commented, 'the Prime Minister was taking a gamble, in the hope that the whole thing would sort itself out with the omission of D'Oliveira.'[13]

For a while it seemed that the gamble might work. D'Oliveira had a disappointing tour of the West Indies in 1967/68 and, although he scored a solid 87 not out in the second innings of the first Ashes Test against Australia in June, he was thereafter dropped from the England team, and his form in county cricket was generally unremarkable. It was his sudden return to the England team for the final Ashes Test in August, and his outstanding performance that obliged Vorster and his Cabinet to make their policy decision on his presence in the MCC team.

Vorster had, much earlier in the year, reached the conclusion that he could not allow an MCC tour with D'Oliveira in it. The MCC, he believed, had forced the issue by ignoring his warning not to pose 'hypothetical' questions and writing to SACA, on the advice of Denis Howell and the recommendation of Billy Griffith, on 5 January to request assurances that no preconditions would be laid down regarding their choice of players and that all members of the MCC team would be accorded the 'normal courtesies'.[14] In Vorster's mind, this constituted a clear sign that the MCC had buckled under pressure from the Labour Government. Not only could he not be seen to capitulate to such outside 'political interference', conducted in the face of his own provisos and warnings, but he also took the request for assurances as a signal that the MCC was so craven that it would include D'Oliveira in the team for South Africa regardless of his form.

It became a persistent source of concern for Vorster and his ministerial colleagues that even D'Oliveira's loss of form would not be enough to rule him out. The player's progress was closely monitored by Frank Waring. On 7 March 1968 Waring wrote to the Prime Minister: 'Should his form not improve, it would seem unlikely that the M.C.C. selection committee could choose him on merit.' SACA vice-president Jack Cheetham had exacerbated this concern when, on his return from a visit to England in March, he had expressed the fear that merit might not be the only consideration. Vorster was informed that Cheetham had 'returned with the opinion that MCC compromised themselves to such an extent with the Labour Government in their statement read in the House of Commons last year that no Selection Committee, which has a majority of MCC Members, would dare not select the person concerned, despite loss of form'.[15] The inclusion of D'Oliveira in the England team for the first Ashes Test against Australia in June seemed to confirm this view. 'They have persevered with him,' Waring reported to Vorster, 'when in fact his record on paper in the West Indies hardly justified this.' Waring added that the MCC had evidently given way to pressure from the Labour Government to cancel the Rhodesian leg of the projected tour to southern Africa.[16] For Vorster and his ministerial colleagues evidence of 'political interference' in the forthcoming MCC tour abounded.

While the circumstances forced Vorster to decide that he could never accept an MCC team with D'Oliveira in it, he also appreciated that a formal ban on the cricketer would be a disaster for South African sport in general, and cricket more particularly, and that consequently what was required was an active strategy to ensure that no such ban became necessary. That meant stalling the MCC on the question of assurances, and taking positive steps to secure D'Oliveira's omission, either through engineering his 'non-availability' or his non-selection, without being seen in public to dictate on matters of selection.

Vorster's strategy took shape in late February and early March 1968 in individual meetings in Cape Town, where Parliament was sitting, with Sir Alec Douglas-Home, the former Conservative British Prime Minister and former MCC president, Arthur Coy and Lord Cobham, a former Governor-General of New Zealand and also a former MCC president.

Vorster and Douglas-Home met on 22 February. Douglas-Home was visiting South Africa and Rhodesia in his capacity as Opposition shadow minister of foreign affairs, and the chief purpose of the South African leg of his visit was to speak to Vorster about his policy towards Rhodesia, which had declared its unilateral independence (UDI) of the British Crown in 1965. But Douglas-Home was also still a member of the MCC Committee, and he had been requested to broach the question of D'Oliveira with Vorster as the committee had received no reply to its request for assurances. From the meeting Douglas-Home concluded that if the MCC pressed Vorster for assurances in advance regarding D'Oliveira, the answer would be 'no'.[17]

When, on 6 March, Vorster met Coy to discuss SACA's response to the MCC's request, he was given a copy of both the MCC's letter of 5 January and SACA's reply of 1 March. Vorster made it clear that he could not allow D'Oliveira to tour with the MCC, and that to safeguard the tour plans were afoot to secure D'Oliveira's 'non-availability' for selection. With D'Oliveira due to coach in South Africa between the end of the tour of the West Indies and the beginning of the English season, a 'well-wisher' was to establish contact with him and offer a lucrative coaching contract in return for his 'non-availability' for the tour.[18] The 'well-wisher' would be linked to the Rembrandt Tobacco Company, headed by Anton Rupert, patron of the South African Sport Foundation and a long-standing friend of Vorster's. During his visit to South Africa, Sir Alec Douglas-Home dined with Rupert in Stellenbosch.[19]

The previous year D'Oliveira's stint coaching coloured cricketers in South Africa had been sponsored by the United Tobacco Company, a rival to Rembrandt, and Vorster had publicly denounced the latter for 'meddling' in sports policy. Vorster now welcomed both Rembrandt's interest in cricket and its money. In the event, D'Oliviera did not come to South Africa after the tour of the West Indies, and it was not until August that 'Tienie' Oosthuizen, the UK manager of the Carreras Tobacco Company, offered him a £40 000 coaching contract with the Sport Foundation on condition that he declared himself unavailable for the MCC tour.[20]

On 12 March Vorster saw Lord Cobham, who had been anxious to talk to the Prime Minister while visiting South Africa and was finally requested to do so.[21] To obviate any misunderstandings at Lord's arising out of his discussions with

Douglas-Home, Vorster was adamant at his 'informal' meeting with Lord Cobham: there could be no D'Oliveira. As a 'wildly indiscreet' Cobham later informed the Reverend David Sheppard, Vorster told him 'that anyone else would be accepted but not D'Oliveira'.[22] Cobham was regarded as an ally of South African cricket and, through his agency, Vorster sent a direct signal to the MCC not to select D'Oliveira. The Prime Minister specifically requested Cobham to convey to the MCC the gist of what he had been told.[23]

Politically, Vorster felt he had no option but to prevent an MCC tour with D'Oliviera in it. As a relative junior in the Nationalist ministerial hierarchy when he became Prime Minister, and widely criticised in the early years of his premiership as a weak leader, he was struggling from the outset of 1968 to establish his leadership and to assert his ascendancy over the *verkramptes*. To allow D'Oliveira into the country as part of an MCC team, and particularly if his inclusion was seen as the product of political pressure from within Britain, would simply galvanise *verkrampte* opposition, possibly imperilling his leadership or provoking a major split in the party.

If the first major test of his new sports policy had been a handful of Maori rugby players, Vorster might have been prepared to stand his ground. But for a South African-born coloured to be the first beneficiary of the policy; for him to parade his prowess and international success on the country's cricket grounds, thereby giving the lie to the standard white claim that 'non-whites' were simply not good enough to represent South Africa; for him to demonstrate that 'non-white' South Africans might still aspire to play white South Africans within South Africa; and for him to do so seemingly at the behest of an actively anti-apartheid Labour Government in Britain was more than the bulk of Nationalists, not merely the *verkramptes*, could tolerate. 'The party, in fact,' as the *Star* was to comment on 20 September 1968, 'is not behind any permissive sports policy at all. It did not want D'Oliviera here in any circumstances.'

Apart from the affront to apartheid that D'Oliveira represented, all Nationalists, and many other whites besides, dreaded the 'hullabaloo' that would accompany him and the unpredictability of the exercise. South Africa would be besieged by the British media, who would cover every aspect of what happened to D'Oliveira, and, almost inevitably, there would be incidents off the field, and perhaps even crowd disturbances at match venues. In the wake of the riots during the second Test between the West Indies and England in Kingston, Jamaica, Arthur Coy in Port

Elizabeth, a city with a significant coloured population, surmised that cricket in South Africa might be 'subjected to possible West Indian behaviour'.[24]

In what the press at the time described as the biggest Cabinet reshuffle in South African history, Vorster, on 12 August asserted his supremacy in the party by removing the leading *verkramptes*, Dr Albert Hertzog and P.M.K. le Roux, from office. In a speech in Heilbron on 16 August, the Prime Minister vigorously defended his *verligte* (enlightened) policies as against the *verkramptes*. However, he was now even less inclined to challenge the dissidents on the D'Oliveira issue. His new sports policy had suffered a humiliating reversal when South Africa's invitation to attend the Mexico Olympics had been withdrawn in late April; sport was consequently not a favourable ground on which to pursue the *verkramptes*, particularly on something as close to home as D'Oliveira. Rather than provide them with a potentially effective rallying-cry Vorster's concern was to cement support for himself among the Nationalist rank-and-file.

The undercurrents at the party's provincial congresses in August and September indicated that the rank-and-file was solidly *verkramp* on the prospect of D'Oliveira touring. At the Transvaal congress in Potchefstroom Louwrens Muller, the new Minister of Police, interrupted his speech to announce that D'Oliveira had not been selected by the MCC, an announcement that was greeted with loud cheers. When Vorster informed the Free State congress in Bloemfontein that he would not accept the last-minute inclusion of D'Oliveira in the MCC team, the applause was prolonged and deafening. As J.H.P. Serfontein, political correspondent of the *Sunday Times*, reported 'Mr Vorster received the most frenzied and enthusiastic ovations a Nationalist Prime Minister has received in many years'. He added: 'I regard this reaction of the audience as evidence of the relief felt by rank-and-file Nationalists who have been worried over stories that Mr Vorster was a "liberal" and that his outward policy would affect apartheid.'

It was Serfontein who revealed at the time, in the *Sunday Times* of 22 September, the government's decision not to allow D'Oliveira to tour with the MCC even if he had been selected in the first instance. He had, he wrote, learned this from Nationalists 'very close to the Party leadership'. Serfontein represented the decision as a strategic political victory for Vorster, making his position as National Party leader 'impregnable'. As one 'key' *verkrampte* told him, 'It [the decision to refuse D'Oliveira entry] has set us back for some years. Mistakenly many *verkrampte* Nationalists will regard this action of Mr Vorster as proof that he is not a liberal but a conservative.' For all that, the D'Oliveira Affair was a significant, if temporary, setback for Vorster's new sports policy. His first attempt at 'liberalisation' had failed, and it was a failure that helped ensure South Africa's cricketing isolation.

What enabled Vorster to disguise his retreat was the MCC's handling of D'Oliveira's selection. Had D'Oliviera been selected in the first instance, Vorster's new sports policy would have been exposed as hollow. Frank Waring had already prepared a statement to announce the cancellation of the tour in the event of D'Oliveira's selection. The statement largely reflected Nationalist paranoia. Its thrust was that 'it would be naïve . . . on anybody's part to maintain that there had been no political intervention, not only in this MCC team but also in cricket generally'. It also asserted that 'the conditions which were laid down by the Prime Minister regarding tours from overseas countries to South Africa have been brushed aside'. To substantiate the claim of political intervention the statement cited Howell's involvement in the affairs of the MCC, and the cancellation of the traditional Rhodesian leg of the MCC tour, allegedly as a consequence of British Government pressure.[25] It was D'Oliveira's belated inclusion in the team, and particularly as the replacement for a specialist bowler, that enabled Vorster to assert it was self-evident the MCC had bowed to political pressure, and to suggest that his hand had been forced by the intervention of South Africa's 'political enemies'. The decision had also put him in a position to lie to the British ambassador, assuring Nicholls that had D'Oliveira been included in the MCC team in the first instance, the tour would have gone ahead. As Nicholls cabled the Foreign and Commonwealth Office on 17 September:

He said that, had D'Oliveira been chosen in the first place, his presence in the side would have caused him a good many headaches but he would have accepted it on the principle that it was not for him to select visiting teams. He had accepted the MCC decision to omit D'Oliveira at its face value – i.e. a decision reached on straight cricketing grounds. But the mounting agitation in the United Kingdom had unfortunately made this into a political issue. If D'Oliveira came, either as a journalist or as a replacement, he would now be the object of demonstrations and counter-demonstrations, and he himself would come under attack from many of his party supporters, who would believe that the MCC had given way to politically motivated agitation.

He attached importance to good relations with the United Kingdom in the field of sport as in every other but it would not be conducive to good relations if D'Oliveira were to come and be used as a political catspaw by the opposing groups in South Africa.[26]

By not selecting D'Oliveira in the first instance, the MCC had let Vorster off a major hook.

D'OLIVEIRA AND THE MCC

At the end of a visit to South Africa in early 1967, which coincided with P.M.K. le Roux's 'idiotic' statement about not permitting 'mixed' teams into South Africa, C.M. Le Quesne, the head of the West and Central African Department of the Foreign and Commonwealth Office, minuted: 'The one thing which we must now hope for is that Mr. D'Oliveira keeps his form, and the MCC their nerve.'[27] He was to be disappointed on both counts, more particularly the latter.

When, on 28 August 1968 the MCC team for South Africa was announced, Doug Insole, the chairman of selectors, explained that D'Oliveira had been left out of the team for cricketing reasons alone. D'Oliveira had been considered purely as a batsman, and the balance of the team required Tom Cartwright's medium-paced bowling skills more than D'Oliveira's batting skills. The claim that D'Oliveira had been omitted for purely cricket reasons was met with general disbelief, and it was widely assumed that the MCC had left him out so as not to imperil the tour. The assumption was that the MCC Committee and selectors had acted in the knowledge, or simply the belief, that if D'Oliveira were included the Vorster Government would disallow the tour. The chief criticism levied by the Reverend David Sheppard, and a group of dissidents within the MCC, was that the MCC Committee had failed to secure in advance a firm commitment from SACA that D'Oliveira would be acceptable, and thus the selectors had been forced to make their choice under duress, realising that his inclusion might well prejudice the tour.

On 5 January 1968 the MCC had, in fact, written to SACA requesting assurances, and Sir Alec Douglas-Home was briefed to assess the situation concerning D'Oliveira during his discussions in February with Vorster and with SACA officials. Hitherto it has always been asserted, including by the MCC, that the MCC never received a reply from SACA to its inquiry. This is not correct. A reply dated 1 March 1968 was taken personally to Lord's by Jack Cheetham. On 6 March a copy was also handed to Vorster by Arthur Coy. The letter stated:

> The South African Cricket Association would never presume to interfere with the manner in which you choose your side to tour South Africa, nor has it during the 80 years of tours between our respective countries. Regarding the treatment of your team whilst on tour in South Africa the South African Cricket Association has no hesitation in advising that it can see no reason why the hospitality and courtesy generally extended to all visiting teams should in any way be changed.[28]

The letter, in short, gave no assurance that any team selected by the MCC would be permitted to tour South Africa. No mention was made of the attitude of the Vorster Government, or whether it had been consulted.

On the advice of Gubby Allen, the letter was never submitted to the MCC Committee, supposedly for fear that its contents 'would be twisted and leaked to the press'. Instead, Cheetham was advised by Allen and Billy Griffith that SACA 'need not answer their letter and it has been agreed to continue with the normal preparations and negotiations that are necessary when a tour is due to take place'.[29] The instruction given to the South African Tour sub-committee, chaired by Doug Insole and responsible for negotiating arrangements for the tour, was that it should proceed with its task but not discuss '(a) Rhodesia, or (b) D'Oliveira', and instead await 'direction from the MCC Committee on both matters'.[30]

At the time, the affairs of the MCC were controlled by a trio comprising Allen, Griffith and Arthur Gilligan, the MCC president. Starting with the letter carried by Cheetham they set themselves up as a filter for the flow of sensitive information from South Africa to the MCC Committee and the selection committee, holding back what they deemed unsuitable for official circulation or wider consumption. The classic instance of their censorship was the 'informal' letter from Lord Cobham, via a senior member of the MCC Committee, advising that Vorster would never accept D'Oliveira.

Allen, the senior figure in the MCC, was the dominant person among the three. A former England captain, chairman of selectors and MCC president, he was firmly established as a powerful influence in the 'backroom' politics of English cricket. Gilligan was likewise a former England captain – he had captained England to victory against South Africa in 1924 – but was otherwise a gentle person with a distaste for conflict. Griffith, as the chief professional administrator in the MCC, was supposedly a 'neutral' figure, and it is not entirely clear where his sympathies lay in the D'Oliveira Affair. He had toured South Africa with George Mann's MCC team in 1948/49, had been appointed assistant secretary of the MCC in 1952, and in 1962 had succeeded Ronald Aird as secretary. From what Coy gathered from Lord Cobham, Griffith was 'very much for' SACA.[31] The Reverend David Sheppard had a different perspective on Griffith. According to him, Griffith had been 'appalled' at what he had seen in South Africa in 1948/49, and it was he who started Sheppard thinking about South Africa.[32] In an interview with Rob Steen, the Rt. Rev. Lord Sheppard recalled of Griffith: 'He saw a lot of things the way we did . . . If he had not been in that post I always thought he would have joined our protesting group.'[33] In private, evidently, Griffith believed the MCC should have continued to press SACA for assurances over D'Oliveira.[34]

At its meeting on 21 February, the MCC Committee had postponed any decision on the South African tour; no reply had been received from SACA concerning pre-conditions of selection, and the committee was awaiting the return of Sir Alec Douglas-Home from his visit to South Africa. At its next meeting, on 21 March, the MCC Committee noted that it had still not received a 'definite reply' from SACA. The question was whether to press for assurances or to proceed with preparations for the tour. On the advice of Douglas-Home, it was decided to proceed with the tour arrangements 'on the assumption that the selected team would be accepted by the South African Government when the time came'. Douglas-Home's intervention was crucial, and his advice thereafter served as the basic guideline for the MCC Committee and its selectors.

Douglas-Home's agenda contained a strong political element; it was by no means simply cricketing. His visit to South Africa and Rhodesia in February represented a venture in bi-partisan foreign policy by the Wilson Government in an effort to bring about a settlement in Rhodesia. In dealing with Vorster, his prime objective was to get the South African Government to apply economic sanctions against Rhodesia. It was a delicate, and as it proved, impossible task. Vorster was already feeling bruised by the British Government's decision to renew the country's arms embargo against South Africa that had been in force since 1963; as the British ambassador reported to the Foreign Office on 19 February 1968, the decision to maintain the arms embargo constituted a 'severe blow' to the South African

Government.[35] In the circumstances Douglas-Home had no intention of adding to the pressures on Vorster by forcing the D'Oliveira issue. As he later told Colin Cowdrey, the England captain, 'We wanted relationships kept as warm as possible in the current climate.'[36] More broadly, Douglas-Home believed it was important to maintain bridges to South Africa in 'that perception and understanding would bring apartheid to an end far more quickly than boycott'.[37]

Douglas-Home left his meeting with Vorster feeling generally pessimistic about the prospects for the MCC tour. He seems to have appreciated that it was a political mistake to ask Vorster for assurances in advance of a 'hypothetical' event, and believed that the tour would be more likely to take place if the MCC waited until the team was actually selected. He put the odds at 5/4 that, if chosen, D'Oliveira might be admitted.[38] Douglas-Home's advice to the MCC Committee was consequently 'that it would be wrong to confront the South African Government with individual possible selections until they were made, as this would undoubtedly result in a refusal to answer hypothetical questions of this nature', and that there would be 'more chance of the selected team being accepted if we waited until the selection was actually made'.[39] This advice from a seasoned politician was accepted unanimously. With D'Oliveira currently experiencing a disappointing Test series against the West Indies it seemed foolhardy to imperil the tour by pressing for assurances on a selection that might never materialise.

Another piece of advice from Douglas-Home, that Rhodesia should not be incorporated in the South African tour, was accepted by the MCC (with one dissenting vote) on 24 April. A month later SACA was informed that the MCC, in consultation with the British Government, had decided not to play in Rhodesia.

The MCC Committee's decision to proceed on the assumption that whatever team was selected would be accepted by the South African Government was never formally reconsidered, even though evidence to the contrary presented itself. No sooner had the Committee decided to act on Douglas-Home's advice than the letter from Lord Cobham reached Griffith advising that his discussion with Vorster indicated that a team that included D'Oliveira would be unacceptable.[40] Griffith consulted with Gilligan and Allen, and they decided against conveying the information to the full Committee. According to an MCC statement on 10 April 1969 they did so because Cobham's message 'appeared not to coincide with the impression which Sir Alec Douglas-Home gained from his discussion with Mr Vorster' and because it might prejudice team selections, which, of course, was Vorster's intention.

Two of the Committee's members, Doug Insole and Peter May, were selectors, and knowledge of Cobham's message would place undue pressure on them, complicating their brief to select the best team.[41] More pointedly, had Cobham's letter been passed on to the Committee it might have felt itself compelled to reconsider the tour.

In late June, at the time of the second Ashes Test, Arthur Coy, fresh from a second meeting with Vorster, appeared at Lord's as the guest of Lord Cobham to conduct consultations 'privately' rather than to make 'formal representations' to the MCC. The message Coy carried was clear, 'that D'Oliveira's selection would endanger the tour'.[42] The primary purpose of Coy's mission to Lord's was to ensure that D'Oliveira was not included in the MCC team, either by securing his 'non-availability' or, failing that, his non-selection. So, far from seeking to challenge Vorster to admit D'Oliveira, if he was chosen, the SACA Board of Control directed its energies to trying to ensure that he was not selected in the first place.

The SACA Board of Control had set up a sub-committee of three, comprising its president, E.R. 'Wally' Hammond; vice-president, Jack Cheetham; and the convenor of selectors and former president, Arthur Coy, to deal with the D'Oliveira question on a 'confidential basis'. The three were the key figures in South African cricket administration. In white South African cricketing circles, both Hammond, managing director of the South African Permanent Building Society, and Cheetham, a director of Roberts Construction and revered as a great Springbok captain of the 1950s, were deemed vaguely 'liberal', but both were solidly of the school that believed that sport should keep out of politics and were extremely wary of crossing the government. Coy, a shrewd and energetic Port Elizabeth businessman who had changed his name from Cohen, was the most conservative of the three. A member of the right wing of the opposition United Party, who had fiercely contested South Africa's adoption of republic status in 1961, he also became a good friend of Vorster. He was considered vital as he had the ear of government, serving as the link between SACA and the Prime Minister. On 4 March, in what is for the historian a marvellously indiscreet letter, Coy wrote to Cheetham, then in London for discussions with the MCC:

I had dinner with Charles [Lord Cobham] last Wednesday night and half-an-hour privately the next morning and here is the gist:-

1. B.G. [Billy Griffith] asked him to contact me re O. [D'Oliveira] question.
2. B.G. is very much for us – is influential outside meetings but hamstrung inside.
3. C. [Cobham] will do almost anything to see that the tour is on.
4. C. agrees that even if O. were allowed to come the obvious problems would be exploited by press and the cricket subjected to possible West Indian behaviour.
5. It was agreed that if P.M. said O. could come it would certainly be qualified by guarantees that there would be no incidents.
6. C. is going to talk to O. with ideas that would suit us.
7. C. hopes to see the P.M. about 12th March before returning to U.K. by sea.
8. I told C of your mission and showed him the letter with which he agreed. I have an appointment at 4p.m. on 6th with P.M. and I will also tell him of the H. [Hammond] lunch and C. discussions.

If you get this letter in time I think you must push point 4 of my discussions with C. when you see Gubby. M.C.C. should surely be more interested in cricket than politics and for the sake of one man would they jeopardise the success and harmony of a tour?

Cheetham's message on his return from England that the MCC would not dare leave D'Oliveira out prompted Coy to write to Vorster: 'In view of this the "non-availability" of this person seems to be more important than ever.'[43]

At the SACA Board of Control meeting on 24 March, after Cheetham's return, Hammond 'reported fully on what had transpired to date', and promised to keep the board informed of developments.[44] Matters thereafter were so confidential that virtually nothing was committed to writing; certainly no reports to the board were minuted. In mid-May the sub-committee decided to send Coy to England, in time for the Lord's Test in late June, to talk to interested parties. The sub-committee's strategy, evidently, was both to try to secure D'Oliveira's 'non-availability' and to 'privately' warn MCC officials of the perils of selecting him. Before departing for England, Coy again saw Vorster to brief the Prime Minister about 'our plans, possible solution and alternatives'.[45]

What that 'possible solution' was is not clear from the documents, but, according to D'Oliveira in his autobiography, he was approached at the dinner prior to the

Lord's Test by a 'top cricket official' who told him 'that the only way the tour could be saved would be if I announced I was unavailable for *England* but would like to play for *South Africa*'. D'Oliveira 'angrily refused', and said 'Either you respect me as an England player or you don't.' The next day an 'eminent cricket writer' put the same proposal to D'Oliveira. In his new biography of D'Oliveira, Peter Oborne has identified the official as Billy Griffith, and the cricket writer as E.W. Swanton. In Oborne's opinion, Griffith and Swanton, 'in their well-meaning quest for a solution', were probably conned into making the proposal, believing that it might help to break down racial barriers in South African cricket, whereas in fact if D'Oliveira had accepted he 'would have been converted overnight into an Uncle Tom'[46]. For the Test itself, D'Oliveira found himself relegated to twelfth man, despite his good performance in the previous Test. The selectors ascribed England's defeat in the first Test to an 'unbalanced' bowling attack, and replaced D'Oliveira with Barry Knight, who proved an instant success.

Whatever the shenanigans surrounding Coy's visit to Lord's, leading officials of the MCC, notably Allen, Gilligan and Griffith, were fully apprised about Vorster's attitude towards an MCC tour with D'Oliveira in it. When Vorster finally announced his ban on D'Oliveira, Hammond told the press: 'We understood the position for some time, and have done everything possible to obviate any misunderstanding.'[47]

The selection committee met at Lord's on the evening of 27 August, following the fifth Test against the Australians at the Oval during which the star performer had been D'Oliveira. After having been omitted for the second, third and fourth Tests, he was a last-minute substitute at the Oval and scored an epic 158 in the first innings. On the way from the Oval to Lord's for the selection meeting, Colin Cowdrey, the England captain, confided to Jack Bailey: 'It's good to have beaten the Aussies. It looks as though we shall have problems with South Africa, though. They can't leave Basil out of the team. Not now.'[48]

Unbeknown to Cowdrey, at the end of D'Oliveira's innings Geoffrey Howard, the secretary at the Oval, had received a call from 'Tienie' Oosthuizen, phoning from the Prime Minister's office in Pretoria. Oosthuizen said he had been trying without luck to get hold of Griffith at Lord's, and that he had a vital message that needed to be conveyed to the selectors: 'Tell them that, if today's centurion is picked, the tour will be off.' Howard duly passed on the message to Doug Insole.[49]

At the heart of the selection committee were the regular selectors: Doug Insole, chairman since 1965; Peter May, who was married to Gilligan's niece and was a strong supporter of South African cricket; Alec Bedser, later a founder member of the conservative Freedom Association, partly funded by South African money, and Don Kenyon, D'Oliveira's former captain of Worcestershire and a good friend of Lord Cobham, likewise a former Worcester captain. Insole, May and Bedser had all toured South Africa as players, and Insole's work in the construction industry took him to South Africa from time to time. To them were added Cowdrey, as England captain; Leslie Ames, as tour manager; and Arthur Gilligan and Gubby Allen as the senior officers of the MCC. The task of the latter two was not to recommend selections, but on behalf of the MCC to rule on the acceptability as tourists of those considered for selection. Billy Griffith and Donald Carr were also present as part of the MCC administration. MCC policy was to preserve and promote cricketing ties with South Africa, and to select the best available teams for overseas tours. Beyond these general guidelines, no specific instructions were given to the selection committee, and the MCC Committee itself had not formally reviewed the situation. 'Thanks for leaving everything to the selectors,' Insole is reputed to have said.[50]

Selection meetings for touring parties are often marathon affairs, and this one went on for five and a half hours, lasting until 1.30 am. With speculation rife as to what might happen if D'Oliveira were selected, and with pressure from Pretoria having intensified, the meeting evidently began with the MCC office-holders, Gilligan and Allen, who were fully aware of the consequences of choosing D'Oliveira, speculating about whether it would be a futile exercise to select a team for South Africa. Insole, respected for his straightforward approach to issues, responded by suggesting that the committee simply get on with the task of selecting a team and, to escape political considerations, imagine it was a team to tour Australia. According to Insole's own recollection, this device worked; it cleared the air and the selection committee was able to proceed with the task of selecting a team on merit.[51] At some point, evidently, Allen made it clear that he believed D'Oliveira would be a bad choice for cricketing reasons, and was reportedly surprised at how many of his co-selectors agreed with him.[52] Whether the selectors ultimately agreed by consensus to leave D'Oliveira out, or whether there was a vote, is unclear. At the MCC Committee meeting on 28 August it was decided that no voting figures should be given to the press, but no one, including the chairman, ever recollected a vote, and Kenyon was evidently the only selector to urge the case for D'Oliveira. Cowdrey, who D'Oliveira believed had promised his support, evidently decided that 'on purely cricketing grounds' D'Oliveira would have to be left out. Cowdrey had gathered from Bill Lawry, the Australian captain, that South African pitches were now a 'seamer's paradise', ideally suited to Tom Cartwright and Barry Knight, whereas D'Oliveira was more 'a batsman who could bowl well'.[53]

Until the Oval Test, D'Oliveira had not featured in the selectors' plans for South Africa. He was not on their original short-list of 30, approved at the meeting of 26 July, and his name was only added after his innings of 158, when Insole asked him whether he would be available for the tour. He replied in the affirmative, even though he was still being pressurised by 'Tienie' Oosthuizen, latterly on the phone from South Africa, who told him that he had it from 'the highest possible source' that he would prove an embarrassment to Mr Vorster, and that reading between the lines he should realise that it was better for him not to go.[54]

In the final analysis, the selectors proved unwilling to revise their plans, at the risk perhaps of jeopardising the tour, and even South Africa's place in international cricket, in the light of D'Oliveira's innings. As Peter May recounted in his autobiography: 'After Basil had made 158 at the Oval we reconsidered the position but, as he had been dropped twice early on, came to the conclusion that his innings, valuable though it had been in its context, did not alter the judgements made over the cricket of the past year.'[55] Sheppard believed that had D'Oliveira been central to the selectors' plans, they would have gritted their teeth and included him.[56] The decision they did take, according to Cowdrey, was to nominate D'Oliveira as first reserve, but the minutes of the meeting, thin as always, simply recorded that Insole and Cowdrey were delegated the task of drawing up a list of reserves for consideration at the committee's next meeting.[57]

Two sets of cricketing considerations led directly to D'Oliveira's exclusion. The one was to view him purely as a batsman, and not as an all-rounder. According to Hugo Young of the London *Sunday Times*, who received his information from 'one of those present' (evidently Insole) the first 'cricketing' decision taken by the selection committee was to select seven batsmen, and the second was that D'Oliveira would be considered purely as a batsman. 'It was at this point,' Young commented, 'that the reasoning got, to an outsider, almost unintelligibly contorted.' D'Oliveira had been drafted by Cowdrey into the England squad for the Oval Test primarily for his medium-paced bowling, but for overseas conditions his bowling was considered of no account. As a batsman, he, along with Colin Milburn, was not considered to be one of England's top seven, and was consequently left out.[58]

A batting place that might have been given to D'Oliveira went instead to a third opener, a greatly relieved Roger Prideaux, the man D'Oliveira had replaced for the Oval Test. Prideaux had pulled out on the grounds of illness but evidently the real reason was that he did not want to risk failure at the Oval and thereby jeopardise his chances of touring South Africa. The selection of three regular openers – the others were the established pair of Geoffrey Boycott and John Edrich – was considered crucial for touring purposes. In the middle order, Keith Fletcher's youth and promise counted against D'Oliveira's age, particularly as the remaining specialist batsmen, Cowdrey, his vice-captain Tom Graveney, and Ken Barrington, a backbone of England's batting in South Africa in 1964/65, were all getting on in years.

Given the dearth of all-rounders available for the tour, and D'Oliveira's later inclusion as an all-rounder, the original decision to consider him purely as a batsman has always been perceived by critics as questionable.[59] The one genuine all-rounder on the selectors' short-list, Barry Knight, was ruled ineligible by Gilligan and Allen as his personal life was in disarray.[60] The place that might otherwise have gone to an all-rounder went to Tom Cartwright, a medium-paced bowler who batted a little. Cartwright had played in none of the Tests against the Australians, having been plagued by injury for much of the season, and had experienced an unimpressive tour to South Africa four years previously, but for all that it was generally accepted he was England's finest bowler, when fit. The other cricketing factor that counted against D'Oliveira was that, following the West Indies tour, he was deemed a 'bad tourist' who did not adjust well to overseas conditions, spent much of his time partying, and generally detracted from team morale.[61] That had been the report of Ames as tour manager.

At the MCC Committee meeting on 28 August to ratify the team for South Africa there was some debate about whether the public would understand the omission of a man who had just scored a match-winning Test century.[62] The Committee none the less accepted the team as selected and, after a discussion about how to handle the press, appointed Insole as spokesman. In response to questions from the press about why D'Oliveira had been omitted, Insole explained that 'we have got players rather better than him in the side'. In a statement that came back to haunt the selectors, he added that from an overseas point of view D'Oliveira had been regarded purely as a batsman, and not as an all-rounder.

When the team was announced Vorster phoned Arthur Coy to congratulate him on the satisfactory resolution of 'our respective problems'. Coy wrote back: 'My information is that "he" was still available and had not withdrawn.'[63]

The exclusion of D'Oliveira, in the immediate wake of his Oval performance, provoked outrage in Britain. 'No one of open mind,' Arlott asserted bluntly, 'will believe that he was left out for valid cricket reasons.'[64] Even Denis Compton, regarded as a special friend of white South African cricket, registered powerful disapproval. 'The omission of Basil D'Oliveira from the party to tour South Africa,' he wrote in the *Sunday Express*, 'will go down as one of the most staggering and shameful decisions in cricket's long history.' Several members of the MCC resigned in protest, while a group of critics, led by Sheppard, demanded a special general meeting of the MCC to consider a vote of no-confidence in the MCC Committee.

At a preliminary meeting on 12 September to discuss the general meeting, Sheppard's four-man delegation found themselves confronted by the full MCC Committee, including Sir Alec Douglas-Home, who had flown down specially from Scotland. In the face of the criticism that the MCC should have secured assurances from the South African Government in advance, Douglas-Home, unaware that Sheppard knew of the Cobham letter, repeatedly insisted 'it was no good asking these people hypothetical questions'. The meeting, chaired by Gubby Allen, failed to persuade the Sheppard delegation to call off its request for a special general meeting.[65] As the MCC Committee sensed, the fundamental division between it and the dissidents was in fact over the question of playing cricket with South Africa at all. The minutes recorded that there was 'a strong feeling among certain Members that, as a matter of principle, there should be no cricket played against South Africa while the South African Government's racial policy existed' and 'that whereas the Committee's actions had sprung from a desire to play cricket against South Africa, if that were at all possible, the Committee's critics had never felt that this would have been a good thing under any circumstances in existing conditions'.[66]

In the midst of the furore over D'Oliveira's omission, the extent of which seems to have taken the selectors altogether by surprise, the selection committee was scheduled to meet again on Monday 16 September to consider reserves. After meeting with the dissidents, and after Vorster had intimated that D'Oliveira would not be welcome as a journalist to cover the tour for the *News of the World*, the MCC Committee, on the recommendation of George Mann, drafted the following message to SACA:

D'Oliveira is a reserve for the England XI. We have always assumed that purely as a cricketer, he will be acceptable. In view of the recent doubts which have arisen about his eligibility to enter South Africa, would you please confirm his acceptance as a cricketer. For obvious reasons, it is important that we have your assurance by the end of the month.[67]

The message was never sent. On 16 September Tom Cartwright dropped out of the team as a consequence of a recurring shoulder injury and, after a brief consultation, the selectors nominated D'Oliviera, as his replacement. 'Ironically enough, on cricketing grounds,' John Arlott commented in the *Guardian*, 'D'Oliveira's selection now is more puzzling than his original omission, for though he is a batsman with big occasion temperament, who can also bowl usefully, he is no adequate substitute for the finest medium seam bowler in England. So the puzzlement grows – whose word so surprisingly swung the position? But it has been swung – in effect if not in final decision – by public feeling.'

The next day Vorster announced he would not accept the 'team of the anti-apartheid movement', thereby forcing cancellation of the tour.

D'OLIVEIRA AND THE ANTI-APARTHEID CAMPAIGN
For the Anti-Apartheid Movement (AAM) and SANROC in Britain, the D'Oliveira Affair came as a godsend. Until then their campaign against Britain's links with apartheid sport in South Africa had sputtered along; the D'Oliveira Affair gave it an entirely new fillip, even if D'Oliveira himself proved something of a disappointment.

As the AAM and SANROC saw it, D'Oliveira should, on principle, never have made himself available for a tour of South Africa that would be run along strictly 'racialistic' lines, with games against white teams only at segregated venues. However, they made no real attempt to persuade D'Oliveira to issue a political statement declaring himself unavailable for the tour; it suited their purposes for him to embarrass the South African Government. On a couple of occasions, Dennis Brutus and Chris de Broglio had canvassed D'Oliveira's support for SANROC, but D'Oliveira had made his attitude clear: he was a sportsman not a politician, who believed he should seize the opportunities given him as a cricketer to break down prejudices against people of colour.[68] Going to South Africa as part of an MCC team represented just such a golden opportunity.

Some time after the cancellation of the tour, eleven 'so-called Cape Coloured' exiles in Britain wrote to D'Oliveira attacking his decision to make himself available for it. In a remarkable onslaught, which was passed on to Dennis Brutus and reported in *The Times* in June 1969, they rejected as 'ridiculous' his view that it was 'necessary for MCC to play South Africa and so maintain contact through which influence and pressure can be brought to bear to bring these racialists to their senses'. After condemning him for his 'unthinking and insensitive attitude', they advised that if he thought in terms of the larger principles involved he would conclude 'that you cannot play cricket with those who have stolen your country, robbed you of your birthright and driven you to live elsewhere'. Instead of making himself available for the tour of South Africa, he should have urged the MCC not to go: 'The hearts of your people would have swollen with pride that a son of theirs had shown such resolution.'[69]

That was not the message D'Oliveira had been hearing prior to the rumpus over his initial non-selection; his own sense was that he was being accused of letting the side down by allowing his chances to slip, and that the talk back home was that he was reluctant 'to spoil things for the white man'. As the likes of Vorster and Coy feared, the expectations of him among the coloured population especially would be huge, and crowd behaviour at games would be unpredictable. He would certainly have received a hero's reception. As Clive Taylor reported in the *Sun* in October 1967, coloured interest in D'Oliveira was massive, stretching far beyond cricket fans: 'To them he is the one who charged the barriers and broke through. It is reasonable to assume that when he returns as a member of the England team the atmosphere will be even more electric.'[70]

D'Oliveira's initial omission from that England team elicited damning statements from both SANROC and the AAM. The central charge of the AAM was that the MCC was not only endorsing apartheid by going to South Africa to play against teams selected on apartheid principles, but had now imported apartheid principles into the selection of its own team. 'Instead of selecting our team on merit alone,' the AAM's press statement asserted, 'we are submitting to apartheid requirements by excluding a player who has been a great asset to English cricket.' On the afternoon of 16 September the AAM sent a deputation, headed by Jeremy Thorpe, the Liberal MP, to see Dennis Howell, the minister responsible for sport, who advised that he had no authority to intervene in the affairs of a private club. Thorpe had just announced to the press that the AAM would be seeking meetings with the Prime Minister, the Foreign Secretary and the MCC itself when the news came that D'Oliveira had been selected as Cartwright's replacement. His selection, the AAM proclaimed in its next press statement, represented 'a great victory for all those who protested at his initial exclusion'.[71]

Vorster's announcement of the ban on D'Oliveira allowed the AAM and SANROC to declare that the argument about building bridges through sport had been dealt a death blow, and they called on the MCC to cancel all further tours to and from South Africa 'until apartheid has been eliminated from sport'. The general outrage provoked by the ban gave a huge new boost to their campaign to cut Britain's ties with apartheid sport, and both warned that it would be madness to attempt to proceed with the 1970 South African tour of England. To their chagrin, however, D'Oliveira indicated his willingness to play against the South Africans in England, thereby opening up a serious breach between himself and the anti-apartheid campaign.

Evidently, though, pressure had to be brought to bear on D'Oliveira to ensure his support for the 1970 tour. On 4 December 1969 Cowdrey took D'Oliveira to see Sir Alec Douglas-Home at the latter's London flat. According to D'Oliveira, who, in his autobiography incorrectly dated the meeting as September 1968, Sir Alec 'was particularly worried that the Springbok tour scheduled for the UK in 1970 was in danger of being called off because he wanted the South African Government to see how their British counterparts could handle law-abiding demonstrations without resorting to violence to break them up'. 'Keep doing it on the cricket field,' Douglas-Home persuaded D'Oliveira. 'Other forces can look after events off the field.' After the meeting a grateful Cowdrey wrote by postcard to Douglas-Home: 'Thank you so much for giving time to see Basil and I yesterday. What a problem! But you helped him enormously and when the time is right, he will reiterate what he has said all the way through.'[72]

On the cricket front, D'Oliveira continued to prove his worth for England, playing in another 28 Tests between the cancellation of the 1968 tour and his last appearance against the Australians at the Oval in August 1972. In total he represented England in 44 Tests, scoring 2 484 runs, including five centuries, at the formidable average of 40.06, and took 47 wickets at an average of 39.55.

CONCLUSION

In retrospect, after more than three decades and the opening of confidential government files, the initial omission of Basil D'Oliveira from the MCC team to tour South Africa in 1968/69 emerges as even more of an elaborate charade than E.W. Swanton, the cricket correspondent of the *Daily Telegraph*, contended at the time.

The charade was directed by B.J. Vorster. His parliamentary address of 11 April 1967 suggested a shift in government policy towards the racial composition of international visiting teams, but was otherwise ambiguous. From at least March 1968, if not before, Vorster's concern was to ensure an MCC tour of South Africa without D'Oliveira, but without being seen to require D'Oliveira's omission. Even after D'Oliveira's eventual selection, and the scrapping of the tour, Vorster maintained the charade with his assurance to the British ambassador that he would have let D'Oliveira in had he been selected in the first instance, and his declaration to the House of Assembly that 'no official communications whatsoever went out from either the Government or the Cricket Association in South Africa' concerning D'Oliveira's selection.[73] Indeed they did not; communications were all 'informal' or 'unofficial'. Vorster also declined to answer the question posed by Sir de Villiers Graaff, the leader of the opposition United Party, in the House of Assembly on 21 April 1969 as to whether he would have admitted D'Oliveira if he had been selected in the first instance:

> If I were to say now that I would have accepted D'Oliveira, or that I would not have accepted him, I would surely be placing myself in a terribly vulnerable position. Then I might, in regard to future tours, be asked whether I would accept A, or whether I would accept B, or whether I would accept C or D. Surely this would lead to an absurd position . . . The attitude I have adopted all along is that I am not prepared to act as the selection committee.[74]

In January 1968 the MCC, at the behest of the Labour Government, had threatened to put an end to the guesswork when it requested from SACA an assurance that D'Oliveira would be admitted if selected, but Douglas-Home had intervened to ensure that the charade continued.

His advice not to press for an assurance was gratefully accepted by the MCC Committee, and the MCC selectors were consequently drawn into the charade. Swanton, along with others, believed that the selectors made their own contribution by attempting to justify the omission of D'Oliveira on purely cricketing grounds. 'To say that there were "several better batsmen" after a Test innings of such calibre,' he asserted in the *Daily Telegraph* of 4 September 1968, 'to assert on the one hand that the South African pitches are expected to be grassy enough to suit Cartwright and on the other that D'Oliveira's bowling did not come into consideration: this in the language of ordinary followers was merely adding insult to injury.'

For some among the more politically sensitive the real complaint against the MCC Committee and their selectors was that they did indeed think in purely cricketing terms; that their vision did not extend beyond the boundary. As the press noted prior to the selection of the team, D'Oliveira's inclusion would represent the first real test of Vorster's new sports policy. By omitting D'Oliveira the MCC was perceived to have evaded the test, and with it the opportunity to begin whittling down apartheid barriers in South African sport. Even the *Star*, the moderate English-language Johannesburg daily, believed the MCC selectors had 'dropped a dolly' and done South African sport a disservice by not putting Vorster's policy to the test. 'Something needed to be proved internally as well as externally,' the *Star* commented on 30 August, 'the inward policy as well as the outward.'

Alan Ross in the *Observer* was more forthright, asserting that 'any sophisticated committee with a healthy sense of priorities' would have made a different choice: 'In a flexible situation the wrong gamble was taken.' Instead of seizing a 'golden opportunity' to confront sporting apartheid and encourage black cricketers in South Africa, the MCC gave comfort to 'the sweating but complacent apostles and fellow-travellers of apartheid'.[75]

More narrowly, the reason for much of the fury directed at the MCC and its selectors over the initial omission of D'Oliveira was that it allowed Vorster to hide his cards. D'Oliveira's belated inclusion in the team forced the South African Prime Minister to play his hand. 'The onus and the odium of excluding D'Oliveira on the grounds of his colour,' the *Guardian* declared, 'is now the South Africans' alone.'[76]

There were also people in cricketing circles in South Africa who were furious at the MCC for its handling of the affair. In a remarkable outburst Louis Duffus, the doyen of South African cricket writers, placed the entire blame for the debacle at D'Oliveira's doorstep, describing it as 'a dagger directed at the heart of South African cricket' and castigating the MCC for their 'blatant ignorance or deliberate ignoring of South African conditions'. He asked: 'Was it to be expected that the

South African Government would change its whole policy for a cricketer?' The MCC had committed 'fratricide upon a younger brother in the prime of life', and all because of one man: 'Because of one cricketer the great players produced in this country and the game itself have both been victimised. Posterity will surely marvel how a player, helped to go overseas by the charitable gesture of white contemporaries, could be the cause of sending the cricket of his benefactors crashing into ruins.'[77]

Geoffrey Chettle countered in an editorial in the *South African Cricket Annual* that it was amazing that South Africans 'should be so lacking in faith in themselves and in their country as to imagine for a single moment that the presence of one man – a clean-living, respectable person who is an accomplished exponent of the game of cricket – should constitute a national hazard'. The awful truth white South African cricket now had to contemplate was that politics did indeed impinge upon sport. As Mike Procter, the Springbok all-rounder, later acknowledged: 'In 1968, it was the South African government which brought politics into sport, not the protestors. In later years, defenders of South Africa's right to play international sport would usually bemoan the blurring of the boundaries between sport and politics, but we have to accept that initially the fault was on South Africa's side.'[78]

The D'Oliveira Affair came at the end of a decade in which the Nationalists had consolidated their hegemony within South Africa. The African National Congress, the Pan Africanist Congress and the South African Communist Party had all been banned, and even liberal organisations were in disarray, most notably with the dissolution of the Liberal Party as a consequence of the Prevention of Political Interference Act of 1968. It was in the international sphere, with the beginnings of the arms embargo and the sports boycott, particularly the exclusion of South Africa from two successive Olympic Games, that the apartheid regime was meeting with mounting if patchy opposition. The significance of the affair was that neither the South African Cricket Association from within the country nor the MCC from without was prepared to take a principled stand against the crassest form of sporting apartheid, the exclusion of 'non-whites' from touring teams to South Africa. Their first concern had been to try to preserve the traditional cricketing links between South Africa and England, and that was to remain their primary concern, even after the D'Oliveira Affair.

South African Team in England, 1955

Standing: Ian Smith, Headley Keith, Trevor Goddard, Paul Winslow, Peter Heine, Neil Adcock, Chris Duckworth, Eddie Fuller, Mich McLennan (scorer)

Seated: Percy Mansell, Roy McLean, Russell Endean, Jack Cheetham (captain), Ken Viljoen (manager), Jack McGlew (vice-captain), Hugh Tayfield, John Waite, Anton Murray

South Africa vs Kenya Asians, December 1956

Standing: E.I. Jeewa (Natal), S. Raziet (Western Province), B. Malamba (Western Province), C. Abrahams (Western Province), S. Abed (Western Province)

Seated: M.R. Varachia (secretary), C. Meyer, B. D'Oliveira (Western Province, captain), A.M. Jassat (manager), A. Variawa (Transvaal, vice-captain), A. Bell (Transvaal), B.D. Pavadai (president)

Front: A.S. Bulbulia (Transvaal), E. Lakay (Western Province, 12th man), H. Abrahams (Transvaal)

B.J. Vorster
(Die Burger)

Basil D'Oliveira in the process of scoring 158 at the Oval, August 1968 (Hulton)

Barbed wire being laid out at Headingley, Leeds, 1970

The Last Springbok Test Team vs Australia, Port Elizabeth, March 1970

Standing: A.M. Short (12th man), P.H.J. Trimborn, B.A. Richards, H.R. Lance, M.J. Procter, A.J. Traicos, B.L. Irvine

Seated: D.T. Lindsay, P.M. Pollock, A. Bacher (captain), E.B. Norton (manager), E.J. Barlow, R.G. Pollock

How cartoonists saw the challenges of Springbok cricket

Above: Knit One, Pearl One (Bob Connolly, *Rand Daily Mail*)

Right: Last Wicket Stand (Robin, *Natal Mercury*, 12 May 1970)

Below: (Collette, *The Australian*, 6 September 1971)

Boon Wallace and Hassan Howa

Rachid Varchia   (The Star)

Dr Piet Koornhof launches 'normal' cricket, 2 October 1976
Dr Koornhof, the Minister of Sport, greets Moosa Mangera, captain of the Crescents club, at the
Wanderers. Looking on is John Waite, the former Springbok wicketkeeper batsman. (Rand Daily Mail)

South African Cricket Union Board of Control, 1977/78

Standing: S.B. Myers, F.B. Gouws, M. Henning, N.E. Markham, F. Brache, D.J. Lewis
Seated: D.V. Dyer, M.R. Varachia (president), B. Wallace (vice-president), J.L. Pamensky
(treasurer)

South Africa vs South African Breweries English XI, Wanderers, March 1982

Standing: Jimmy Cook, Ray Jennings, Steve Jefferies, Alan Kourie, Kevin McKenzie, Garth le Roux
Seated: Peter Kirsten, Barry Richards, Graeme Pollock, Mike Procter (captain), Ronnie Ericson
(manager), Clive Rice, Vintcent van der Byl

6

How the Seventy Tour was Stopped

IN 1960 South African teams, composed entirely of whites, had competed internationally in all major sports. South Africa had participated at the Olympic Games in Rome, the Springbok rugby team had hosted a visit by the New Zealand All Blacks and embarked on a tour of the British Isles and France, and the Springbok cricketers had toured England. By the end of 1970, as a consequence of the sports boycott, the picture was very different – the world of white South African sport had been turned upside down.

The first year of the new decade was one of stunning success for the boycott campaign. South Africa, excluded from the 1964 Tokyo Olympics and the 1968 Mexico City Olympics, was finally expelled altogether from the Olympic Games movement, the first country ever to suffer such humiliation. The suspension later in the year by the International Amateur Athletics Federation of South African athletes from international competition meant that South African sportsmen were now banned from participating in international competition in virtually all the Olympic codes. In tennis, while South Africa survived the attempt to expel it from the International Lawn Tennis Federation, it was suspended from the Davis Cup competition, and the annual South African tennis championship lost its Grand Prix status. In cricket, the projected tour of South Africa to England was cancelled. In the following year the tour to Australia was likewise cancelled, leaving the country effectively excluded from international Test-match cricket. Among the major team sports, rugby alone survived the onslaught of the sports boycott. Despite organised opposition and protest within New Zealand, the All Black rugby tour of South Africa went ahead in 1970, with the inclusion for the first time of Maoris in the touring party.

The banishment of South African cricket did not follow immediately on the D'Oliveira Affair and, in the end, was imposed on the international cricket establishment rather than imposed by it.[1] Unlike in the case of other sports, South Africa's expulsion from international Test cricket was the achievement of protest from below, rather than committee decisions from above.

Even in the wake of the D'Oliveira Affair, the cricket administrators of South Africa's two major rivals and co-founders of the ICC, England and Australia, were generally reluctant to cut playing ties with the country; they ultimately capitulated before the threat of militant popular action, and, in the instance of England, at the behest of the government. Although the MCC tour of South Africa for 1968/69 was called off the Cricket Council, the successor to the MCC as the governing body of English cricket, maintained the invitation for South Africa to tour England in 1970. However, the widespread sense of outrage that the ban on D'Oliveira had caused in Britain enabled anti-apartheid groups to mobilise formidable opposition to the tour, with militants threatening to physically disrupt games.

Vorster's blatantly political interference in the selection of the MCC team when cricket was trying desperately to assert that it was 'above politics', and the crass racism of his ban on D'Oliveira offended sporting instincts, generating the outrage that militants capitalised on to pose a direct threat to the tour. In this climate, and with African, Asian and Caribbean countries threatening to boycott the Commonwealth Games in Edinburgh and a general election pending, the Labour Government of Harold Wilson, which had all along sought to avoid intervening directly, finally found itself obliged to step in. A fortnight before the tour was due to begin, the government formally requested the Cricket Council to call it off 'on grounds of broad public policy'. This it did on 22 May 1970.

Ironically, in a final bid to save the tour from disruption and recognising that it had become impractical to continue playing with 'apartheid cricket', the Cricket Council had already taken the decision that would prove truly fatal to white South Africa's cricketing relationship with England. There would be no further tours to or from South Africa until cricket there was played on a 'multi-racial' basis, and its national team selected on merit.

Hitherto both the MCC and the Cricket Council had urged that 'cricket in South Africa should be given the longest possible time to bring about conditions in which all cricketers in their own country, regardless of their origin, are able to play and be selected on equal terms'.[2] The Cricket Council's decision of May 1970 regarding future tours signified that it could no longer hold the ring for SACA, and that the time had arrived for South African cricket to advance towards non-racialism, or accept ostracism. SACA's own signal failure to have made any real progress since the 1960 Springbok tour of England, when it had simply brushed aside suggestions about the inclusion of 'non-whites' in the team, helped ensure that the 1970 tour never took place, and that South African cricket entered its era of isolation.

THE ROAD TO CANCELLATION

As *The Times* came to contend retrospectively, the moment that the invitation to South Africa to tour England in 1970 should have been withdrawn was when Vorster refused to allow D'Oliveira into South Africa as a member of the MCC team. Such a move would have been seen by everyone as a fair riposte, and would have made it absolutely plain to the South African Government that its political interference in the selection of British teams would not be tolerated.[3] It would, by extension, have left the Vorster Government carrying the direct responsibility for wrecking South Africa's cricketing relationship with England. But in the wake of Vorster's intervention the fundamental concern of both SACA and the MCC was to save that relationship, and persevering with the 1970 tour was seen as crucial to this objective.

After Vorster's statement Jack Cheetham and Arthur Coy flew incognito to London in a desperate effort intended not as much to salvage the MCC tour but future cricket relations with England. Both addressed a special meeting of the MCC Committee on 24 September, stressing that 'there was nothing they could do to alter the fact that the MCC side, as constituted, was unacceptable to the South African Government, and it was evident that the matter had been taken out of their hands'. Their hope was that 'present circumstances would not affect future relationships', more particularly the 1970 tour. The pair held that if that tour was cancelled the link would be broken, and South African cricket would be doomed to isolation, with disastrous consequences for the game within the country. The MCC Committee thereupon took the inevitable decision to cancel its tour to South Africa, underlining that cancellation had been forced on it by the policy of the South

African Government, and not by SACA. The question of future relationships was to be the subject of a special general meeting called for by the Reverend David Sheppard and his rebel group.[4]

The special general meeting, attended by over a thousand members, was finally held at Church House, Westminster, on 5 December 1968. Three resolutions were put to the meeting by Sheppard, a former England captain, and seconded by Mike Brearley, a future England captain. The first expressed 'regret' at the MCC Committee's 'mishandling of affairs' leading up to the selection of the team to tour South Africa, the second moved that there should be no further tours to or from South Africa until 'actual progress' was made in that country towards 'non-racial cricket', and the third that a special committee be established to monitor such progress. 'Our protest,' Sheppard declared, 'is against tolerating racialism in cricket. We object to the fact that politics have entered into cricket.'

Ronald Aird, who was now president of the MCC and, as such, presided over the meeting, sought to put a different spin on the issues at stake. To cries of 'shame', he declared that the fundamental difference between the Sheppard group and the MCC Committee was that the committee wanted to send a team to South Africa, and the others did not because of their political opposition to apartheid. Thereafter, as *The Times* reported, the temperature at the meeting rose considerably. The meeting lasted almost four hours, and in Sheppard's recollection was 'the most fraught' he had ever attended.[5]

All three of Sheppard and Brierley's resolutions were defeated at the meeting; by substantial margins when the postal votes were added. At the beginning of the following year the MCC Cricket Council, or Cricket Council as it came to be renamed, and the Test and County Cricket Board (TCCB), the new governing and administrative bodies of English cricket, unanimously decided to proceed with the South African tour of England in 1970 in accordance with the Council's policy 'to play and foster the game as widely as possible, both at home and overseas'. The itinerary for the tour, released in September, provided for five Tests and matches against all the counties over four months from 2 May to 8 September 1970. The decision to proceed was confirmed, again unanimously, by the TCCB on 10–11 December 1969.

By then it was evident that the tour would prove bitterly divisive and generate massive protests. To the dismay of the cricketing authorities, the D'Oliveira Affair had kept on unravelling. In April 1969 two startling revelations were made. The first was about 'Tienie' Oosthuizen's clandestine approach to D'Oliveira with a 'fantastic' offer for him to coach in South Africa on condition that he render himself unavailable for the MCC tour. The second, that Lord Cobham had informed Lord's of Vorster's attitude, proved directly damaging to the reputation of the MCC leadership.

Organised pressure against the tour mounted relentlessly, initially spearheaded by SANROC. As far back as December 1968 Dennis Brutus had written to the Cricket Council and to all seventeen county cricket clubs, asking them not to endorse the tour. The reply he received from Wilfred Wooller, the Glamorgan secretary and former captain known for his right-wing views, was, as Brutus described it, 'brusque and discourteous':

We have no sympathy with your cause in any shape or form and regard you as an utter nuisance. You do far more damage than good, and I have yet to come across any first-class cricketer, active in the game at present, who has any use for your activities. Furthermore, I personally suspect your motives and your background.[6]

In May 1969 Brutus asked the ICC to intervene to stop the tour, only to be informed by Billy Griffith, in his capacity as ICC secretary, that the ICC could not 'properly discuss the matter of South Africa, or the South African Tour to the United Kingdom in 1970', as SACA was not a member of the ICC: 'It remains, therefore, a matter for each individual country to decide whether or not they will play cricket against South Africa.'[7]

By way of public pressure, SANROC held a meeting in London in May 1969 to discuss plans for securing a cancellation of the tour. It was at this meeting that Peter Hain, the young South African exile now vice-chairman of the left-wing Young Liberals, made the suggestion that direct action be employed to stop the tour. According to Hain, Brutus was 'very supportive'. In September, a meeting between SANROC, the Young Liberals and various left-wing organisations set up the Stop the Seventy Tour (STST) Committee, with the forceful Hain as chairman.[8] Unlike the symbolic protests, characterised by peaceful, orderly picketing, that had met the Springbok cricketers in 1960 and 1965, the STST campaign was designed to force the Cricket Council to abandon the tour.

The D'Oliveira Affair had rocked the English cricket scene at the very moment that Britain, as elsewhere, was hit by an upsurge in left-wing student protest with mainly educated middle class youth rebelling against complacency, conformity and authority. It was the era of what conservative Britons considered 'permissiveness' and of the 'long-haired protester'. The protest movements had myriad targets, ranging from university administrations to the American presence in Vietnam to the actions of hated regimes across the world, including South Africa. The modes of protest were militant and sometimes violent, encompassing sit-ins, mass demonstrations and clashes with the police.[9] 'Direct action techniques' provided the mould for the STST campaign, and rebellious students the core of its militant support. In Hain's reckoning, picketing did little to concentrate minds at Lord's; the strategy was to force cancellation by threatening a massive campaign of 'non-violent' direct action designed to disrupt or prevent matches.[10]

Initially, the leadership of both the African National Congress and the Anti-Apartheid Movement (AAM) in London were wary of Hain and his campaign. Hain's student militancy did not square with the more respectable middle-aged, middle-class constituency targeted by the AAM's leadership, or with the movement's more traditional modes of protest. As David Steel, the Liberal MP and president of the AAM, impressed on its National Committee, 'The policy of the Movement must be to demonstrate, but the Movement should not itself organise disruptive demonstrations. The Movement is essentially a propaganda organisation.' Personally, Steel thoroughly disapproved of Hain's tactics, believing the antagonism they provoked to be counter-productive to the overall anti-apartheid cause.[11] Richard Crossman, the Labour Cabinet minister, concurred, noting in his diary after the harassment during the Springbok rugby tour that 'there is no doubt whatsoever that the demonstrators have damaged their own anti-apartheid cause'. In his assessment, 'they have strengthened racialism and turned sportsmen against them'.[12] Even Hassan Howa, the president of the 'non-racial' South African Cricket Board of Control, had major reservations about Hain's tactics. 'It is not cricket,' he told Michael Melford of the *Daily Telegraph*, 'it is an invasion of freedom which we hold very dear.'[13]

Hain nonetheless had powerful support among the AAM's rank-and-file. One resolution adopted at the AAM's annual general meeting at the National Liberal Club on 26 October 1969 warned the MCC that if it proceeded with the tour matches would 'inevitably be disrupted'; another went so far as to assert that 'this Annual General Meeting, aware of the effectiveness of direct action in the sphere of sport, urges an extension of this kind of activity to other fields'. The stand ultimately taken by the AAM on the STST campaign was that while 'the Movement sympathised with the objectives of those who disrupted matches and many AAM members took part in such activities, the Movement as an organisation had not organised disruptive demonstrations'. The *Daily Express* accused the AAM's leadership of effectively giving a nod and a wink to the militants while at the same time saying, 'Don't associate us publicly with this'.[14]

The campaign mounted by the AAM itself centred on a petition, signed by over 12 000 people, submitted to the TCCB in February 1970, and it planned its 'biggest-ever demonstration' for the first Test at Lord's. In the end this campaign served to complement that of the STST, and Hain won the movement's plaudits for having 'handled publicity in the Press and on television outstandingly well'.[15]

In the winter months, as a 'dummy run' for the cricket tour, STST demonstrators dogged the 1969/70 Springbok rugby tour, invading pitches and disrupting play. Over Christmas the demoralised rugby players voted to go home, but were ordered by management to continue. At the end of the tour the Springbok manager, Corrie Bornman, confessed: 'The last three months have been an ordeal to which I would never again subject young sportsmen.' Cheetham and Coy, who were in London for discussions with the Cricket Council, saw the Springboks play England at Twickenham with Jack Bailey, the MCC assistant secretary, and Raman Subba Row. According to Bailey, 'Cheetham and Coy watched it all and showed no misgivings about the forthcoming tour', while in Subba Row's recollection the match made it 'painfully clear that the cricket tour was impossible'.[16]

Painfully clear or not, the immediate effect of the threat of direct action was to heighten the resolve of the cricket establishment to proceed with the South African tour; the national pastime of the Britain they identified with was under assault from the 'great unwashed'. At its December 1969 meeting, the TCCB agreed unanimously not only that it was in the interests of cricket for the tour to be confirmed but that 'it was the duty of the Board, as a National Body, to uphold the rights of the individual to play and watch cricket'.[17] For the cricket establishment, mounting the South African tour had become something of a crusade for defending, in the words of the Cricket Council, 'civilised pursuits' against 'a minority who seek to impose their views by violent demonstration'. As one county secretary said to the *Observer* of the county chairmen who sat and voted on the TCCB, 'This was their opportunity to apply all their dislike and loathing of permissiveness, demonstrators and long hair. Staging matches is their chance to make a stand against these things.'[18]

To contend with the threat of direct action, the Cricket Council's Emergency Executive Committee, under its chairman, the normally relaxed Maurice Allom, the former Surrey and England bowler, was authorised to examine fully all the problems connected with the tour and make recommendations. The brief included the feasibility of protecting grounds and matches and the possibility of shortening the tour. To highlight for the committee the vulnerability of grounds, about a dozen county grounds were sabotaged on the night of 19 January 1970 in what Hain later described as 'a carefully timed bombshell'. 'Everyone had been caught by surprise,' Hain recalled, 'and the widespread strength of the movement had been starkly revealed in an operation carried out with almost military precision.'[19]

On the advice of Quintin Hogg, the 'shadow' Home Secretary and MP for Marylebone, which included Lord's, Allom's committee thereupon sent a deputation representing 'Cricket' to see the Home Secretary, Jim Callaghan, on 29 January to discuss police protection and its costs. Callaghan's own view, expressed at a departmental briefing, was that it would be impossible for police to keep a cricket match in progress against 'determined opposition', and he explained to the deputation how easy it would be to disrupt a match by creating noise, shining mirrors, and other such tricks. He also emphasised that the hire of policemen for special occasions was hugely expensive and that there were limits to 'how far the police could be withdrawn from their normal duties in order to attend a cricket match'. Callaghan's demeanour was, evidently, dismissive and, according to Jack Bailey, 'he was somewhat surprised at just how resolute we were'. The deputation responded that they were 'reasonably confident' they could prevent demonstrators from stopping play once it was under way. Their main concern, they said, was damage to property and to the pitches.[20]

At a special Cricket Council meeting at Lord's on 12 February, the Emergency Executive Committee recommended a drastically curtailed tour itinerary – from twenty-eight matches to twelve, and those restricted to eight 'defensible' grounds; that matches be made all-ticket affairs so as to keep demonstrators out; and that an appeal for funds be launched to cover the exceptional costs of the tour. For the protection of grounds prior to matches the committee suggested such extraordinary measures as barbed wire fencing, floodlights, alarm systems and police dogs; and for matches themselves it recommended the erection of fences between the spectators and the playing area as well as the employment of stewards. Artificial pitches were to be prepared for use in the event of damage to the regular pitch. However, the ultimate responsibility for the maintenance of law and order in the face of threats lay with the police. Insurance against cancellation of the tour, it was reported, was only possible if it were cancelled after the South African team had arrived in England.[21] In accordance with the Emergency Executive Committee's recommendations, the Cricket Council voted 23-0, with one abstention, to proceed with the tour. The South Africans were scheduled to arrive on 1 June.

The thinking behind the decision to proceed was summed up in a memorandum prepared by Jack Bailey, who, as MCC assistant secretary, had special responsibility for the press and public relations; and Raman Subba Row (the man Vorster had once claimed was never chosen to tour South Africa because of his colour), who was in charge of the public relations campaign to counter opposition to the tour:

The decision on our part was made because:
a) They are traditional opponents.
b) We are satisfied that the SACA are making every possible effort to further the cause of multi-racial cricket.
c) No minority group should be allowed to dictate to the majority in this country. No amount of blackmail or pressure should influence this decision.
d) The Tour is practicable and profitable within the terms of the revised itinerary.
e) The ultimate good of all cricketers in South Africa is best served by the Tour taking place.
f) In the interest of world cricket in the long term, expediency, however desirable it might seem in the short term, should not be a consideration.
g) Public opinion is on our side and therefore the majority of people would be disappointed if the Tour did not take place. Furthermore, it would be difficult for them to reconcile our constantly stated intention with any change of heart.

In a pamphlet issued by the Cricket Council in support of the decision to proceed, it emphasised its own fundamental opposition to apartheid in sport and spelled out its 'underlying' philosophy that continuing contact would do more to promote multi-racial sport in South Africa than would boycott, which would almost certainly prove counter-productive. 'The effect of total isolation,' the Council declared, 'would serve to make those who are already inward-looking even more so.'[22]

As a result of a security lapse, Peter Hain was present at Lord's for the announcement of the Council's decision to proceed with the tour, and he responded that the Council had made 'a declaration of war'.[23] With Lord's itself already surrounded by barbed wire, and floodlit by night, it was clear that the tour would take place under siege conditions, a prospect that gravely troubled the Wilson Government.

With a general election due in either the summer or autumn of 1970, the government was particularly anxious to avert a prolonged and bitter public disturbance over an apartheid cricket tour, especially with its potential to inflame fragile race relations in an era in which Britain was struggling to come to terms with the fact that it had become a multi-racial society and Enoch Powell had provocatively conjured up visions of 'rivers of blood' flowing through Britain's cities as a consequence of Asian and West Indian immigration. But for a number of reasons the government was equally anxious to avoid taking direct action to stop the tour. Direct political intervention in international sporting affairs was contrary to British tradition and to oft-stated government policy; to take such action might complicate relations with South Africa to the detriment of British trade, which was still heavily reliant on South Africa as its third largest market; and the government simply did not want to be seen as capitulating to the protesters, a move that might provide the Conservatives with a handy election issue. On 2 February, Ted Heath, the Conservative leader, had said on television that the tour should go ahead, and an integral part of Conservative election strategy was to highlight 'law and order' issues. The Conservatives could be expected to pounce on any suggestion that the government capitulated to the threat of 'mob rule'.

Though making it clear throughout that it thoroughly disapproved of the tour, government's official policy was consequently to allow the cricket authorities to decide for themselves whether or not to continue. The formal request the Wilson Government ultimately made to the Cricket Council to cancel the tour represented a sudden reversal of policy.

From the government's standpoint the rational thing for the Cricket Council to do was to abandon the tour, and it consequently regarded the decision to proceed with some suspicion, particularly given the Council's links with the Conservative Party leadership. As Callaghan put it to his advisers on 27 January, he 'thought that the Cricket Council would be relieved if the tour were cancelled, but would prefer a situation in which they could claim that the Government had compelled them to cancel it'. Such a move, he insisted, should be avoided. Instead, he sought to encourage other pressures on the Cricket Council to cancel, making the rather impolitic suggestion that 'it might be possible for the Foreign and Commonwealth Office to mobilise opinion in other countries such as the West Indies'.[24] The government's objective, as Callaghan later put it to the Prime Minister, 'was to intensify the pressures by all the unofficial means we can find in the hope that the nerve of the Cricket Council will crack'.[25] But the Cricket Council held its nerve, adopting the attitude that if the government wanted the tour stopped it would have to stop it.

From early April the political pressures on the Cricket Council to cancel intensified hugely. In an ITV interview on 16 April Harold Wilson denounced the decision to invite the South Africans as 'ill-judged' and a mistake, as they had placed themselves 'outside the pale of civilised cricket', and he controversially encouraged everyone to feel free to demonstrate against the tour, though he was careful to add they should not resort to violent methods or to 'nasty sneaky little things, like sort of mirrors to deflect the sunshine into batsmen's eyes'. From the perspective of Lord's this prime ministerial 'incitement to demonstrate' amounted to 'blackmail', prompting Jack Bailey to issue a press statement saying that if 'the Prime Minister believes that the tour by the South Africans should not go ahead, then he should come out and say so, to the South African government'.[26]

A week later the Supreme Council for Sport in Africa threatened that African countries would boycott the Commonwealth Games, scheduled for Edinburgh in July, should the tour go ahead. Cricket was placed in the awkward position of seeming to sabotage the Commonwealth Games if it stubbornly proceeded with the tour. The threat was resented at Lord's as a crude attempt at political blackmail and, as the Foreign and Commonwealth Office submitted in a note to the Cabinet, it could not be expected that the Cricket Council would back down in the face of the African threat: 'They would be criticized bitterly by their supporters for giving into black blackmail after having held out against strong white pressures and threats.'[27]

The real challenge of the African boycott threat was to the government, already sensitive to the unhappiness of Commonwealth African countries about its failure to deal effectively with Ian Smith's UDI regime in Rhodesia and it was this threat that put the whole question of the South African tour on the Cabinet agenda.

The boycott threat was orchestrated by SANROC, operating in conjunction with the STST campaign. At the 7 March national conference of the STST campaign held in London, SANROC had been delegated to lobby for Afro-Asian support. In late March two SANROC delegates, Chris de Broglio and Wilfrid Brutus had attended the General Assembly of the Supreme Council of Sport in Africa in Cairo as observers, lobbying behind the scenes for action against the cricket tour. The General Assembly reached the 'informal' decision 'that no African team would attend the Games unless the MCC's decision to invite a South African cricket team were reversed'.[28] To the chagrin of the British Government and the Commonwealth Games officials this 'informal' decision was withheld until word of it was released to the press on 23 April. Although criticised as ill-judged and illogical – the Commonwealth Games and cricket had nothing to do with one another – the threat was a reality the government simply could not ignore. Wilson consequently asked Denis Howell, the minister responsible for sport, to set up a ministerial committee of the departments concerned to review the situation and advise the Cabinet.

At its meeting on 30 April, the Cabinet discussed the threats posed by the cricket tour to both the Commonwealth Games and to public order. For Wilson, a major concern was that support for the boycott might spread to other 'non-white' Commonwealth countries, creating the prospect of a preponderantly 'white' Commonwealth Games, which 'raised implications which went beyond the sphere of sport'. Callaghan reported that the Commissioner of Police for the Metropolis was confident that the Metropolitan Police could deal with any demonstrations at matches in London, though he personally feared this was 'too optimistic a forecast'. What particularly irked him was a letter from Hain asking for assurances that the police would not adopt 'discriminatory methods' in dealing with demonstrations; to rebut such insinuations Callaghan proposed 'a firm reply' indicating that no such assurances were necessary. This was followed by some talk of taking pre-emptive legal action against the militant opponents of the tour on the basis they might open themselves to 'prosecution for conspiracy' even before their plans for disrupting matches were put into operation. That possibility was not ruled out by the Cabinet, but it was appreciated that 'a prosecution for conspiracy was less likely to be effective than one based on an actual breach of the peace'. The conspiracy charge later brought against Hain by an English barrister, Francis Bennion, proved that.

Despite the misgivings voiced by Wilson and Callaghan, the Cabinet reached 'general agreement' that it would be inadvisable for the government to take direct action to stop the tour. Instead, it followed the recommendation of the Howell committee to encourage pressure on the Cricket Council from other sources, including possibly Sir Alec Douglas-Home, who was a Scot and consequently had an interest in avoiding a debacle in Edinburgh.[29] In the assessment of Richard Crossman 'Harold and Jim have handled this issue extremely adroitly in a way that is simultaneously liberal, fair-minded and pro-sport.'[30] In a TV interview after the Cabinet meeting, Wilson appealed to the Cricket Council to reconsider its decision.

When the Cabinet next discussed the cricket tour, at its meeting on 7 May, there had been a distinct deterioration in the situation, with the Indian Government prohibiting Indian participation in the Commonwealth Games should the cricket tour proceed. The Games organisers, Howell reported in a memorandum to the Cabinet, had not been 'unduly worried if only African States were to withdraw', but the ban on Indian participation increased the possibility of a widespread boycott. Indirect attempts to pressurise the Cricket Council had borne no fruit. Douglas-Home had advised that the Council would only be likely to call off the tour in response to a direct government request, and Sheppard had received a blunt 'no' when he asked the Council on 5 May whether they 'would like the Government to get them "off the hook" '. Given this situation, the Cabinet considered, but rejected, the possibility of making a direct appeal to the Cricket Council to cancel the tour. A formal approach, especially from the Prime Minister himself, would amount to direct political intervention in sport, and there was a risk that it would be rebuffed, giving rise to 'an intolerable situation'. Legal advice was that it would be impracticable to ban the entry of the South African team as 'undesirable aliens'; such a move would require amendments to the instructions to Immigration Officers, which would have to be laid before the House of Commons, where 'it would be difficult to avoid a major debate, with unpredictable consequences'. The Cabinet consequently decided to persist with its policy of encouraging pressure on the Cricket Council by 'appropriate individuals and organisations, who might usefully emphasise that to persist with the tour might put at risk future Test series with the West Indians and other non-white cricketing countries'.

The recommendation of the Howell committee was that ministers should watch developments for the following week or so to see if 'a significant change of circumstances' warranted a change of policy. The committee also observed that while a formal request to the Cricket Council would probably raise vociferous protest from certain sections of the public, 'it might be short-lived and in any case much less serious than the prospect of disturbances over a period of two months or more if the tour goes on'.[31]

On 21 May the Wilson Government, without further consultation with the Cabinet, formally requested the Cricket Council to cancel the tour. The trigger for the Government's intervention was the secret emergency meeting of the Council at Lord's on the afternoon of Monday 18 May, and its announcement the next day that the tour was still on. One of the factors that had prompted the meeting itself was the intervention of David Sheppard, now Bishop of Woolwich and chairman of the newly-formed Fair Cricket Campaign. Intended as a 'moderate' alternative to the STST campaign, the Fair Cricket Campaign had Sir Edward Boyle, the Conservative MP and former Cabinet minister, and Reginald Prentice, the Labour MP and former Cabinet minister, as its vice-chairmen. On 5 May it sent a delegation to Lord's. Sheppard was shocked to discover that everything relating to the tour had been delegated to the Emergency Executive Committee, and he consequently asked for a meeting of the whole Council.[32] Another development that prompted the meeting was a three-hour emergency debate in the House of Commons on 14 May in which Callaghan told the Council 'squarely' that if it failed to call off the tour, it would be responsible for the consequences. The Cricket Council meeting was subsequently summoned 'in the greatest possible secrecy' so as to put 'the least possible pressure' on the members of the Council.

Prior to the meeting, two crucial steps had been taken to help secure the Council's finances against various eventualities. First, in early April, a policy had been negotiated providing indemnity cover of £140 000 should the tour be called off 'solely and directly in consequence of riots, civil commotions, vandalism, malicious damage and/or acts of demonstrators' *after* the South African touring team had arrived in the United Kingdom. Second, on 23 April 'The 1970 Cricket Fund' had been launched at Lord's, with the approval of the Cricket Council. Under the chairmanship of Lt-Col Charles Newman, VC, it aimed to raise a minimum of £200 000 to help pay for police protection at grounds and for insurance cover. The one contingency that could not be provided for financially was cancellation *before* the rioting and civil commotion began.[33]

As Allom detailed in his comprehensive report to the Council, the pressure to cancel was multi-pronged. In addition to 'mounting pressure of a political nature', including threats by various organisations to disrupt matches, virtually every organisation concerned with community and race relations had made representations against the tour, as had the British Commonwealth Games Federation and the British Sports Council. The International Olympic Committee's decision of the previous day to expel South Africa from the Olympic movement likewise added to the pressure on the Cricket Council; it meant that South Africa was now 'excluded from international competition in all but two games, cricket and rugby football'. There was also pressure on the cricket front itself to cancel. Domestically, while it was evident that the vast majority of cricketers and cricket followers were in favour of the tour, it was also evident that the South Africans were 'likely to have a disturbed and unhappy tour', and that, together with the prospect of a potentially ruinous police bill, would mean that 'the adverse financial effect of the tour upon English cricket would be considerable'.

Internationally, the black cricket-playing countries had recently brought considerable pressure to bear. In April Howell had bemoaned the unwillingness of other members of the ICC to exert any pressure on the Cricket Council 'not-withstanding the political views of their own Governments'.[34] In May that had changed. As Allom reported, the Pakistan Board of Control for Cricket had cancelled the tour of the United Kingdom by its under-25 team; the West Indies Board of Control had urged cancellation of the South African tour 'in the interests of future cricket relationships between the West Indies and England'; and the Indian Cricket Board had advised all Indian cricketers playing for English counties not to participate in any matches against the South Africans.

There was one other major inducement to cancel – the likelihood of a general election in the midst of the tour. Billy Griffith, the MCC and Cricket Council secretary, had twice consulted Douglas-Home about the imminent general election. Sir Alec had said that his personal view was that the tour should be cancelled, but 'only after discussion with the Prime Minister, giving the Prime Minister the option of himself asking for cancellation'. He added that the right thing to do in the national interest was to 'avoid the Tour – and its immense difficulties – clashing with the General Election'. As it happened, while the Council was meeting, the Prime Minister gave notice that the election would be held on 18 June, the scheduled opening day of the first Test at Lord's.

Summing up, Allom stressed that the basic concern of the Council was the best interests of cricket, both in the short and the long term. The decision whether or not to proceed with the tour, he impressed on the Council, was 'perhaps the most important cricket decision that the Council would ever have to take'.[35]

Despite all the pressures to cancel, and the looming threat of a major split between black and white cricket-playing countries, the Council voted by 18 to 8 to go ahead with the tour, but added one crucial rider. In a seemingly desperate bid to avert large-scale disruption of the tour, but more significantly as a signal to SACA that it could no longer continue to dodge the question of racialism in South African cricket, the Council resolved that 'no further Test tours will take place between South Africa and this country until such time as Test cricket is played and tours are selected on a multi-racial basis in South Africa'.

The next day, the Council's decision was announced at a press conference at Lord's. Journalists, according to the *Guardian* reporter, arrived expecting to hear the tour had been cancelled, and listened with 'mounting incredulity' as it became clear that that was not the case. The tour was immediately put in doubt again on the following day, Wednesday 20 May, when Callaghan invited representatives of the Cricket Council to meet him at the Home Office. He and Wilson had finally decided to formally request the Council to cancel the tour in the fairly confident expectation – gained from discreet soundings in banking circles – that the Council would agree. On the Wednesday morning, at Callaghan's behest, Sir Leslie O'Brien, the Governor of the Bank of England and a friend of Callaghan's from his Treasury days, approached Sir Cyril Hawker, president-elect of the Cricket Council and chairman of the Standard Chartered Bank, which had major South African connections, 'to discover on what terms the Cricket Council were prepared to cancel the Tour'. Hawker told O'Brien that 'cancellation would only be considered if a formal request was received from Her Majesty's Government'. That was the green light for Callaghan, who, that afternoon, made the formal request. As Callaghan informed the Prime Minister in a late-night telephone conversation, he had 'discussed the matter with Sir Leslie O'Brien who had advised him, in the light of his contacts, that there was a good chance that the Cricket Council would respond to an appeal'.[36]

In making the decision on 18 May to proceed with the tour, the Cricket Council had quite clearly rebuffed the government, but it had also signalled its readiness to surrender. Its members were no longer unanimous in support of the tour, future apartheid cricket tours had been ruled out, and the Council had stated outright that it saw its responsibilities as being restricted to cricket and sport, deeming 'matters of a public and political nature' to be 'the responsibility of Government who are best equipped to judge and act upon them'. The latter was an open invitation for the government to intervene, if it so chose.

The imperatives were on the government to change its policy and accept the invitation, confident now there would be no rebuff. The 'fiasco' of an all-white Commonwealth Games was becoming more of a reality as the boycott movement continued to gather pace, with Pakistan, Malaysia and Jamaica joining it, and Labour backbenchers had shown themselves anxious for the government to act. The challenge to law-and-order, moreover, was mounting, as policemen, many of them shaken by the anti-Vietnam War demonstrations and resentful of the burdens placed on them of protecting the Springbok rugby tour, made it evident at the annual Police Federation conference that they would not volunteer for extra duty for fear of sustaining serious injuries. But the key new ingredient in the situation was the government's own decision, finalised on 14 May, to hold the general election on 18 June, so that it might be staged before the progress of England, the defending champions, in the soccer World Cup in Mexico became too great a distraction.[37] To allow for the potential of riots over an apartheid cricket tour in the midst of a general election was simply not feasible – not only would the situation be well beyond the capacity of the police to handle, it might prove dangerously damaging to the Labour campaign.

At his three-hour meeting with Allom and Griffith on 21 May, Callaghan's demeanour was quite different from what it had been during their previous encounter; there were no bullying tactics, and dismissiveness gave way to inclusiveness. The Home Secretary impressed on them 'the wider considerations' of the tour, notably its implications for race relations, the Commonwealth Games and the police, and 'the divisive effect it would have on the community generally', and asked what the Cricket Council's reaction would be 'to a formal request from the Government that the invitation to the South African tour should be withdrawn on these grounds'. What he stressed was that he had no power 'to prevent the tour from taking place without the consent of the Cricket Council'. Allom responded that 'if such a request were made it would be virtually impossible for the Cricket Council not to accede to it'. Losing no time, Callaghan thereupon had a draft letter prepared requesting that the tour be called off 'on grounds of broad public policy'. Once the terms had been finalised, Callaghan signed a formal letter and handed it to Allom for submission to the Cricket Council. There followed a discussion of the financial losses to the Council and the county clubs from gate receipts and BBC coverage, with Callaghan intimating that he would consult his colleagues about providing 'limited assistance'.[38] An ex gratia payment of £75 054 was duly made to the Cricket Council by the subsequent Conservative Government.

On 22 May the Cricket Council announced, with deep regret, that the tour was cancelled. No vote was taken; only two diehards insisted that the Council should attempt to hold out and force the government to cancel the tour. 'I think those of us close to the centre of things had all realized that to sustain a tour would be virtually impossible,' Jack Bailey later conceded. He added: 'But at least we had got so far as ensuring that the government had become closely involved in the cancellation.'[39] Both the government and the Cricket Council had saved face, though the latter lost any claim on its insurance cover.

While opposed in principle to the tour, the Wilson Government's policy all along was that it wanted the Cricket Council to cancel of its own accord, which it stubbornly refused to do. In truth, the Cricket Council had staked out a position where it could not cancel of its own volition. Even when its members recognised that the situation had become too fraught for the tour to proceed, voluntary cancellation was not seen as an option.

The Cricket Council's refusal to cancel the tour of its own accord can be put down to the perception that such a decision would have represented a craven capitulation to what the *Daily Telegraph* described as 'a fascist-minded anti-democratic minority', and to a hypocritical government that asked them to stop playing cricket with South Africa while it actively promoted trade with the country. Voluntary cancellation would also have represented a betrayal of the cricketers and spectators who were looking forward to the tour, and of majority public opinion that wanted the tour. However, the Council already had contingency plans in place in case it was forced to call off the tour – a series against a World XI would replace the series against South Africa.

Cancellation was a triumph for the determination of Hain and the STST campaign he had run from his parents' home in Putney, London. The prospect of tens of thousands of demonstrators besieging fortified cricket grounds, battling police and severely disrupting or preventing games was the key factor leading to cancellation. Although there were many other layers in opposition to the tour, including the active assistance of the Anti-Apartheid Movement and the West Indian

Campaign against Apartheid Cricket, headed by Jeff Crawford, which targeted a particular constituency, in the end, as a headline in the *Guardian* proclaimed, it was truly a matter of 'Hain Stopped Play'. It was a triumph that launched Hain on a political career that was to lead ultimately to the Cabinet.

Even in South Africa there were some sighs of relief when the tour was cancelled, given mounting concerns about the injuries demonstrators might inflict on the Springbok cricketers. In its anxiety to preserve the tour and South Africa's position in international cricket SACA, it seemed to some, had wilfully ignored the lessons of the rugby tour of the British Isles. Kevin Craig warned in the *Sunday Times* that South Africa's cricketers would be exposed 'to physical danger and maybe death'. Ben Schoeman, Transvaal leader of the National Party, and Morris Zimmerman, a Progressive Party politician, both urged that the tour be called off for the sake of the cricketers themselves.

Pretoria had been forewarned about the cancellation of the tour when Michael Stewart, the British Foreign Secretary, cabled the British ambassador on 21 May with instructions to inform the South African Government of the meeting between Callaghan and the Cricket Council representatives.[40] Vorster's public response on hearing of the cancellation was predictable. It was not cricket or sport that had lost, he declared, but the forces of law and order: 'For a Government to submit so easily and so willingly to open blackmail is to me unbelievable,' he said, adding defiantly, 'This particular cricket relationship between South Africa and Great Britain was a relationship of the MCC with white South Africans.' Frank Waring's response was equally defiant. The South African Government, he declared in a press statement on 27 May, would not be intimidated into permitting 'integrated multiracial sport' in South Africa. 'It is now abundantly clear to all,' he went on, 'that sport is being employed by anti-South African political organisations to bring South Africa to her knees.' At the same time both Vorster and Waring welcomed the arrival of the first-ever mixed All Blacks team in South Africa. The All Blacks were pronounced a rugby team, not a political team.

SOUTH AFRICAN CRICKET

A major complaint at Lord's during the negotiations over the aborted 1970 tour was that SACA was leaden-footed in its own cause, proffering little to help counter the image of racialism in South African cricket. While officials at Lord's generally perceived SACA as a victim of South African Government policy over D'Oliveira, and had sought to offer it a life-line by confirming the invitation for the 1970 tour, there was a strong sense that the time had come for white South African cricket administrators and players to assist themselves by taking forceful steps against racialism in the sport. Instead, it appeared to those in London, timidity continued to prevail in white South African cricket circles. 'It is sad,' E.W. Swanton commented in the *Daily Telegraph* on April 1969, 'that there is so little evidence from South Africa of an appreciation of the strength of feeling against apartheid in sport.' Swanton believed that the only chance the South Africans had of making themselves welcome in England in 1970 was for SACA to do 'whatever it could, within the laws of South Africa, to recognise and help non-European cricket in their country', and also to arrange for mixed teams to tour outside of South Africa. A little more than a year later, after the collapse of attempts to salvage the 1970 tour, the *Rand Daily Mail* reported that several members of the Cricket Council had become thoroughly irritated and exasperated with their South African counterparts. A member of the Cricket Council was quoted as stating that 'we thought they could have helped us a bit more'. Impatience with Cheetham was evidently particularly acute; he had gained a reputation as a vacillator and fence-sitter.[41]

White South African cricket continued to be guided by the trio of Hammond, Cheetham and Coy, with Cheetham taking over as SACA president in September 1969. A highly efficient administrator, with a strong cricket background as a former Springbok captain, Cheetham was not a particularly political person. In white cricketing circles he was considered vaguely liberal, though the 'non-racial' cricketing world had a less favourable view of him, regarding him as an opportunist motivated purely by a concern for white cricket rather than 'the interests of all South African cricketers'.[42] He and SACBOC consequently never got on well. In late November 1969, and again in late January 1970, Cheetham and Coy travelled to Lord's to discuss arrangements for the 1970 tour and to report on progress towards breaking down racial barriers in South African cricket. On both occasions they had little by way of progress, or even the prospect thereof, to report.

Swanton's view on the need for mixed race touring teams was shared at Lord's. While it was accepted that SACA could not defy the country's laws, it was believed that it could explore a range of opportunities within the law in an effort to prove its good faith on the racial front. One of these would be to include black players in overseas touring teams; not only was there no law to prohibit it, but Vorster himself had allowed for a 'multi-racial' team to represent South Africa at the Olympic Games. Subba Row, chairman of the TCCB's Public Relations and Promotion sub-committee, in a letter to Billy Griffith on 22 October 1969, suggested that SACA might issue a public statement that 'coloured' players worthy of selection would be chosen for overseas tours, and proceed from there to include a 'coloured' player in the team to tour England, to appoint a 'coloured' manager or assistant manager, and to provide for a tour of the United Kingdom by 'a mixed side of lesser ability'. Another suggestion mooted at Lord's was that, to side-step government obstacles, SACA might invite one or two 'coloured' South African cricketers who were playing league cricket in the United Kingdom to join the Springbok team when it arrived.[43]

Within SACA it was fully recognised that there was a need for some change if South Africa was to save the tour and salvage its position in international cricket, but the national cricket body remained fundamentally constrained by its entrenched policy of not only accepting the law of the land but also of attempting to work with rather than against government. As a consequence of this policy SACA emerged from its negotiations with government unable to offer any prospect of changing the racial composition of South African touring teams. Its one dramatic new initiative was to be seen to be doing something positive to promote black cricket in South Africa, which meant that it engaged for the first time in negotiations with SACBOC. To its consternation, however, SACA discovered SACBOC to be no more pliable than Pretoria.

Until the tribulations over D'Oliveira, SACA had, to all intents and purposes, ignored black cricket. This was something it now sought to rectify, embarking on a survey of black cricket in all the provinces. 'We must get on with this,' Arthur Coy urged, 'so that we can have a case to forward to MCC to assist them when constant and increasing pressures will be brought to bear on them in the near future to cease cricket relationship with South Africa.'[44] At the December 1968 meeting of the SACA Board of Control it was established that there were two governing bodies for black cricket; SACBOC, with its headquarters in Cape Town, for coloured and Indian cricket, with about 7 000 registered players, roughly a third of the number in senior white cricket; and the South African African Cricket Board of Control, with its headquarters in Johannesburg, for 'Bantu' cricket. Both suffered from a 'lack of facilities, coaching and umpiring knowledge', with black cricket still being played overwhelmingly on sub-standard fields with matting wickets. 'After lengthy discussion' it was agreed that members of the Board should interview top members of the two controlling bodies.[45]

Coy, who had the ear of the Prime Minister, was careful to keep Vorster fully apprised of what SACA was contemplating, and, in conversation over the Christmas holidays, impressed on him that SACA 'considered it essential that they improve their image overseas and help Non-European cricket'. It was a policy with which Vorster 'thoroughly agreed', though he cautioned against being 'too benevolent in the way of money unless it was on a quid pro quo basis'. As Coy put Vorster's explanation: 'The reason for this was that these people do not appreciate anything they do not have to work for themselves.'[46]

Despite Vorster's warnings about over-generosity, the heart of SACA's initiative lay in providing financial assistance to black cricket, in the form of a considerable R50 000 (£25 000) trust fund that the Board of Control approved in principle at its meeting of 25 April 1969. The fund was intended to 'assist the development of non-Europeans', and particularly 'to develop non-white junior cricket'. As a public relations manoeuvre however, the trust fund was a failure in that it was ultimately rejected by SACBOC as a 'bribe'.

SACA's approaches to SACBOC proved scratchy throughout. SACBOC's initial response was that it was difficult to reconcile 'almost a century of indifference' on SACA's part with the 'almost indecent haste with which the present approach is being made', but it was prepared for the two executives to meet. Since the mid-1960s the control of SACBOC had moved from the Transvaal to the more radical Cape, and the first meeting between the SACBOC leadership and white cricket officials was in Cape Town. In January 1969 two representatives of the Western Province Cricket Union, Clive van Ryneveld and Bryan 'Boon' Wallace, met the SACBOC trio of Dirk van Harte (president), Hassan Howa (vice-president), and A.J.E. Jordaan (secretary), at Van Harte's Athlone home, and were informed that their help was not needed.[47] For the first meeting of the two national executives at Newlands on 16 March, SACBOC was ready with positive proposals for integrated cricket as well as for a trial match in Rhodesia between SACA and SACBOC XIs so the team that would tour England could be selected on the basis of merit. The SACA executive rejected these proposals as 'impossible' in the existing political climate, but did undertake to investigate whether SACBOC would be allowed to affiliate to SACA. The legal opinion given SACA was that its constitution did not allow SACBOC's affiliation as the latter was not a provincial or district union. A major point made by SACBOC at the meeting was that SACA officials refused even to object to government policy requiring discrimination in sport.[48] For the next meeting, on 13 July, the SACA executive was equipped with its proposals for a trust fund, but the SACBOC executive was dismissive of the suggestion, reserving final judgement until its next bi-annual general meeting. As Howa put it to Hammond, two thousand years ago the bribe had been 30 pieces of silver; now it had been raised to R50 000.[49]

Arthur Coy's response was that even if it was rejected by SACBOC, the trust fund should still be established for the benefit of the South African African Cricket Board (SAACB), which had broken from SACBOC when it embraced non-racial cricket, citing 'pressure exerted by other races'. With African cricket in a state of acute decline in many parts of the country, the SAACB was grateful for the assistance offered.[50] Beginning in January 1971 the trust served to finance an annual South African African schoolboys tournament, generally known as the Passmore week after the trustee, John Passmore, who organised it.

Abroad, the composition of South African touring teams was considered the cutting edge of any progress towards 'multi-racial' cricket. In his *Daily Telegraph* articles and his communications with South African cricket organisers, E.W. Swanton kept up the pressure for mixed race touring teams. His 1968 Christmas proposal to Wilfred Isaacs, the Johannesburg property tycoon and cricket patron, was that the Isaacs invitation team to tour England the following year should include a couple of black players. Isaacs promptly went to the Minister of Sport and Recreation, Frank Waring, and his department for advice, on the grounds that he feared a trap, and they told him to reply that his team had already been selected on merit and it was too late to make any changes.[51] To the chagrin of SACA, it was not even consulted. In the event, the tour of England by an all-white Isaacs invitation team provided Peter Hain and the Young Liberals with their first opportunity to experiment with demonstrations designed to disrupt play.

More disconcerting for SACA was that Isaacs, in his capacity as chairman of the South African Schoolboys Cricket Overseas Tour Fund, when inviting an MCC Schoolboys team to tour South Africa at the end of 1969 had apparently intimated that there would be no objection to 'non-whites' being included in the team 'provided the government was satisfied that there were no ulterior motives in their choice'. No black had played for England Schoolboys in several years, but SACA officials were alarmed to learn of a 'dark Indian schoolboy who is captain of

Harrow and is playing very well'. On 3 February 1969 Billy Griffith wrote to SACA, with a copy to Isaacs, intimating that the MCC would be delighted to accept the invitation provided that no pre-conditions would be imposed on the selection of the team, and that every member of the team would receive exactly the same treatment. The SACA executive, and particularly Coy, were outraged that Isaacs should have 'prejudiced' them over a schoolboys team.

'What these people don't realise,' Coy fulminated, 'is that Vorster's outward look was to protect international matches.'[52] The upshot was that SACA Board of Control decided at its meeting of 25 April 1969 to postpone the MCC Schoolboys tour 'for a season or two'. At its next bi-monthly meeting, on 21 June, it decided that the time had arrived 'to get clear instructions from the Government' and that a deputation should consult the government 'concerning the Association's future policy in regard to non-white cricket'. On 8 August four members of the SACA executive – Hammond, Cheetham, Coy and Dennis Dyer – met with the Prime Minister himself. It was the first of a series of essentially unfruitful meetings and negotiations.

To the question of whether 'non-whites' could be included in Springbok touring teams, the SACA delegation received a straightforward answer of 'No'. In the Olympic arena Vorster had conceded the principle of a mixed South African team, but for him international competition in team sports like cricket and rugby constituted a different category. In those sports, he insisted, South Africa's relations with the outside world were purely white, which was another way of saying that he would never compromise the all-white status of Springbok rugby. With regard to cricket, moreover, he was adamantly opposed to anything that might lead to mixed trials or mixed nets. However, when asked whether South African 'non-whites' in the Lancashire League might be permitted to play for South Africa in the United Kingdom, the Prime Minister said he 'would prefer to consider this point'. The possibility of 'mixed teams below international standard' touring abroad was ruled out; such teams would 'not be permitted to leave this country for tours of any nature'.

In the case of future international tours to South Africa by its traditional opponents, England, Australia and New Zealand, the Prime Minister accepted that 'non-whites' might be included, but only on condition that they were 'born in the country from which the tour emanates'. It was a formula that ruled out D'Oliveira, but that accepted Maoris and Aborigines and recognised that it was only a matter of time before the cricketing sons of West Indian and Asian immigrants might be playing for England. To the question of whether visiting international sides might play a South African 'non-white' side in South Africa, Vorster gave 'a qualified Yes'. Such games were not to be encouraged, unless specifically asked for, and were to be played on white grounds with 'proper segregation of the spectators, as is done at present'. Vorster also seems to have allowed for the possibility of 'mixed teams below international level' to tour South Africa 'subject to the same birth qualifications already mentioned'.

With regard to SACA's attempts to assist black cricket, Vorster pledged to bring pressure to bear on provincial and divisional councils and municipalities to provide better facilities, but on the question of whether a 'non-white' body, specifically SACBOC, could affiliate to SACA he said he would need to look at the terms of such an affiliation.[53]

Despite Vorster's rejection of the notion of including 'non-whites' in Springbok touring teams, SACA requested and received permission from SACBOC to send two of its national selectors to the SACBOC tournament in Kimberley at the end of the year. In November that invitation was 'retracted irrevocably' when Hammond was quoted by the *Diamond Fields Advertiser* as stating that the selectors 'would attend the tournament with a view to assisting the non-White body in the distribution of the R50 000 granted to the non-White association'. Hammond claimed that he had been misquoted, but the damage was done; SACBOC had never accepted the grant, and its invitation to the SACA selectors had been to look at cricket talent, nothing more. On 15 November Hassan Howa, the SACBOC vice-president, told the *Star* his Board would reject the money as it had been offered 'as a bribe to keep us quiet on the real issue, which is our drive to have our cricketers recognised and given a chance of selection for a Springbok side'.

Cheetham and Coy consequently had a public relations disaster rather than a breakthrough on their hands when they flew to London to consult with the Cricket Council in late November 1969. Subba Row's advice to the Council was that 'the seriousness of the situation' would have to be impressed on the SACA representatives: 'They must be made fully aware of the danger of the tour being abandoned and they must be prepared to be frank about their position.'[54] The urgent need for positive action was duly brought home to Cheetham, who, on his return to South Africa, announced that in future South African teams would be selected 'on merit' alone, 'irrespective of colour considerations'. He was promptly repudiated by the Prime Minister in his New Year's address. 'To make futile promises solves nothing,' Vorster declared, 'and in the long run creates more ill-feeling than the doubtful advantages it has for the moment.' This prime ministerial 'slapping down', as the British Embassy in South Africa described it, did little to encourage Cheetham to stick his neck out again in the near future.[55]

It was an inauspicious opening to 1970, and worse quickly followed as Vorster took a hardline stance on sporting matters. In September 1969, in the first major split in the National Party since it had come to power, Albert Hertzog and three other *verkrampte* MPs had finally seceded to form the Herstigte Nasionale Party (HNP), with opposition to Vorster's new sports policy constituting one of their key issues. To crush the HNP at the outset Vorster called a general election for April 1970, and his method of confronting the right once more entailed establishing his own hardline credentials. In January the South African Government refused visas to Arthur Ashe, the black American tennis star who had applied to enter the South African tennis championship, and to Sueo Masuzawa, the Japanese jockey. Had Vorster given in to American pressure over Ashe, the British Embassy in South Africa reported to the Foreign and Commonwealth Office, as many as 20 Nationalist MPs might have crossed the floor to the HNP.[56]

The split was consequently contained, and the HNP roundly defeated in the April general election, but with the result that the *verkramptes* remained a powerful force within the National Party.

In a murky episode, SACA also turned down an International Cricket Cavaliers tour of South Africa that would have included black players, among them Gary Sobers, on the grounds that visas would not be forthcoming. Evidently the SACA Board did not consult the government but rejected the tour of its own accord; the Board minutes record simply 'that in view of the circumstances the Board could not support the pursuance of this tour'.[57] Altogether the episode undermined SACA's international credibility, leaving the impression that it was enforcing, not contesting, sporting apartheid. At the very moment that the greatest ever Springbok cricket team, captained by Dr Ali Bacher, was proving its prowess in thrashing the touring Australians 4-0 in the last Test series before South Africa's exclusion from Test cricket, the administrators appeared to have capitulated completely to the politicians.

At the end of January, between Test matches against the Australians, Cheetham and Coy flew to London for consultations with the Cricket Council's Emergency

Executive Committee who again impressed upon them that there was a vital 'necessity for improving the image of the SACA in the UK'. Cheetham's statement on merit selection had helped, but had promptly been undermined by the controversy over the Cavaliers. Cheetham and Coy responded that in view of the forthcoming general election 'in which colour in sport is likely to become a major issue, their present Government may be positively unhelpful in the next few months'. Nevertheless they were urged to do 'all in their power' to improve SACA's image by means such as arranging a tour of the United Kingdom by a multi-racial junior team and securing the representation of 'non-white' cricket bodies on SACA, thereby leading to representation on the ICC. The committee minutes recorded: '[W]e were offered little hope that any progress in either direction would be made in the immediate future.'[58]

Realising that SACA was not going to make any meaningful changes before the tour, the Cricket Council pressed it at least to make a major statement against apartheid in sport. As Billy Griffith reported to the emergency meeting of the Council on 18 May, earlier in the month he had told Cheetham 'that a strong statement of the SACA's attitude to multi-racial sport in their own country in the future would be helpful'. Only such a statement, the *Rand Daily Mail* urged, might save the tour. None was forthcoming from either the administration or the players. 'It will amaze and disgust future generations of South Africans when they come to read of this phase of our cricket history,' Donald Woods's *Daily Dispatch* asserted, 'to find that the prevailing response from our officials and cricketers in the game's great hour of need was: "No comment"'.

None of the thirteen players selected for the tour considered withdrawing in the light of what had happened to their compatriots on the rugby field. The one star of South African cricket who had signified that he was unavailable for the tour was Colin Bland, unquestionably the world's greatest fielder of the 1960s. Bland was a Rhodesian, and in August 1968 had been turned back at London Airport because he held a UDI passport. The inclusion of Bland, or other Rhodesians, in the South African team to tour England raised the prospect of a D'Oliveira Affair in reverse, should the British Government refuse to admit them.

In a secret memorandum written in July 1969 to his departmental secretary, Frank Waring rejected the proposal that any Rhodesians selected should be given South African passports, but also abandoned his earlier opinion that it would be 'weak-kneed' simply to leave Rhodesians out of the team: 'I am now inclined to think that we must not give the British Government anything which might justify the cancellation of the tour.'[59] Bland's form by 1970 did not warrant his inclusion in the team, but John Traicos, the Rhodesian off-spinner, was selected. This selection, however, was not likely to cause an incident. It was all a matter of passports: Traicos, who was born in Egypt of Greek parents, travelled on a Greek not a Rhodesian passport.

CONSEQUENCES OF CANCELLATION

The intervention of the Wilson Government in the 1970 tour debacle represented a major departure from the long tradition in Britain of relative government detachment from international sporting relations.[60] From that point onwards, cricket journalist, Christopher Martin-Jenkins, contended, politicians proved more powerful than sportsmen in determining sporting relations with South Africa.[61]

Ironically, the cancellation of the 1970 tour probably proved less damaging to Anglo-South African relations than might have been the situation had the tour gone ahead. The British ambassador to South Africa, Sir Arthur Snelling, had predicted that June would prove a 'rough' month, and there would be 'a sharp deterioration in our relations with South Africa' if the Springbok cricketers were given 'a beastly time' in Britain.[62] That did not happen but June indeed proved to be a 'rough' month for the Labour Party and Vorster watched with satisfaction as Wilson slid to defeat in the general election on 18 June and the anti-apartheid Labour Government gave way to a potentially more friendly Conservative Government. Ted Heath, the new Prime Minister, even promised to lift the arms embargo.

Labour's defeat at the polls cannot be ascribed in any measure to the cancellation of the cricket tour. In both sporting and Conservative circles the cancellation of the tour was met with a burst of real indignation and anger, with opinion polls suggesting that a majority of the public were against cancellation. According to the National Opinion Poll published by the *Daily Mail* on 9 May, 53 per cent of people thought the tour should go on, 28 per cent that it should be cancelled, and 82 per cent disapproved of the protest demonstrations. None the less, there seems to have been general relief at escaping a summer of conflict and in public the bitter debate over the tour soon gave way to a resounding silence. In the immediate wake of the cancellation, Quintin Hogg blamed the Labour Government for bowing to threats and yielding to blackmail, but the tour did not thereafter feature as a major election issue. Labour's shock defeat was generally ascribed to an exceptionally low Labour and comparatively high Conservative turnout, and the latter was related to matters other than irritation at the cancellation of the tour, such as concerns about trade union power and the wider immigration issue. Had the tour gone ahead, and been accompanied by mass demonstrations and clashes with the police, cricket might well have made matters worse for Labour.[63] 'Whatever claims might be made about Waterloo, and the playing-fields of Eton,' Harold Wilson later recalled, 'our opponents hoped that the General Election of 1970 would be fought and won on and around the cricket-pitch at Lord's.'[64]

For proponents of the sports boycott, and for the anti-apartheid movement more generally, the cancellation of the 1970 South African tour of England represented a major breakthrough. For the first time, grass-roots agitation and demonstration had forced the cancellation of a major sporting engagement involving South Africa. In the retrospective assessment of the AAM, the campaign against the tour provided a huge fillip and proved a 'vital educational force' in Britain. Thereafter the movement regularly found that the sports boycott generated 'more controversy and greater press interest than any other aspect of the AAM's work'.[65]

The cancellation and the Cricket Council's decision that there would be no more tours until South African cricket had become 'multi-racial' were to prove fatal set-backs for South Africa's place in international cricket. An outraged Arthur Coy wrote to Donald Carr at Lord's: 'I cannot reconcile myself to the fact that, soft-soaping the non-white members of the Commonwealth, by interfering with the way of life in South Africa, can be covered by the Council's constitution. This statement has done cricket no good whatsoever, and the general opinion is that cricket between our countries is now finished.'[66]

The prospect that this might be true finally persuaded leading South African cricketers to begin speaking out against discrimination. Dennis Gamsy, the Springbok wicketkeeper, took the lead in calling on the government to set up a commission of inquiry to investigate ways of introducing non-racial sport in South Africa, stating that the time had come 'to examine more closely the policies which make South Africa repugnant to the outside world', and in this he received the support of Ali Bacher and the cricketing brothers, Peter and Graeme Pollock.[67]

7

No Tour to Australia

AFTER eighty years of Test match contests, the cancellation of the 1970 tour effectively placed cricket relations between England and South Africa on hold. That left Australia and New Zealand as the remaining redoubts for South African international cricket. New Zealand soon proved totally unreliable. In April 1971 the South African Cricket Association (SACA) wrote to the New Zealand Cricket Council (NZCC) inviting it to send a team to tour South Africa in 1973/74, but never received a reply. The NZCC, under the chairmanship of the very Gordon Leggat who had so strenuously defended New Zealand's tour of South Africa in 1961/62, had ceased official communication with SACA.[1] The Australian Board of Control for International Cricket (ABC), however, was of a different mind. Despite the D'Oliveira Affair and the cancellation of the tour of England, the ABC, under the chairmanship of Sir Donald Bradman, decided to proceed with its invitation for South Africa to tour in 1971/72. As in England, it would be the threat of militant protest action to disrupt the tour that ultimately forced its cancellation.

While there is extensive literature on the D'Oliveira Affair and the cancellation of the tour of England, there is relatively little on the cancellation of the tour of Australia. There are several reasons for this. The primary one is that England had already set a precedent. But there is another major reason. Unlike its English and South African counterparts, the governing body now called the Australian Cricket Board (ACB) resolutely denies researchers access to its 'confidential' records, regardless even of the 30-year convention. The ACB, evidently, does not consider itself part of the public domain, and has no interest in serious contemporary history of cricket 'beyond the boundary'.

146

The application of the thirty-year rule does, however, mean that the records of the Australian Government relating to the cancellation of the tour are now available, and these serve to answer certain questions. In particular, they indicate that, unlike in Britain, there was no government pressure on Australian administrators to cancel the tour. The decision to cancel was entirely that of the ABC under Bradman's chairmanship.

In his celebrated biography of Bradman, Charles Williams suggests that the great cricketer and his colleagues were blind to political realities when they confirmed the invitation to South Africa to tour in the wake of the debacle over the England tour and simply invited a repeat of the English experience. Given the emergence of militant protest action in response to Australia's involvement in the Vietnam War, and the hostility of 'the heavyweights of the Australian establishment, the bishops and the universities', it was politically inevitable that the tour would have to be called off: 'It was only Bradman and his colleagues on the Board, all of whom wanted the tour to go ahead, who had been trying to find a way round the political realities in the first place.'[2]

Bradman's other major biographers concur that he and his board were not deterred by the cancellation of South Africa's tour of England. In their view, Bradman and the ABC were determined to have the Springboks, who were the best team in the world, offering the prospect of exciting cricket and vast crowds, and they were also strongly of the opinion that 'politics' should be kept out of sport. Virtually until the very end, it is claimed, Bradman worked to save the tour, and it was only after witnessing first hand the violent demonstrations against the touring Springbok rugby team that he realised that the cricket tour would be an impossibility.[3]

Records now available suggest that matters were rather more complicated than that. Bradman and his colleagues were more politically attuned than is generally believed – at least one Labour member of the Board was positively opposed to the tour on political grounds – and throughout they were much less inclined than their counterparts on the Cricket Council in England to contemplate staging a cricket tour under siege conditions. In fact, the invitation to South Africa was confirmed in the face of fierce controversy. As Bradman advised Cheetham in late 1970, 'not every member of the Australian Board of Control agreed that the tour should take place'.[4]

Bradman also warned Cheetham that the tour would be in jeopardy unless there was a change in the 'political attitude' in South Africa. The message was clear – if

South Africa insisted, as in the past, on sending an all-white team, there would probably be no tour.

Despite SACA's plea that if it could not make some concession South Africa faced complete isolation from world cricket, the Vorster Government held firmly to the position the Prime Minister had adopted in April 1967 that he would rather accept South Africa's sporting isolation than capitulate to the ultimatum 'that our Springbok team would not be welcome unless it included all race groups'.

THE DECISION

While captaining the Australians in South Africa in early 1970, Bill Lawry had told his hosts there was 'no chance' the Springbok tour of Australia would ever be cancelled. History suggested he would be right, as Australia, still attached to its White Australia immigration policy, had traditionally been sympathetic to South Africa. Australia was even regarded as a bastion of economic and moral support for white Rhodesia in its unilateral declaration of independence from Britain in 1965.[5] Time and events, however, were to prove Lawry wrong.

With the precedent having already been set in Britain, the pattern of events that led to the cancellation of the tour of Australia proved distinctly familiar. The projected cricket tour, scheduled to begin in October 1971, was preceded by a Springbok rugby tour in July and August. Demonstrators, organised under the auspices of the Campaign Against Racialism in Sport (CARIS), founded two years previously, mounted militant opposition, besieging matches and interrupting play.[6] This was a foretaste of what lay in wait for the cricketers; Australian protest methods had been sharpened by the demonstrations against involvement in the Vietnam War.

An added ingredient in the Australian situation was the direct involvement of the trade union movement in the harassment of the Springboks. Under its militant new president, Bob Hawke, the Australian Council of Trade Unions advised its affiliate unions to withhold their services from the South Africans 'as an act of conscience'. As a result the airlines and railways declined to transport the Springboks, and many trade unionists refused to staff the hotels in which the South Africans stayed. The South African players were consequently moved around in secret in small planes and private cars, and accommodated in the homes of sympathisers. They were met with silent vigils as well as virtual battles at matches in Adelaide and Sydney. In Queensland police were put through special training, and on 14 July a state of emergency, labelled by the Brisbane *Courier Mail* a 'state of absurdity', was declared. One of the reasons was to empower the state government of Joh Bjelke-Petersen to commandeer an appropriate ground for the match, but wide powers were also assumed over food distribution and transport. The Bjelke-Petersen Government behaved as if it was a sovereign state, going so far as to use army facilities in the face of federal government opposition. The ground was surrounded by a six-foot high fence with welded uprights creating a twelve-foot drop. Baton charges on demonstrators and intimidation of the press persuaded some Australians that a Springbok cricket tour would inevitably be accompanied by police state methods and disruption of the social cohesion of Australia. Some extremists, however, still wanted the cricket tour to go ahead in order that they might disrupt it and create more propaganda against apartheid.[7]

Where Australia differed fundamentally from Britain was in the absence of active federal government pressure to cancel. Australia's Liberal/Country Party Government, traditionally friendly to South Africa, remained formally attached to the policy marked out by Sir Robert Menzies during his long tenure as Prime Minister (1949–66) that politics had no place in sport. Consequently, it 'raised no objection' to the tour.[8] The Government's position was summed up in notes prepared by the Department of the Prime Minister and Cabinet for William McMahon when he took over from John Gorton as Prime Minister in March 1971:

> This Government believes strongly that sport should be divorced from politics and that the business of selecting sporting teams and arranging their visits should be left to the sporting bodies themselves. The concept that a government should interfere in these arrangements runs directly counter to our beliefs.[9]

After Menzies retired Australia experienced a run of short-term Liberal premiers in Harold Holt (1966–67), Gorton (1968–71) and McMahon (1971–72), the latter two having to contend with the matter of Springbok tours. When approached by Bradman as to his attitude, Gorton gave the assurance that the government would not wish to prevent a South African cricket tour from taking place, and this assurance was confirmed by McMahon immediately on assuming office. On 25 March 1971 Bradman was advised that there would be no change in the government's policy.[10] On 6 April, after the South African Government formally prohibited the inclusion of blacks in the Springbok touring party, McMahon relayed to Vorster his regret and disappointment at the decision, but declined to revise his government's policy towards the tour. In Decision No 70 for 1971, McMahon's Cabinet reaffirmed 'that sporting exchanges between countries should be conducted with as little political interference as possible'.[11] In an interview with the BBC, McMahon went so far as to assert that it would be 'a strange thing' to prevent the South African cricketers, 'who dislike this policy of separation in sport just as much as we do', from playing in Australia. When in July Jack Cheetham confided in the Australian ambassador, T.W. Cutts, that he would rather call the tour off 'if it were to result in grievous problems for the host organisation or political embarrassment for the Australian government', Cutts reassured him that the Prime Minister had 'expressed himself in favour of the tour' and that he had no doubt 'weighed the political and other consequences of this stand'.[12]

In August, in the wake of the Springbok rugby tour and in the face of mounting pressure against the cricket tour, Bradman sought a meeting with the Prime Minister to discuss the position and role of the federal government. For the rugby tour, McMahon had offered Royal Australian Air Force aircraft to transport the Springboks, and Bradman wanted to know what support, if any, the Prime Minister would give to the cricket tour. After the experience of the rugby tour McMahon was not inclined to offer any, and Bradman found himself 'constantly fobbed off' by the Prime Minister's staff, who told him McMahon did not think a meeting would be helpful.[13] Bradman ultimately wrote to the Prime Minister 'asking for any views or advice the Commonwealth Government might wish to give'. McMahon declined to give a positive lead. In a discussion not recorded in the regular minutes, McMahon's Cabinet decided at its meeting on 24 August not to take a formal decision about the tour, but the general sense was that it favoured a neutral stance. The separate 'secret' minute recorded:

> The general reaction was that the judgement whether to continue with the tour or not had to be left to the Board of Control and that the Commonwealth should not itself take any position of endorsing or opposing the tour.

At the same time, the Cabinet accepted that it had to respond to Bradman, 'avoiding initiatives but reacting to specific issues raised'. In its discussion the Cabinet took stock of what it perceived to be the dilemma confronting it. On the one hand the government had to 'sustain its authority in the face of challenge', on the other it had to recognise that it would be immensely difficult to sustain a cricket tour in the face of 'demonstrations on the rugby tour scale'. The Cabinet also appreciated that 'if the tour were once embarked upon, the Commonwealth would not want to be in a position of not seeing it through'. In other words, if the ABC decided to proceed with the tour an ugly situation was likely to develop, requiring federal government intervention. Even so, the Cabinet could not bring itself to break from declared principle and recommend cancellation. The discussion none the less reflected a shift from McMahon's perceived public stance in that positive endorsement of the tour had been replaced by neutrality. The minute concluded: 'The matter was left without decision and with an indication that knowledge of the discussion should be closely held.'[14]

The Cabinet's attitude was evidently conveyed to Bradman in a letter prepared by Sir John Bunting, secretary of the Prime Minister's Department, and was described by Bradman himself as 'wishy-washy'. Its gist was that the government wanted no part in deciding whether the South African cricketers toured, and that it had no plans to assist the tour.[15]

Politically, it was virtually impossible for McMahon's Government to reverse its stance and advocate cancellation of the tour, but the coded message was that it would welcome the ABC cancelling it. As the South African ambassador reported to Pretoria, while there was good support in government ranks for the principle of not yielding to blackmail, in practice 'even these Members of Parliament would probably heave a sigh of relief if the tour were abandoned'.[16] That was not, however, the way the opposition Labour Party represented it. It believed that the Liberal/Country Party Government was, in fact, anxious for the tour to go ahead as the prelude to a 'law and order' general election. Norman Foster, the Labour member for Sturt in South Australia, told the House of Representatives on 7 September: 'The Government expects to win on the basis of cricket grounds ringed with barbed wire over a 5-day period.'[17]

The ABC was left to its own devices, more particularly since a West Indian attempt to persuade the International Cricket Conference (ICC) to prohibit the tour had been thwarted. At its July 1971 meeting, T.N. Peirce, the delegate of the West Indies Board of Control, called on the ICC to take 'definite action' to restrict 'member countries in their cricket relations with South Africa', but the white member associations resisted any such ruling. As Ben Barnett, the Australian delegate, told the press: 'We should be left to play whom we want.'[18] The threat of massive direct action, however, was already determining that Australia would not be playing South Africa in the coming season.

Australian cricket administrators were generally more chary than their English counterparts about the prospect of playing cricket behind barbed wire and, should the tour take place, it was likely that they would have to do so. All the ingredients were there for the STST example to be followed. Student rebellion had already engulfed Australian campuses, race was surfacing as a major issue in Australian politics, and CARIS was flexing its muscles, demonstrating against South African women netball players.[19]

To further complicate matters, the ABC, unlike the Cricket Council in England, was divided along political lines, encompassing a broad range of political identities and positions. Bradman himself, who epitomised conservative, suburban Protestant Australia, identified with the right wing of the governing Liberal Party, while at the other end of the party political spectrum Clem Jones, the Lord Mayor of Brisbane, was a prominent member of the anti-apartheid opposition Labour Party.

On the question of apartheid, as Jones recollects, 'there were some very strong and differing views held by various members of the Board'. In September 1970, in the first of a series of 'determining discussions' on the tour, Jones led opposition within the board to proceeding with the invitation to South Africa: 'I and others were extremely vocal and in many cases comments were specifically excluded from the Minutes. I think this was quite understandable and Bradman in particular, being imbued as he was with the protection of the good name of Cricket from every aspect, was party to this.'[20] As Cheetham later learnt from Bradman, 'The opposition to the Tour within the Board – a very senior man in the Australian Labour Party – has gone on record as saying that he will do everything possible to prevent the Tour taking place.'[21]

Bradman's letter intimating that his board was divided over the tour came as a huge shock to SACA. It arrived in response to Cheetham's proposal that SACA delegates should meet members of the ACB during that summer's England tour to Australia to bring to 'fruition' plans for the South African tour. Bradman not only recommended against SACA sending a delegation, he insisted that 'there must be a change in the political attitude in South Africa'. The ABC was next due to meet on 26 January 1971 to review the tour. As Cheetham advised his board at its meeting on 29 November 1970, it 'was obvious from Sir Donald's letter that the tour was in jeopardy'. The upshot was that the SACA Board gave Cheetham an 'open mandate' to visit Australia and engage in dialogue with Bradman. If after the discussions it was decided that the tour should be called off, 'this should be by mutual agreement and a joint announcement made simultaneously by both Boards'.[22]

Cheetham ultimately held discussions with Bradman in Adelaide over three days, 19–21 February 1971, after the ACB had met, and was told that 'The Australian Board by a majority decision, made purely in the light of their cricket requirements, wish the Tour to proceed'. None the less, with opposition to the tour mounting, there was 'growing unease' among members of the board that the tour might prove 'impractical to stage', and Bradman conveyed to Cheetham his own view, shared by the board, that it would prove hugely destructive to the game of cricket to attempt to play it under siege conditions. 'The Australian Board', he made quite clear, 'will not countenance having to play the Tour under the type of security conditions which became evident in England during the South African Rugby Tour in 1969.'[23] To assess whether it would be feasible to stage the tour the ABC had in fact set up an ad hoc committee, comprising Bradman as chairman, Syd Webb and Bob Parish.

On 8 September, at an all-day meeting in Sydney's Cricket House, the ABC unanimously endorsed the recommendation of the ad hoc committee that the tour be cancelled.[24] The proposals made by SACA, desperate to retain some international connection, that the full tour be replaced either by a shortened South African tour of Australia or an Australian tour of South Africa, were set aside.[25] Instead the Springboks were to be replaced by a series against a World XI, the plans for which had been devised by Parish.

One of Bradman's characteristics was that he did his 'homework' thoroughly, and this was certainly the case with the South African tour. In addition to listening to his own board and attempting to sound out the Prime Minister, he consulted the state premiers, police commissioners, cricket administrators and groundsmen. The states were crucial for it was they, and not the federal government, who provided policing. While the state premiers promised their support, whether 'qualified or enthusiastic', the general message was that police forces would struggle to protect grounds adequately against invasion. Bradman also met Bob Hawke to assess trade union opposition to the tour, and concluded that if the trade unions took all the steps open to them, the tour could not proceed. The 'final act' that decided the issue for Bradman was the rugby test between the Wallabies and the Springboks in Sydney, where he witnessed first-hand the mayhem caused by the protestors, despite a formidable police presence. He was also impressed by the effectiveness of the trade union blackballing of the match; no food or drink was available. In Bradman's assessment 'conditions were impossible', and so too was a cricket tour under such conditions. This confirmed what he had told Cheetham in February. In his report to the board, Bradman also emphasised growing public concern over the possible repercussions of the tour.[26] In the end the government's decision to stay out of the debate proved to be a godsend; support from the government for the principle of the tour would only have complicated an otherwise straightforward decision.

Announcing the decision Bradman gave three major reasons: the tour would tear Australian society apart through the inevitable bitterness it would engender between rival groups; it would expose the police forces to a 'severe ordeal'; and it would impose unfair strain on the South African cricketers themselves. The underlying cause of cancellation, however, was 'the widespread disapproval of the South African Government's racial policy which restricted selection of South Africa's team'; his board earnestly hoped that in the near future the South African Government would 'so relax its laws that the cricketers of South Africa may once again take their place as full participants in the international field'.

Bradman might earlier have favoured proceeding with the tour on the grounds that 'politics' should be kept out of sport but now he blamed the cancellation on the South African Government 'for bringing politics into sport'. Had Vorster allowed two 'coloured' players to join the Springbok cricketers, Bradman allegedly told the journalist Jack Fingleton, the tour would not have been cancelled.[27]

Vorster, for his part, accused Bradman of talking through his hat, and represented the cancellation as a triumph for the 'riff-raff' elements in Australia that 'threatened violence and committed violence'. Apparently oblivious to the contradictions of his own position, he warned: 'It is time that democracies take note that minorities are trying to force their will on majorities.'[28]

END GAME

The inclusion in the projected touring team of the two 'coloured' players to whom Bradman had referred might have saved the tour but the intransigence of the government and, indeed, of SACBOC, removed that one last hope.

The cancellation of the tour of England and the Cricket Council's intimation that there would be no further tours until cricket in South Africa was 'multi-racial' had caused a crisis in SACA. At a minimum, SACA appreciated that if South Africa was to preserve any connection with Test cricket it had to counter the charge that

Springbok teams were not representative of the country as a whole and therefore did not qualify for international competition. Cheetham and his colleagues consequently turned to putting some flesh on the pledge made in the effort to save the England tour – that future teams would be selected on merit. This involved tackling the government. After canvassing the views of the provinces, the SACA Board of Control determined at its meeting on 26 July 1970 that 'every effort should be made to perpetuate overseas cricket tours' and its first approach would have to be to the Prime Minister to 'ascertain his views on the future of international tours to and from this country'.

As Eric Rowan, the former Springbok batsman and a member of the Transvaal Cricket Union (TCU) Board, warned Vorster, SACA was seeking 'to do all in their power to keep in the international sphere', though with the caveat, insisted on by the TCU, that they do so 'within the laws of the country'. While Rowan thought some of SACA's ideas 'quite reasonable' he personally could not support the notion of integration in sport: 'I am not in favour and I must say that I find it hard to visualize sports integration without social integration. History has proved that social integration leads to sexual intercourse with the majority gradually taking over until the minority is finally submerged.'[29]

At a confidential meeting after the SACA annual general meeting on 27 September 1970, provincial delegates presented the Board of Control with a unanimous recommendation 'that the Prime Minister and Cabinet be approached for leave to select South African teams for domestic and overseas tours on merit, regardless of race, creed or colour' and that they give 'serious consideration' to allowing 'multi-racial' trials.[30]

The SACA Board of Control duly made several representations to Vorster and Waring for permission to stage mixed trials for the Australian tour, but the pair were inflexible in their rejection of the idea. SACA, as Cheetham complained to the Board at its meeting of 29 November 1970, was doing everything possible to get the government to budge but was getting nowhere, to the point where 'it was difficult to bear the political frustration any longer'.[31] As Cheetham explained it to the Australian ambassador, the government was disinclined to make any concessions to cricket which might prove embarrassing in relation to rugby, the sport of the 'Afrikaner *volk*' and whose leading players 'were not keen to play with non-whites'.[32]

So it was that Cheetham could report no change in 'the political attitude in South Africa' when he met Bradman in February 1971, but the message he came back with was clear: the only real hope of salvaging the tour of Australia, and South Africa's place in international cricket, was through the inclusion of two black players in the Springbok team. Such a move, Bradman urged, would 'effectively counter the protests from organisations which insist that the South African Team is selected from only 18% of the population'. Without such assistance from South Africa, Bradman underlined, the tour would at least have to be postponed.

SACA came up with one last desperate proposal at its board meeting on 27 February 1971. With mixed trials prohibited, and SACA selectors excluded from SACBOC's tournaments, the proposal was that SACBOC should select two of its own players on merit for inclusion as 'full and corporate members' of the touring party. As SACA tried to persuade the government, it was in the national interest to make the concessions necessary to keep cricket alive: 'Cricket has contributed to the building of our Nation, through its common cause between the Afrikaans and English language groups,' it argued. The postponement or cancellation of the tour, SACA warned, would 'mean the complete isolation of our cricket in this Country, and the sport will not then be allowed to emerge until full multi-racialism has taken place in this Country'.[33]

The proposal was rejected both by government and by SACBOC, whose president, Hassan Howa, rejected SACA's 'gesture' once it was made public, declaring that he would have 'nothing to do with two token non-whites in the team, like dummies in a shop window'. He was only interested in merit selection, based on mixed trials, even if this resulted in an all-white team. As Howa had told *The Times* in the previous year: 'What we don't want is a method of selection which requires the inclusion in the national team of four whites, four Coloureds, two Africans and an Indian.'[34]

In fact, Howa had not even been consulted about SACA's proposal. Evidently Cheetham had indirectly sounded out two veteran SACBOC players, the all-rounder Sulaiman 'Dik' Abed and the left-arm spinner Owen Williams, about joining the team. As Cheetham told the Australian ambassador, he hoped that Howa would 'come under pressure from his players to co-operate'.[35] But Abed, in his prime one of SACBOC's greatest-ever cricketers, and Williams, would have nothing to do with the proposal. 'I want to be selected on merit – and not as a glorified baggage master,' was Williams's rejoinder, echoing the plight of 'Krom' Hendricks some eighty years previously.[36]

From the government side, Waring was totally unsympathetic. After meeting representatives of SACA on Sunday 21 March, he concluded that Bradman and Cheetham were 'trying to exaggerate the position'. He wrote to his secretary, Beyers Hoek:

> Quite frankly I think the Australian Cricket authorities and their public must sooner or later wake up to the fact that the demonstrations go far beyond the sports argument and although we may be in the front line at present, Australia will be forced into this in due course on the basis of its White Australia immigration policy.

Hoek, in his advice to the minister, summed up the government's attitude with his statement that any concession would represent 'the thin end of the wedge and open the door for mixed sport in South Africa'. In broader terms, he reminded the minister: 'The policy of South Africa is separate development, which also applies to sport. This traditional policy and principle cannot be sacrificed for the sake of sport and to satisfy our enemies. Any concession in the direction of mixed trials and mixed teams may be interpreted as a backward step in our policy of separate development and a victory for the integrationists.' Hoek accepted that 'cancellation of this tour will mean complete isolation of S.A. Cricket'.[37]

At its meeting on 24 March 1971, the Cabinet resolved that any cricket team that went to Australia must be white – '*slegs 'n blanke span*'.[38] On 2 April Cheetham made the Cabinet's ruling public.

In response to Cheetham's announcement of the government veto, South Africa's top white cricketers staged a celebrated walk-off at Newlands on 3 April. The occasion was the match between the Currie Cup champions, Transvaal, and a Rest of South Africa XI as part of the Republic Sports Festival celebrating the tenth anniversary of South Africa becoming a republic. After Mike Procter had bowled the first ball, the players walked off the field to hand in a statement to the press box, and then returned to continue the match. The statement was as brief as the protest:

> We cricketers feel that the time has come for an expression of our views. We fully support the South African Cricket Association's application to include non-whites on the tour to Australia if good enough and, furthermore, subscribe to merit being the only criterion on the cricket field.

Waring's immediate response was to cancel the post-game *braaivleis* (barbecue), and to challenge white cricket clubs to open their doors to black players, believing that this would reveal the inherent racialism of South African cricket. When clubs began to demonstrate support for mixed cricket, Waring dismissed their resolutions as 'hollow' and, with the Australian tour still in the balance, affirmed that no 'multi-racial' matches would be allowed at any level.[39]

White South African cricketers had mounted their first political protest against apartheid sport, but it was not enough to save their tour of Australia. The world champions, as the South African press liked to call them, had no one left to play against.

8

Towards 'Normal' Cricket

A T THE START of the 1970s, white South African sport was in crisis; only rugby seemed exempt from the relentless slide into isolation. By the latter part of the decade, rugby had lost its exemption, and a multi-pronged crisis had overtaken the apartheid state itself.

For South Africa, 1974 to 1977 were 'watershed' years.[1] Economically, the profits of apartheid seemed to dry up as the prosperity of the 1960s gave way to deep recession. Regionally, the sudden overthrow of the fascist regime in Portugal in 1974 and the subsequent abandonment by Portugal of its African colonies, Mozambique and Angola, to Marxist regimes revolutionised the strategic situation in southern Africa. The independence of Mozambique led directly to the downfall of Rhodesia by 1980 and an end to the ring of white-ruled buffer states that had protected South Africa's borders from hostile incursion. Domestically, the Soweto uprising of June 1976 ushered in a new era of endemic urban unrest and, internationally, it prompted intensified sanctions and pressure on the apartheid regime as international outrage against apartheid reached new levels. The regime was now confronted simultaneously by growing black internal resistance to white political power, and growing international isolation.

In 1977 the United Nations imposed a mandatory arms embargo against South Africa and issued its international declaration against apartheid in sports. In the same year the Commonwealth heads of government signed the Gleneagles Agreement, stating that it was 'the urgent duty of each of their governments vigorously to combat the evil of apartheid by withholding any form of support for, and by taking every practical step to discourage contact or competition by their nationals with sporting organisations, teams or sportsmen from South Africa or from any other country where sports are organised on the basis of race, colour or ethnic origin'.

In response to the gathering sense of crisis, and also to the changing nature of its support base consequent on the rapid rise of Afrikaner capital and the progress of Afrikaners into the urban middle classes, the Nationalist Government tilted increasingly to its *verligte* wing. After 1976, narrowly based 'reforms' gave way to a more concerted process for 'reforming' or 'modernising' apartheid so as to adjust it to changing circumstances. When P.W. Botha replaced B.J. Vorster as Prime Minister in 1978, 'reform' became an integral part of his strategy for countering the 'total onslaught' against white South Africa.[2]

A pioneer area of reform was sport, in an effort to counter both South Africa's rapid slide into sporting isolation, which increasingly troubled local sportsmen, and the broader movement towards sanctions against the Republic. By projecting a 'reformist' image through sport the apartheid state sought to regain some international respectability and reverse the trend to isolation. In the assessment of the political scientist, Jon Gemmell, 'sport increasingly proved a means by which the government chose to display to the international community that it was prepared to adapt and reform'.[3] In the 1970s the government did an almost complete about-face, abandoning its total ban on 'multi-racial' sport for a policy of extending autonomy to sports bodies and, in so doing, attempting to de-racialise and, in its own view, de-politicise sport.[4]

The Minister of Sport and Recreation who presided over much of the change, Dr Piet Koornhof, a former Secretary of the Broederbond, came to see himself as driving the process towards 'normalising' sport. As he plaintively told a South African Cricket Union delegation in December 1977: 'He refuted the idea popularly believed in England, that it is the sportsmen alone, who have taken the lead in normalising sport in South Africa. He himself, had, in the first instance, taken the matter to the Cabinet who were now fully in support of his sports policy.'[5]

In 1972 Vorster had personally selected Koornhof to replace the inept English-speaking Frank Waring, and had given him a simple brief: 'See what you can do to remedy the situation.'[6] From the outset, the political complication was to convince international sporting bodies that reforms were being put in place to 'normalise' South African sport – a euphemistic formula, evidently devised by Rachid Varachia, that suggested sport was being de-racialised[7] – so as to warrant South Africa's readmission, while at the same time reassuring the *verkramptes*, the bulk of whom remained within the National Party, that apartheid policy remained intact.

Although Koornhof failed entirely in his attempt to breach the sports boycott, the 'reformist' thrust of his tenure as Vorster's Minister of Sport and Recreation (1972–78) facilitated South African cricket's first attempt at unity and integration. On 18 September 1977 the white South African Cricket Association (SACA); the 'non-racial' South African Cricket Board of Control (SACBOC), which was largely coloured and Indian, but which had acquired significant African support in the Eastern Cape; and the South African African Cricket Board merged to form the South African Cricket Union (SACU) as the country's sole official cricketing body, with a constitution that banned any form of discrimination based on race, creed or colour.

From the outset, SACU's experiment in 'normalising' cricket was fatally flawed in terms of motivation, content and timing. Its engagement in unity and the 'normalisation' of cricket was driven by its determination to see South Africa back in its 'rightful' place in Test cricket, and the very transparency of its motives aroused suspicion among black cricket administrators that they were somehow being conned. Motives aside, the underlying problem was that no amount of constitution-making could wish away the discriminatory legislation that affected the playing of sport and condemned black cricketers to return to a society based on race, creed and colour immediately a game was over.

As Hassan Howa averred, the very notion of 'normal' sport implied that the remainder of apartheid society was abnormal; that 'normal' cricket required black players to contend with the contradiction that they might play 'normal' sport for a day and return to the abnormal life structured by apartheid laws for the rest of the week. On top of that, black players generally found 'normal' cricket itself riddled with racism and racial slights, particularly when it came to access to white clubhouses and change rooms. The timing of the launch of 'normal' cricket undercut its chances of success. The fact that the launch took place in the immediate wake of the Soweto uprising virtually doomed the experiment to be overtaken by political developments, given the political radicalisation of the 'non-racial' sports movement and the sports boycott that followed the events in Soweto. A week after the formation of SACU Hassan Howa and the Western Province Cricket Board led a revolt that was to result in the formation of a rival 'non-racial' body, the South African Cricket Board (SACB), committed to the philosophy that apartheid had to be abolished before there could be any normal sport and a return to international competition. By 1982, when the last of the teams from Lenasia, the Indian group area on the outskirts of Johannesburg, abandoned the Transvaal League, the experiment in 'normal' cricket was effectively over. Throughout the country, Indian and coloured cricket was now overwhelmingly under the control of the SACB.

GOVERNMENT POLICY

Between 1971 and 1976 the Vorster Government's sports policy underwent a fundamental shift, embracing the concept of 'multi-nationalism'. In Vorster's own estimation his premiership represented the third phase of apartheid, the 'multi-national' phase, following the earlier phases of segregation and separate development.[8] Under Verwoerd, South Africa had been officially perceived not as a multi-racial but as a 'multi-national' country, comprising a total of eleven minority nations – one white, one coloured, one Indian, and eight African – and all were entitled to their own separate development. Vorster took the Verwoerdian logic a step further, and formally offered the African 'nations' 'independence' based on their homeland 'states'. The Transkei was the first to achieve 'independence' in 1976. On the sporting front, Vorster and Koornhof sought to employ the 'multi-national' formula to counter the sports boycott and assist white sports administrators in their efforts to maintain or restore international sporting contacts.

In doing so, they confirmed the feelings of the then British Consul General in Johannesburg, A.P.W. Northey, expressed in a report to the Foreign and Commonwealth Office in April 1972, in which he conceded: 'One is, perhaps reluctantly, edged towards the conclusion that sport is the soft underbelly of apartheid and that boycotts work. Sport – international sport – is probably more important to South Africans than to any other people and Peter Hain and the rest have certainly been right to concentrate on it.'[9]

While the government continued to insist it would not permit 'multi-racial' sport, it was prepared to allow 'multi-national' sport. It thereby provided sports administrators with something new – space within which to manoeuvre. Under the rubric of 'multi-nationalism' the first steps were taken towards 'normalising' sport in South Africa.

Vorster announced the new sports policy in the House of Assembly on 22 April 1971, a year after the rout of the HNP at the polls and immediately after the protest by South African cricketers at Newlands. In his effort to avert triggering a right-wing backlash, Vorster had invoked the help of the Broederbond in formulating a strategy that would seek to satisfy international opinion without deviating from the policy of separate development. The magic formula produced was 'multi-nationalism'.[10]

In a speech, described by the *Natal Witness* as 'as clear as mud', Vorster signalled two major changes in the government's sports policy in terms of this extraordinary formulation. First, multi-racial teams from South Africa's traditional opponents in sports such as rugby and cricket could not only tour but would in future be permitted to play against black teams, at segregated venues, so as to provide black players with the opportunity to participate in international sport. Vorster said he trusted this policy would influence England's Cricket Council to alter its decision not to play South Africa until its cricket had become 'multi-racial'; a 'decision which they took under pressure from the Wilson government'. Second, blacks, local as well as foreign, might compete as individuals against whites at certain 'open international' competitions in South Africa, provided the local black sportsmen were members of sports bodies affiliated to white federations. These 'open internationals' were chiefly in Olympic sports such as athletics.

Mixed or multi-racial sport at club, provincial or national level remained off-limits, and, as in the past, mixed teams would not be allowed to represent South Africa internationally, except in special cases, notably the Olympics, the Canada Cup golf competition, and the Davis Cup and Federation Cup tennis competitions. These mixed teams would be regarded as South African, but not as Springboks, as Springbok teams and blazers belonged exclusively to whites. 'The Springbok rugby team is not representative of the whole of South Africa,' Vorster asserted, confirming the message Dennis Brutus conveyed abroad. 'It has never been that . . . It is representative of the Whites of South Africa.'[11]

Vorster justified dealing with different sports in different ways on the grounds that they had developed independently, and different considerations applied, but it was not an approach that did much to help cricket, with the tour of Australia still very much in the balance. Cricket Tests ranked as ordinary internationals.

The progress of this 'multi-national' sports policy was tortuous in the extreme. As the *Daily News* described it in 1973, the policy was 'like a drunken man staggering on a slippery slope, one step forward, one sideways, one back'.[12] Although Vorster and Koornhof were anxious to assist sports administrators to rescue South Africa from sporting isolation they were equally anxious not to provoke rebellion among the *verkramptes* in the party ranks. Koornhof, who became known as 'Piet Promises', developed his own peculiar brand of 'double talk', seeking both to send encouraging signals to sports administrators at home and abroad that the government's sports policy was in the process of fundamental change and to reassure *verkramptes* that the essentials of apartheid remained in place, even in sport. As he was later to crack: 'When I explained my sports policy in parliament, they thought I was joking; and when I was joking, they thought I was explaining the sports policy.'[13]

Under the new policy every 'approved' encounter between black and white sportsmen in South Africa required a stamp of approval from the Cabinet, on the recommendation of the Minister of Sport and Recreation. In March and April 1973, at the 'open international' South African Games in Pretoria, black and white South African athletes competed against one another and against six hundred foreign competitors, and Cabinet permission was given for the staging of soccer matches, even though FIFA prompted all the foreign teams to withdraw. The matches, however, were moved from Pretoria to Johannesburg.[14]

The 'multi-national' formulation, the Broederbond believed, constituted 'a signpost rather than a map'. Koornhof saw it as a 'developing' rather than a static policy, and during his tenure it was constantly being adjusted as the sports boycott grew ever tighter – in 1973 the Springbok rugby tour of New Zealand was cancelled – and as South Africa plunged into internal disorder. In 1974 Koornhof announced that South African sports bodies under suspension by international federations would be permitted to stage 'multi-national' rather than 'open international' events, in which South African blacks might compete, thereby substantially increasing the number of 'multi-national' sporting events. The truly radical shift came in September 1976, in the wake of the Soweto uprising, when Koornhof announced the extension of the 'multi-national' principle to club level and declared that mixed teams might represent South Africa in all sports. As he explained in November, this meant that for international sporting events all South African teams would in future be selected on merit, on the basis of racially mixed trials, and those selected would be eligible to play in Springbok colours. The government had finally conceded the principle that Springbok teams should be representative of the country as a whole, and not simply of the white population.

These announcements represented an ideological about-turn in government thinking. Mixed sport, previously represented as a recipe for racial conflict and as the 'thin end of the wedge' that would imperil the whole apartheid project, was now perceived as a potential source of social cohesion and a mechanism for shoring up the beleaguered apartheid state. As the Broederbond Executive sought to convince its branches, 'the recent drastic changes in the internal security situation' made 'the promotion of internal peace and good relations between whites and non-whites essential'. The change in sports policy was consequently 'seen as an important step to prevent or decrease tension and promote goodwill among large sectors of the population'. A significant degree of mixed sport would assist the government in its efforts to project a reformist image, so as to ease international as well as domestic pressure on the apartheid state, and help counter South Africa's pariah status by securing a return to international competition. As the Broederbond Executive put it in a 1975 circular, 'international sporting ties, especially in rugby and cricket, have serious implications at this critical stage for our country, regarding international trade, national trade, military relationships and armaments and strategic industrial development'.[15]

In Koornhof's view the major reason for change was the need to combat the sports boycott. In a discussion with Donald Woods Koornhof agreed 'that non-racial sport would help build useful bridges between South Africa's alienated communities, and that this was a good thing in itself for the sake of racial peace', but he 'saw it mainly as a means of buying time for his Government's general policies'. For as long as the country remained excluded from international sport 'this constituted a political pressure-point against the whole Afrikaner Nationalist regime and the main body of political apartheid'. Ridding sport of apartheid, in short, had become essential to propping up apartheid elsewhere. As Woods recalled: 'I wanted to end sports apartheid in order to *hasten* the breakdown of general apartheid, while he wanted to end sports apartheid in order to *prolong* general apartheid.'[16]

Mixed signals about mixed sports thereafter proliferated as Koornhof sought to sell and explain the government's new sports policy to hugely different constituencies at home and abroad. The heart of the matter was whether the 'multi-national' formula at club level might allow mixed clubs and teams. At the Cape National Party congress in Cape Town in August 1977, Koornhof gave the assurance that 'mixed sport at club level remains contrary to party policy' and that the government's sports policy would 'in no way threaten the identity or self-determination of the race groups'. Yet in *Panorama*, a Department of Information magazine designed for distribution abroad, he was quoted as affirming that 'there is no law prohibiting mixed race clubs in any sport in South Africa', and that 'a club has the right to decide at all times who shall and who shall not be allowed to join that club'. 'It is all now crystal clear,' the *Sunday Tribune* commented. 'Mixed sports clubs are not illegal. They are just against National Party policy.'[17] As summed up by Archer and Bouillon, ' "multi-nationalism" is a policy which, by prohibiting without banning, and tolerating without authorizing, is calculated to satisfy the irreconcilable demands of its critics at home and abroad'. The former were assured that apartheid was still intact, the latter that sport was being 'normalised'.[18]

Following the resignation of Vorster in 1978 as a result of a major financial scandal, and the election of P.W. Botha as his successor as party leader and Prime Minister, the Nationalist Government took its final steps towards 'normalising' sport in South Africa. It abandoned the increasingly awkward juggling act required to reconcile the irreconcilable, and adopted a policy of non-interference in sport. On the recommendation of F.W. de Klerk, Minister of Sport and Recreation from 1979 to 1980, that 'something dramatic' had to be done if South Africa was ever to end its sporting isolation, Botha's Cabinet agreed to 'recognize the full autonomy of sports organizations and sports people to conduct their affairs as they saw fit and to play with whomever they wanted'.[19] After three decades of government intervention, the Nationalists finally moved to allow sports bodies to administer their own affairs free from government interference. However, as David Dalling, the Progressive Federal Party MP, underlined in Parliament, while the government proclaimed the policy of sports autonomy, the practice of sport did not bear the policy out. The discriminatory laws that affected the playing of sport – the Group Areas Act, the Reservation of Separate Amenities Act, the Urban Areas Act, and the Liquor Act – remained on the statute book, and had to be circumvented by administrative instruction. In 1981–82 the Botha Government, in accordance with the recommendations of a Human Sciences Research Council inquiry into sport, amended the Group Areas Act, the Liquor Act, and the Black (Urban Areas) Con-solidation Act so that they no longer impinged on the playing of sport.

But if the government, in its own eyes, was now moving towards de-politicising sport, the opposite was true of its radical opponents involved in the sports boycott.

THE SPORTS BOYCOTT

For some of the architects of the sports boycott, notably Peter Hain, the primary goal of and political justification for the boycott was to eliminate apartheid from sport, and they held it should retain that focus by confining its demands to sport, even if the ultimate objective was to undermine the whole apartheid system. White South Africa, in Hain's belief, might be placed 'once more on the defensive' by a campaign for changes in the law designed to 'exempt' sport from apartheid.[20] The dominant mood in the ranks of the sports boycotters, however, was very different. With sports apartheid showing signs of crumbling, and anger at the apartheid regime mounting in the wake of the Soweto uprising, apartheid itself now became the direct target. Driven internally by the South African Council on Sport (SACOS) and externally by the South African Non-Racial Olympic Committee (SANROC), the sports boycott radicalised itself in terms of both goals and methods during the 1970s. The direct goal became the destruction of apartheid, and the methods embraced third party boycotts and the personal ostracism of 'collaborators' with the apartheid regime.[21]

SACOS had been founded in 1973 in response to the South African Games. As was to become a pattern, attempts to preserve white domination by 'reforming' apartheid provoked new modes of opposition. At a conference in Durban in March 1973 nine 'non-racial' sporting organisations – largely Indian and coloured – that refused to affiliate to white federations and participate in 'open internationals' formed the body to organise opposition to 'multi-national' sport as an illegitimate substitute for 'non-racial' sport. Norman Middleton, the president of the South African Soccer Federation, was elected president, and Hassan Howa vice-president.

Initially, the SACOS agenda was essentially sporting. The target was apartheid sport, to be fought externally through the international sports boycott and undermined internally by negotiations with white sports bodies to bring them within the framework of 'non-racial' sport at every level from school sport upwards. In a major development in December 1976 SACOS became a fully-fledged member of the Supreme Council for Sport in Africa, which effectively set up SACOS and its international ally, SANROC, along with the Supreme Council, as the only conduits through which sports bodies in South Africa could regain membership of the international federations from which they had been expelled.[22]

As became evident in the next year, these were to be closed conduits. In July 1977 Howa, now president, formally took SACOS and the sports boycott in a radical new direction by announcing that SACOS would no longer be satisfied with the 'normalisation' of sport in isolation from the rest of society. There could be 'no normal sport in an abnormal society'; there could be no co-operation with white sports bodies until there was equality more generally for blacks. As Howa explained, 'People questioned how you could be a white man's equal playing sport at weekends, and for the rest of the week be his inferior.'[23]

In short, the destruction of apartheid itself, and not simply sports apartheid, was now the declared goal of SACOS and the sports boycott. 'The sole objective of the international community's boycott was to integrate South African sport,' Douglas Booth observed. 'SACOS turned the boycott into a strategy against apartheid *per se*.'[24] Sport was to be forged into a major political weapon to enable a disenfranchised constituency to force radical change.

Howa's announcement came in response to some fundamental shifts in the wider landscape. The brutal suppression of the Soweto uprising was itself a radicalising influence – in Howa's words, 'the unrest hardened attitudes' – while the government's extension of the 'multi-national' principle to club level gave a new edge to already scratchy negotiations between the 'non-racial' and white sports bodies seeking to 'normalise' sport. The announcement also represented the outcome of a power struggle within SACOS, when the inaugural president, Norman Middleton, was forced to resign in February. Middleton, who was vice-president of the Coloured Labour Party and a member of the uniracial Coloured Persons Representative Council, set up by the Government in 1969, was targeted for his ties with 'government-created institutions' and was generally considered 'too soft' in his approach to white sports bodies. Middleton's stance was that SACOS should exploit 'the legal platforms provided by the system . . . to confront and embarrass the whole system', but for the radicals in SACOS that amounted to the path of collaboration.

Howa's home base, the Western Cape, birthplace of the left-wing Non-European Unity Movement of the 1940s, had a long tradition of non-collaboration, and Howa's own father, an Indian Muslim who had settled in South Africa in 1904, had been linked to that tradition as president of the Cape Indian Congress. Non-collaboration now became in effect a watchword of SACOS. In 1977 its tactics as well as its goals were radicalised with the adoption of the so-called double-standards resolution to enforce the policy. The SACOS executive resolved in April 1977 that there was to be a complete boycott of 'racial' and 'multi-national' sport; individuals who indulged in any collaboration with such sport could no longer belong to a SACOS affiliated organisation. The double standards resolution was applied particularly strenuously to cricket, with SACOS calling for a total boycott of all SACU activity. In a 1979 addendum adopted by the third biennial conference of SACOS non-collaboration was extended to 'all forms of government bodies designed to entrench and/or promote the separateness of people'.[25] The addendum was specifically directed at Norman Middleton, whose Soccer Federation was temporarily expelled from SACOS for collaborating with 'multi-nationalism' by unconditionally including white teams in its professional league.

Internationally, the sports boycott was likewise intensified by the adoption of a strategy of third party boycotts in order to secure the total isolation of South African sport. In July 1976, in the immediate wake of Soweto, some 20 African nations walked out of the Montreal Olympics, refusing to compete against New Zealand which was then in the middle of a rugby tour of South Africa. Initially SANROC, at the behest of Sam Ramsamy, and Jean-Claude Ganga, the president of the Supreme Council for Sport in Africa, attempted to engineer New Zealand's exclusion, but the International Olympic Committee refused, claiming it had no jurisdiction over rugby. As Dennis Brutus had contended all along, it proved easier to persuade the African countries to withdraw.[26] It was to help avert the threat of a similar boycott of the Commonwealth Games in Edmonton, Canada, in 1978 that the Commonwealth heads of government adopted, in June 1977, the Gleneagles Agreement that governments should do their utmost to ensure that their sportsmen did not engage in sporting contact with South Africa.

The divergence over tactics at Montreal proved the parting of the way between Brutus and Ramsamy, who took over as executive chairman of SANROC later in 1976. Ramsamy, a physical education teacher who had fled South Africa in 1972, extended the SANROC network to include all anti-apartheid groups around the world, and establish SANROC as the co-ordinator of the sports boycott in accordance with the new SACOS philosophy that there could be no normal sport in an abnormal society.

It was in this context that the South African Cricket Union was formed in September 1977.

SACA AND UNITY
SACA's chief goal was to secure South Africa's return to Test cricket. To do so in accordance with the Cricket Council's ruling of May 1970 cricket in South Africa had to become 'multi-racial', whatever that meant, and its teams had to be selected

on merit so as to make them representative. To this both the Cricket Council in 1973 and the International Cricket Conference (ICC) in 1974 added the rider that the three governing bodies of cricket in South Africa should come together in a single representative body. With the introduction of 'multi-racial' cricket at club level and the formation of SACU in 1977, SACA officials were convinced they had 'more than met' all the requirements.[27]

Despite the cancellation of the 1968/69, 1970, and 1971/72 tours, South Africa had remained on the ICC tour roster, with the Springboks due to tour England in 1975, Australia to tour South Africa in 1975/76, and England South Africa in 1976/77. Prior to the D'Oliveira Affair, the MCC had been pivotal in holding the ring for SACA in the ICC; in the 1970s the Cricket Council served as white South Africa's main link to international cricket, keeping open the lines of communication, and keeping alive SACA's hopes of a return to Test cricket. It was the Cricket Council that had effectively set the terms for the re-entry of South Africa, and it continued to encourage and monitor SACA's progress. Until 1976 what most distressed the Cricket Council was SACA's relative lack of progress, resulting in the cancellation of tours involving England.

At the outset, the prospect of South Africa ever meeting the criteria set for its return to Test cricket seemed remote. The Vorster Government was adamantly opposed to multi-racial sport, and SACBOC likewise showed itself adamantly opposed to co-operating with the policy of 'multi-national' sport. The note struck by Jack Cheetham in his last two presidential addresses – in September 1971 and 1972 – was decidedly pessimistic. As he advised, representations to government made it 'abundantly clear' there 'can be no change in the official Sports Policy of this country in the foreseeable future', and there was nothing much SACA could do about it, despite the pressure for change from leading players, notably Ali Bacher, in the wake of the cancellation of the Australian tour. SACA was not prepared to 'act in a manner contrary to the laws of the land', nor was it its brief to step into the political field and lead 'a crusade against present legislation, joining its forces with others'. The only hope Cheetham could hold out was that SACA would 'continue to strive towards the selection of national teams by means of trial matches in which all cricketers who merit inclusion will be recognised in this manner'.[28] Durban's *Daily News* complained that the 'tame acquiescence by officials like Mr Cheetham . . . is swiftly diminishing South Africa's chances of ever playing international cricket', while the *Rand Daily Mail* called for 'a new militancy' to replace the 'desperate timidity' that prevailed among the game's white administrators. The *Star* made the point that Cheetham advised cricketers to respect a law that did not exist; there was no law to prevent people of different races playing games together, provided the venue was private.[29]

Militancy never became a watchword of SACA, which studiously refrained from confronting government and its apartheid policy. None the less, during the three-year tenure (1972–75) of Cheetham's successor, Bryan 'Boon' Wallace of Western Province, a subtle change of approach became evident. In accordance with legal advice SACA remained committed to acting within the law, but ceased to conflate government policy with the law. As SACA struggled to find a way forward for a return to international cricket, it determined to go beyond the confines of government policy in shaping its own policy, and its policy became one of promoting 'multi-racial' cricket. As Wallace delicately phrased it in his presidential address of 28 September 1974, it would 'get all of us nowhere to have a confrontation with the Government on the issue of multi-racial cricket at Club level, much as we wish to play such cricket', but SACA would none the less 'work progressively towards multi-racial cricket at Club level'. In Howa's unflattering retrospective view, Wallace, a former Western Province batsman, was 'a man of a thousand words and a few deeds when it comes to normal cricket'.[30]

Under Cheetham, SACA's goal had been the attainment of mixed trials and merit selection for the national team; during Wallace's tenure it shifted to the introduction of 'multi-racial' club cricket. But the shift only came after the failure to negotiate with SACBOC a 'multi-national international' formula, that conformed to government policy, for the selection of Springbok teams on merit.

On 21 May 1971 Cheetham wrote to the Cricket Council asking it to clarify its criteria for 'multi-racial' cricket for the purpose of the resumption of Test matches between South Africa and England, hoping that the Cricket Council would be able to say it was 'willing to accept a team from South Africa which is chosen on merit through trials at top level'. The reply he received was non-committal. The Council did not presume 'to define the extent or degree to which multi-racial cricket should be played in South Africa', and waited hopefully for positive steps 'which will enable a side to be selected which is truly representative of all cricketers in South Africa of whatever race'.[31] During 1972–73 SACA sought, in a series of negotiations with the 'non-racial' SACBOC and the South African African Cricket Board (SAACB), to devise, within the constraints of the 'multi-national' sports policy, a mechanism for selecting such a team on merit. At the end of May 1973 the negotiations collapsed, prompting the Cricket Council finally to call off the 1975 tour of England and make provision instead for the first Cricket World Cup.

In April 1972, Cheetham convened an historic first meeting between the three cricketing bodies at the Jan Smuts Holiday Inn, Johannesburg, 'to consider the promotion of cricket under the prevailing sports policy'. A common strategy at the time was for white sports officials to initiate the formation of multi-national 'umbrella' sporting associations, and what Cheetham proposed was that the three bodies come together in such an association, with the prospect that representative teams from each might participate in 'multi-national international tournaments' as a move to-wards merit selection. Hassan Howa and the SACBOC delegation rejected such tournaments as racialist, and as a device to enable SACA to resume playing international cricket. At this meeting the soft-spoken Howa advocated a moratorium on tours and the introduction of mixed cricket at Currie Cup level, from which they could work upwards to national and downwards to club. The aim at the national level was non-racial merit selection, which, for Howa, meant that 'South Africa must be represented by the eleven best cricketers in the country', even if that resulted in an all-white Springbok side: 'If our best player which we regard as best is coloured – if he is not as good as the 12th man who is white, he has no right to wear Springbok colours. That would be gaining honours because he is black.' Where SACBOC and SACA differed fundamentally was on how to get to merit selection, with SACBOC confident that time was on the side of the 'non-racial' route.

The SACBOC delegation left the meeting early, declining to affiliate as a racial group to the proposed new 'multi-national' association. The British Embassy, which carefully monitored the proceedings, reported back to the Foreign and Commonwealth Office: 'The reasons for the rupture between the Coloured and White associations lie of course much deeper than cricket. The Coloureds are now convinced that they have been used in the past by Whites for the Whites' own ends, not only in cricket. This awareness is symptomatic of the growing division between Coloureds and Whites as a whole.'[32] The SAACB delegation, by contrast, agreed to the establishment of the new association. Led by its president, Harrison Butshingi, it made it clear that whites had done far more for African cricket than SACBOC had – Lennox Mlonzi, the secretary, complained that the Howa group 'have never stretched out their arms to the African' – and that unlike SACBOC they were not prepared to wait for the laws of the land to change. 'Let us remember,' Ashton Dunjwa cautioned, with some percipience, 'this Government might be in power for the next 25 years and we are not going to fold our arms and not play cricket.'[33] On 3 March of the following year SACA and SAACB formally established the Cricket Council of South Africa.

At the behest of SACBOC, which regarded Wallace as more progressive than Cheetham, the three national bodies met again at the Heerengracht Hotel, Cape Town, on 25 March 1973 to consider 'arriving at a workable solution on the basis of merit'. At that stage 'workable' for Wallace still meant operating within the boundaries set by the law and government policy, and settling for the immediately attainable rather than aiming at a 'total solution'. When the talks broke down, the mainstream white media generally blamed Howa for his inflexible 'all or nothing' approach, rather than Wallace for his caution.[34] Thereafter, Howa was consistently vilified by the white media and white cricket officials as the primary obstacle to the return of the Springboks to Test cricket.

On this occasion Howa proposed that the 'normalisation' of sport begin with mixed cricket at club level, and work up to an apex, regardless of the practical obstacles imposed by apartheid legislation. Passionate about the game, Howa urged 'even if we have to change in cars and behind bushes, let's play cricket'. According to Wallace, SACA's standpoint was that there were fewer obstacles to merit selection at 'top level as opposed to starting at club level'. He recommended the formation of a select committee to examine a way forward. A representative committee was consequently set up, with Wallace as convenor, to devise within two months a blueprint for 'a workable solution for the basis of merit selection'. The goal was not only merit selection at national level, but also at provincial and schools levels, the latter intended to produce a representative South African Schools team.[35]

While the committee was considering options, Koornhof announced that the government would allow an open international cricket tournament to be held in the country, in which black teams from South Africa might compete, but that no inter-racial cricket would be allowed at club level. Wallace had, earlier in the year, held 'an amiable and encouraging' meeting with Koornhof, who now, in effect, gave the government's stamp of approval to SACA's formula – open international tournaments, for merit selection.[36] That was the kiss of death for the SACA blueprint, represented by Wallace as a 'short term immediately practicable means of implementing our goals'. At the acrimonious next meeting of the three national bodies at Jan Smuts Airport on 27 May 1973, after the select committee had failed to reach any consensus, Howa accused Wallace of colluding with the government, and rejected out of hand the SACA and SAACB proposals for matches between white, African and coloured teams, from which representative teams could be selected, and for the Cricket Council to serve as an umbrella organisation for the three national bodies. The blueprint Howa offered for genuine merit selection was for a series of 'super leagues' in various centres, comprising the best black and white sides and using private grounds, but Wallace foresaw major practical difficulties with the plan, including government disapproval. For Howa Wallace's negative attitude put the three bodies back at 'minus zero' and SACBOC withdrew from further discussions: 'As soon as the Minister says we can play non-racial cricket at all levels, send us a telegram, and we'll come in with you. Until then there is no point talking about it.'[37]

The failure even to devise a formula for merit selection had instant repercussions abroad, with the Cricket Council calling off South Africa's projected 1975 tour of England.

Ever since its June 1970 ruling on the exclusion of South Africa until 'multi-racial' cricket was played there, the Cricket Council had given regular consideration to the terms on which playing ties with South Africa might be resumed. At the end of 1971 the Council divided over whether to sanction Colin Cowdrey, the former England captain, who had accepted SACA's invitation to undertake early in the next year a 'private' tour of South Africa in accordance with Vorster's new 'multi-national' policy. The tour, which Cowdrey discussed with Edward Heath, the Conservative Prime Minister and a personal friend, was designed to begin the international rehabilitation of South African cricket.[38] Cowdrey's team, which would include D'Oliveira, would be the first 'multi-racial' cricket team allowed into the country, and it would play separately against African, coloured and Indian as well as white teams, but not against a 'multi-racial' team. The Prime Minister gave the assurance that 'D'Oliveira and any other coloured cricketers would be granted the full privileges of the country'. According to Waring, the government's intention was to help 'break the ice' after the Cricket Council's ruling on tours.

A special meeting of the full Cricket Council was summoned on 30 December 1971 to deal with the matter, by which time D'Oliveira was signalling that he no longer supported the tour. Having flown to South Africa to sound out opinion he was stunned by the hostility he had encountered among SACBOC officials both to himself and to the very idea of the tour. He promptly advised Lord's that he was not inclined to join the tour: 'He feels it is the wrong time, far too explosive an issue in the present circumstances and would cause him considerable trouble.' At a follow-up meeting on 6 January 1972 the Cricket Council decided by 'a small majority' that if D'Oliveira confirmed he was not available, the tour should not take place; this despite SACA's plea that 'a courageous step should be taken now'.[39] D'Oliveira, who was heckled throughout when he and Howa addressed a SACBOC symposium on apartheid and cricket, subsequently pronounced himself unavailable, and the tour was called off. [40]

For Raman Subba Row cancellation came as a 'relief' in that 'solid foundations' did not yet exist for 'any real progress to be made towards our agreed objective' in South African cricket. That was certainly the assessment of Jack Bailey, assistant secretary to the MCC and the Test and County Cricket Board, in the memorandum he prepared for the Cricket Council on 'Tours to and from South Africa'. He posed the fundamental question: 'By resuming cricket relations under conditions laid down by the South African Government, would the Council be undoing some of the good work already achieved?'

After the Cowdrey tour had fallen through, the Cricket Council became rather more tough-minded in considering the terms on which tours involving South Africa might be resumed, especially as the next scheduled tour was of South Africa to England in 1975. As early as December 1972 the Council advised SACA that, given the 'virtually unchanged' situation in South Africa, it felt it 'must start making other arrangements for the summer of 1975'. In a follow-up letter of 2 February 1973 the Council unsettled SACA by laying down the terms to be met if it was to give, not a guarantee, but 'serious consideration' to resuming Test matches with South Africa. These included the formation of a Cricket Council of South Africa, representing all national cricket organisations in the country, the staging of multi-racial trials, and an assurance from the new body that 'a genuine beginning of multi-racial cricket in South Africa had been made'. Wallace's plea that SACA was currently engaged in negotiations with SACBOC and SAACB, and the intervention of Billy Griffith, the MCC and Council secretary, prompted the Council to delay its decision on the 1975 tour until July. 'I know just how much you contributed to the decision,' a grateful Wallace wrote to Griffith, 'and can only say how lucky we are to have you at Lord's.'

Following the breakdown of negotiations with SACBOC, Wallace visited Lord's in June to discuss the situation, and was advised by Gubby Allen and Griffith that SACA clearly remained incapable of producing a team 'fully representative of and selected from all persons who play cricket in South Africa'. Any tour was consequently likely to be disrupted, and should therefore be cancelled. Cricket in South Africa, they further observed, seemed to lag behind other codes in progressing towards multi-racial sport. At its July meeting, the Cricket Council cancelled the 1975 tour. None the less, the England tour of South Africa in 1976/77 remained on the roster, giving SACA two and a half years to make real progress towards multi-racial cricket before a final decision was made on that tour.[41]

On the ground, some changes were effected during 1973. Exploiting the opportunities offered by the government's 'multi-national' policy, Springbok Lee Irvine together with Robin Binckes Promotions organised an 'open international' double-wicket competition at the Wanderers in September that included two Africans, Edward Habane and Edmund Ntikinca. And with government permission, Younis Ahmed of Pakistan and John Shepherd of the West Indies toured South Africa with the team organised by Derrick Robins, a British entrepreneur, which played against a SAACB team in Soweto in October.

In conflict with government policy, the Aurora Cricket Club, comprising an ethnically diverse group of cricketers, was admitted in September 1973 to the second division of the Maritzburg Cricket Union (MCU) in Natal, thereby becoming the country's first mixed side in white league cricket. Aurora's application to the MCU represented a challenge both to white cricket administrators, suspected of 'hiding behind the skirts of government', and to government itself. The essence of its challenge was that mixed cricket was not, in fact, illegal, provided certain conditions were met. Aurora's contention was that the provisions of the Group Areas Act did not cover the short time spent on a cricket field, and that no other laws would be infringed if games were played on private grounds or those owned by the municipal corporation, only members were admitted as spectators, and the team carried its own refreshments to grounds with licensed premises. After Koornhof had summoned three officials from Aurora to Pretoria, the government issued a proclamation in terms of the Group Areas Act that threatened 'any disqualified person in or upon land or premises in a controlled area or in a group area for a substantial period of time'. Legal advice was that the proclamation, which failed to mention sport, was so loosely worded as to be meaningless. Koornhof also summoned SACA delegates to his home in Pretoria, and threatened new legislation if they did not act to stop Aurora from playing league cricket.[42] The SACA Board of Control, which had taken legal opinion, decided to 'take no direct action' and to 'wait on events', accepting in effect that the admission of Aurora to the MCU was a matter for local decision. Government continued to threaten, and police harassed Aurora's opening games, but for fear of fatally compromising its reformist image, and any chances of South Africa's return to Test cricket, the government did not act on its threat to legislate. SACBOC, for its part, dismissed Aurora for playing in a racial league, and pressed its black players to return to their original clubs.[43]

In a surprise move in November 1973, Koornhof intervened personally in an effort to bridge the gap between SACA and SACBOC and salvage the next Australian tour. He invited Howa to a private meeting, and set before him a three-year plan that supposedly envisaged fully integrated cricket at all levels in the third year. In the first year Australia would be invited to undertake a Test tour that would include games against the SACBOC national team; for the second year New Zealand would be invited to tour and play provincial matches against black and white teams and Tests against a South African national team selected on merit. The third year would see fully integrated cricket at all levels, club as well as provincial. A major problem, however, was that the plan did not include Africans, as they were 'a different nation', and it was consequently rejected by Howa.[44] In July 1974, for the second successive year, the government refused Howa a passport to attend the ICC annual meeting to put the case for SACBOC's admission to the international body. In the event, it was at the meeting Howa was unable to attend that the ICC concluded that SACBOC was simply not representative of South African cricket and that only when there was 'a single body representative of all cricket in that country' could South Africa take its place at the Conference.

With SACA's top-down, gradualist multi-national approach to mixed cricket having so clearly failed, white cricket administrators finally began to appreciate that unless they broke away from the constraints of government policy and began to introduce mixed cricket at club level, South African cricket was doomed to permanent isolation from Test cricket.

The initiative for multi-racial club cricket came from the Transvaal, where, since 1972, the Transvaal Cricket Union (TCU) had provided for the coaching of Soweto schoolboys and for several years College Old Boys, the Transvaal's leading Indian team, captained by Abdul Bhamjee, had pressed to join the TCU. In August 1974 Joe Pamensky, in his annual address as TCU chairman, challenged the government to open the way for 'multi-racial' cricket. One of white cricket's more perceptive administrators, Pamensky sensed that the time had come to work with Indian and coloured clubs, having already succeeded in establishing personal relations with several of their chairmen and captains. He also believed that it might now be possible to move the government forward. In the April 1974 general election the governing National Party had successfully seen off the challenge of the far right and had watched the advance of the liberal Progressive Party, hitherto represented in Parliament solely by Helen Suzman, which captured six urban seats from an enfeebled and more conservative United Party.

Early in September an historic first meeting was held between the TCU board and members of the Transvaal Cricket Federation (TCF), chaired by Rachid Varachia. In January 1975 the TCU, after canvassing legal opinion and the views of senior players and clubs, announced that the two boards had agreed to organise mixed club cricket for the next season 'in such a manner that games will be played on a league basis within the laws of the country'. For the first time, white cricket administrators had moved ahead of government's official policy, and Koornhof promptly reprimanded them for their 'violation and disregard of the policy of the Government', adding that it was regarded in a serious light. But Varachia and his board had likewise moved ahead of their constituency, and the TCF subsequently backed out of the scheme. A clearly frustrated Pamensky blamed the erratic behaviour of the TCF on 'influences unconnected with cricket administration' intent on 'making the game a tool for the achievement of broader political aspirations'.[45]

In March 1975 Sedick Conrad and Edward Habane became the first blacks to play in a mixed South African first-class team, when they were included, with government permission, in the President's XI that met the Derrick Robins tourists at Newlands, but otherwise South African cricket officials had little tangible progress towards 'multi-racial' cricket to demonstrate in the effort to salvage the scheduled Australian tour for the following season, and England for the season thereafter.

Despite SACA's assurances of 'merit selection', both the Australian Cricket Board (ACB), under the chairmanship of Tim Caldwell, and the Cricket Council, under the chairmanship of F.R. 'Freddie' Brown, cancelled the tours. In contradistinction to what happened in 1970/71, the ACB cancelled in deference to government, and the Cricket Council cancelled of its own volition. Unlike the

McMahon Government, the Labour Government of Gough Whitlam was powerfully anti-apartheid, and, in December 1974, advised the ACB of its opposition to the tour. The ACB had previously decided it 'had no wish to tour South Africa if such action would be opposed by the Australian Government', and in February 1975 it cancelled, after Boon Wallace had been denied a visa to enter Australia to present SACA's case.[46] On 22 July the Cricket Council, six months ahead of its own initial schedule, likewise cancelled on the recommendation of its Emergency Executive Committee. In the Council's view there was little prospect in the 'foreseeable future' that South Africa could satisfy what it saw as the two basic criteria for the resumption of tours, namely that the three governing bodies for cricket in South Africa should come together in a single representative body, and that 'multi-racial cricket should be played in South Africa and representative teams both at National and Provincial level should be selected on merit'. Wallace was promptly informed by telephone of the decision to cancel, which was made public in September, following a meeting with the SACA executive.

Koornhof was outraged by both cancellations, particularly the decision of the Cricket Council, which he represented as a 'volte face'. During the course of 1974 he had held discussions with both Lord Caccia, then the Cricket Council president, and Freddie Brown when they had visited South Africa, and evidently believed that his assurances about 'merit selection' in the future had ensured the tour. Wallace was likewise hugely disappointed by the Cricket Council's cancellation, detecting 'a hardening of attitude towards sticking to the letter of the statement of May 1970', while John Woodcock, the cricket correspondent of *The Times*, believed the Council's decision was a mistake in that it ignored 'the cricket winds of change' sweeping South Africa.[47] The cancellations were to prove fatal to SACA's hopes of securing South Africa's return to Test cricket for the fundamental changes that came thereafter in the field of sport were rapidly overwhelmed by the radicalisation of the wider situation in the wake of the Soweto uprising.

In September 1975, in his final annual address as SACA president, Wallace declared his belief that mixed cricket was coming and his conviction that cricket was a game that would go far to promote 'harmony between the various race groups in our country'. At least four provincial unions, he announced, were investigating ways and means of establishing integrated leagues, and the government was aware of this. Rashid Varachia, who had succeeded to the presidency after Howa's surprise resignation in August 1974, was evidently so impressed by Wallace's declarations that he promptly met with W.C.B. 'Billy' Woodin, the new SACA president, to seek unity in South African cricket. 'If my too ambitious and over enthusiastic colleagues fail to respond to the winds of change, and if we choose rhetoric over reality,' Varachia proclaimed, 'our great goal of returning to international cricket will be submerged in common failure.'[48]

From the outset, Varachia, a wealthy Johannesburg Indian businessman, was regarded as more pragmatic and flexible than his predecessor. The Bombay-born, South African-educated Varachia had played for Transvaal Indians in the late 1940s and early 1950s as a middle-order batsman and was a founder member of SACBOC. It appears that two major considerations prompted him to work for unity in South African cricket. One was that he had come to believe that the way to promote both black cricket and change in South Africa was by working from within, rather than against, a system that was finding itself compelled to change. The other was that he possessed a distinct taste for the international game and had a passionate desire to see South Africa back in international cricket. In negotiating for cricket unity in 1976–77 Varachia never sought to disguise that his primary cricketing goals were 'firstly to provide the greatest opportunity for each cricketer to attain the highest honour, secondly, to break our isolation and re-enter into the International Arena'.[49]

As SACBOC secretary he had travelled to India in 1951 in an effort to arrange a tour that would include three 'Tests', and was centrally involved in the attempt to mount a West Indies tour in 1959. In his capacity as president of the TCF he again travelled to India, and also to Pakistan, in an unsuccessful attempt to persuade their national teams to tour South Africa. In July 1968, to the outrage of the Anti-Apartheid Movement in Britain, he invited Khalad 'Billy' Ibadulla, the Pakistan and Warwickshire cricketer, to bring out a team that included five Test players for a tour that would include three 'Tests'. The tour was called off when visas were not forthcoming.[50]

Despite some hiccups, notably resentment among African administrators at the lack of consultation, the upshot of Varachia's new initiative was an historic 'summit' on 18 January 1976 at the President Hotel in Johannesburg of the three governing bodies of South African cricket to discuss 'the control, administration and playing of normal cricket in South Africa'. The meeting was unanimous that 'normal' cricket – a concept both more flexible and less intimidating for whites than 'non-racial' – would be introduced at club level, and that the game would be administered under a single governing body. A nine-man motivating committee, with three members from each body, was installed under Varachia's chairmanship to oversee the introduction of 'normal' cricket, and to arrange for the formation of a new national body under a non-racial constitution.

Virtually from the outset the committee's proceedings were bedevilled by controversy. The match it sought to arrange for mid-February between a multi-racial South African Invitation XI and the touring Derrick Robins team had to be scrapped after a revolt within SACBOC against 'the playing of isolated, "window-dressing" games at national level'. In March, similar controversy dogged the inclusion of SACBOC players in matches against the International Wanderers team, managed by Richie Benaud and captained by Greg Chappell, which had been brought out by SACA. There was also dissatisfaction among certain SACA officials. After the South African Invitation XI, including three black players, had been roundly defeated by the Wanderers at both Newlands and Port Elizabeth, one prominent official complained to Benaud 'that it was the last bloody time they would allow themselves to be forced into choosing three non-white players', that in future it would be a test of strength.[51] Abdulatief 'Tiefie' Barnes and Ismail 'Baboo' Ebrahim starred thereafter in games against the tourists at the Wanderers and Kingsmead, with Ebrahim capturing 6 for 66 in the second innings to give the South African Invitation XI victory in Durban.

The real crisis came on 11 October 1976 when, after Edward Habane had been blocked from playing for Balfour Guild, Billy Woodin told the *Rand Daily Mail* that cricket administrators and the Minister of Sport and Recreation had reached an agreement that there might be cricket between clubs of different races, but that they had never agreed to 'multi-racial clubs'. In short, according to Woodin, the introduction of mixed leagues at the club level was to conform with the 'multi-national' formula for league sport announced by Koornhof on 23 September. The outcry was immediate; the non-racial SACBOC could never subscribe to 'multi-national' cricket, and Mark Henning, the chairman of the TCU, announced that the TCU would hold to its agreement with the TCF and the Transvaal African Cricket Association for the implementation of 'multi-racial' cricket.[52]

Throughout its deliberations, and the preparations it oversaw for the introduction of mixed club cricket in all the provinces for the 1976/77 season, the motivating committee had taken particular care to get Koornhof on board, and to secure government sanction. Their approach to Koornhof was purposefully non-confrontational, emphasising that their agenda was cricketing and not political, and that they were intent on operating within the law.[53] At a meeting with Koornhof on 1 July 1976, the Minister of Sport and Recreation conveyed that he had discussed the 'proposed basis for normalising cricket', namely to allow 'participation of and competition between all cricketers regardless of race, creed or colour' at club level, with the Prime Minister, and that 'to his surprise' Vorster had broken completely from his historic objections and agreed to extend the principle of normal cricket to 'provincial and national levels as well'.[54] The drama occurred on 18 August when, with the provinces having drawn up their plans for 'normal' cricket for the forth-coming season, Koornhof intimated that he required Cabinet sanction for mixed cricket at club level as a change in government policy was involved. At its meeting on 24 August the Cabinet resolved that, because of the wider implications that extended far beyond cricket, it could not give its stamp of approval before consulting the annual National Party congresses, which met in September.[55]

After a delay that was almost unbearable for the cricket administrators, Koornhof finally provided government's answer in his policy statement on 23 September; that in team games like cricket ministerial permission might be given for 'leagues or matches enabling teams from different racial groups to compete'. The following day the motivating committee saw Koornhof, who gave the go ahead for mixed cricket at club level. 'The Minister accepted our blueprint for normal cricket without one comma being changed,' Varachia informed the annual general meeting of the TCF on 26 September, and that blueprint was for integrated, not multi-national, cricket without government restriction. Koornhof had given the assurance that blanket dispensation would be granted from the provision of those Acts which would otherwise make 'normal' cricket illegal, on the sole condition that provinces made application to his Department, providing fixtures and venues for the season.[56]

At an extraordinary general meeting of SACBOC at the President Hotel, Jo-hannesburg, over the weekend 2–3 October, Varachia repeated the assurance, 'When it comes to normalising cricket, all the Departments have been given instructions that the Group Areas Act will not apply; the Liquor Act will not apply; the Separate Amenities Act will not apply; you are free to do what you want to do. But you must tell them where you are playing.' That Saturday, 2 October, mixed cricket at the club level got under way around the country, except in the SACBOC strongholds of Western Province and Natal, where the various provincial bodies had not negotiated 'normal' cricket agreements. The two Soweto teams in the Transvaal lower leagues were unable to play at home because of 'the present unrest'.

Woodin, nervous and conservative, almost managed to derail the whole movement towards 'normal' cricket and unity. Woodin, a protégé of Arthur Coy's from Port Elizabeth, earned a reputation early in his presidency for 'knocking down his wicket' on sensitive issues, as when in October 1975 he meekly succumbed to Koornhof's ruling that the African XI invited to participate in the Gillette Cup would be restricted to a single game against the reigning champions, Natal.[57] In his alleged 'somersault' over mixed clubs, Woodin broke a fundamental rule of the negotiations with Koornhof, that public controversy was to be avoided at all costs, and sabotaged SACBOC's fundamental stand, that 'normal' cricket was to be 'non-racial' and not 'multi-national'. Varachia responded: 'In the interests of all cricketers in this country it is better that we in SACBOC regretfully terminate our happy working relationship for the protection of our integrity and dignity.' It took the intervention of Joe Pamensky to bring Varachia, Woodin and Koornhof back together, resulting in a joint statement urging all cricketers to continue playing and reassuring them that all differences had been settled. Koornhof seems to have agreed to '5% movement of top Non Whites to White Clubs'.[58] Major problems, none the less, continued to bedevil the introduction of 'normal' cricket, with the key Western Province Cricket Board (WPCB) declining to participate at all.

The man who took the lead against 'normal' cricket was the charismatic and mercurial Hassan Howa, who, earlier in 1976 had returned from his self-imposed exile to resume, in what amounted to a coup, the presidency of the WPCB. Initially, Howa lent his support to 'normal' cricket, but by the time of the annual general meeting of the WPCB on 10 September he had come out firmly against it. By his own account, what he had been 'fighting for for twenty years' was in sight, but he questioned the integrity of his counterparts in the Western Province Cricket Union (WPCU), who seemed more intent on not antagonising the government than on driving the unity process forward, and in the wake of the Soweto uprising had modified his own stand. As Howa now perceived it, the 'normal' cricket being contemplated was purely cosmetic, and would do nothing to counter the structural racial inequality that made it impossible for a young cricketer from the African townships of Soweto to compete on an equal footing with his counterpart from the all-white elite Johannesburg suburb of Houghton: 'For true merit selection every one has to be given the same opportunity to develop his latent talent.' In short, he had come to appreciate that cricket could not be isolated from the rest of South African society; that 'normal' cricket could never be possible in an 'abnormal' society, and that he had been wrong 'to think only about cricket'. There were bigger issues than cricket, and the struggle had to go beyond the sport. As a member of the relatively small Malay community, he did not then envisage a society based on a universal franchise – 'with approximately 20 million Africans and only 4 million other people it cannot work, it cannot be a viable proposition' – but he at least wanted a society based on equal opportunity. At heart, Howa was a non-collaborationist, who believed that boycotts and isolation from the outside world were the best mechanisms to force real change. The last thing he wanted was for white cricketers 'to use us to get back into international cricket'.[59]

On 10 October the WPCB voted not to join forces with the WPCU in a 'normal' cricket arrangement, and, in November Varachia declined to attempt to heal the breach by attending a WPCB meeting to clarify 'normal' cricket. Relations between Varachia and Howa, never cordial, had reached breaking point. 'Mr Howa,' Varachia exploded, 'jumps from spot to spot always finding excuses', and could never be satisfied: 'He belongs on a political platform not a cricket field.'[60] In Natal, another SACBOC stronghold, 'normal' cricket on any scale was short-lived, with the 'non-racial' Natal Cricket Board (NCB) belatedly joining the process and then soon abandoning it, in late February 1977.

During the course of 1977 the actions and deliberations of the nine-man motivating committee failed to bring the WPCB and the NCB on board. On 22 February, the draft constitution for the new national body, drawn up by David Lewis of SACA and Pat Naidoo of SACBOC, was submitted to a special meeting of SACBOC. After accepting an amendment that rejected the allegedly 'multi-national' character of the proposed new union and asserted instead its commitment to 'the principles of non-racialism' Varachia claimed he had obtained the approval of SACBOC. He thereafter turned down requests that he summon the regular annual general meeting of SACBOC to make the final decision on whether or not it should dissolve and join the new union, claiming he had already been given his mandate.[61] Among his critics, Varachia instantly became regarded as a 'sell-out' who had failed to consult his own constituency; and his move lost him the support even of his vice-president, Pat Naidoo, one of the architects of the new constitution.[62]

At a meeting at the Wanderers in Johannesburg on 18 September 1977, SACA, SACBOC and SAACB, merged to form the South African Cricket Union

(SACU), under a constitution that affirmed that it 'would enable participation in it of all inhabitants without distinction of colour, race or creed'. Varachia was elected president, Wallace vice-president, and Pamensky treasurer. Although there were no Africans on the SACU Board – Frank Brache, D'Oliveira's brother-in-law, was the only other black member – cricket had become the first of the team sports in South Africa to negotiate full unification and install a black president. On 13 November 1977, at a meeting in Johannesburg, a rival 'non-racial' South African Cricket Board (SACB) was set up as an affiliate of SACOS, with Hassan Howa as president.

'NORMAL' CRICKET

'Normal' cricket never got under way on any scale in the Western Province as a consequence of the opposition of the WPCB, although some clubs and a substantial number of leading players deserted to the WPCU, and Langa, the only African club in the province, played in the WPCU.[63] In Natal the experiment lasted for only a few months; in February 1977 the NCB, under the chairmanship of Krish Mackerdhuj, a Howa protégé, withdrew after the Natal Cricket Association refused to reschedule its one-day limited overs competition to cater for NCB clubs. At the end of the season Aurora moved across to the NCB on the grounds that non-racial sport in South Africa could only be 'effectively realised' through SACOS.[64] In the Eastern Province, 'normal' cricket caused a major split in the ranks of the Eastern Province Cricket Association (EPCA). Eight EPCA clubs joined the new dispensation, seven others refused from the outset.[65] That left the Transvaal as the main stronghold and testing ground for 'normal' cricket, but even there it had effectively collapsed by 1982.

In the final analysis, the venture into 'normal' cricket proved Howa's point that an abnormal society was not well suited to normal sport. Although, as André Odendaal underlines, the early 1970s witnessed major advances for SACBOC cricket, with the introduction of a three-day, home-and-away competition for the Dadabhay Trophy; the importation of top overseas professionals; and the organisation of special invitational matches to recognise players at a national level, the meeting between white and black cricket was inherently unequal from the outset.[66] The discrepancies between the two in terms of facilities, finances and coaching remained huge. The experiment in 'normal' cricket, moreover, exposed many of the fault-lines and pathologies of late apartheid South Africa.

From the beginning, the most positive atmosphere existed in the Transvaal, which pioneered unification with the launch of the Transvaal Cricket Council (TCC) on 11 August 1977. The powerful commitment of both Varachia and Mark Henning, the TCC chairman, to unity and 'normal' cricket ensured a generally co-operative climate on the TCC Board. The TCC was clearly determined to make 'normal' cricket work, which translated at times into a patronising attitude among white administrators towards black clubs. Altogether in the TCC leagues there were some 30 teams from the Indian group area of Lenasia, the various coloured townships, and from Soweto. Ismail 'Morris' Garda and Solly Chotia became the first cricketers of colour since C.B. Llewellyn to play in the Currie Cup when they represented Transvaal 'B'. Despite these efforts, within six years unity was dead and 'normal' cricket effectively a thing of the past. For the 1982/83 season the last of the Lenasia teams abandoned the TCC for the rival, 'non-racial' and SACOS-aligned Transvaal Cricket Board (TCB).

'Normal' cricket was something negotiated from above, although senior players generally gave their approval. The players most in favour, in the Transvaal as elsewhere, were the elite – whites who had a vested interest in South Africa's return to international cricket, if only to play against touring teams, and blacks who wished to prove their worth and improve their games. The general understanding among black administrators and players was that their participation in 'normal' cricket would serve as a catalyst for change, leading to the complete dismantling of apartheid in sport.

To begin with, the three Lenasia teams, Crescents, Kohinoor and Rangers, struggled to find their feet in what was a powerful Premier League, accentuating the reservations of some coloured and Indian players about the whole enterprise. These reservations were heightened by the inclusion in the Premier League of Varachia's team, Kohinoor, ahead of Abdul Bhamjee's College Old Boys, the traditional powerhouse of Indian cricket in the Transvaal. For the 1977/78 season three prominent white provincial cricketers, David Dyer, Peter de Vaal, and David van der Knaap, were recruited to strengthen Kohinoor. Former Springbok Colin Wesley had previously joined Crescents, which also gave a home to the African all-rounder, Duncan Stamper, making it the most distinctly 'non-racial' of the Transvaal teams. Ali Bacher, the last Springbok Test captain, had a season with Rangers as player-coach. Habane finally made his debut for Balfour-Guild in the 1977/78 season.

In the lower leagues, as the minutes of a rather busy disciplinary committee make evident, racial stereotyping was rampant, with blacks often sensing they were unwanted and uncatered for, while white and Indian players regularly operated on the assumption that player-umpires from the other group cheated. The advent of sledging did not help ease racial tensions on the field.[67] There were also a couple of instances when white headmasters stopped league games from going ahead on school grounds because a black team was involved. To this cocktail was added pressure on black teams and players from the Transvaal Council on Sport (TRACOS), the provincial division of SACOS, headed by the hard-line Reggie Feldman, headmaster of a coloured high school in Bosmont. The message was that by playing 'normal' cricket players were participating in a 'multi-national' fraud rather than contributing to change, and that, as blacks, their struggle extended far beyond the cricket boundary. Certainly, it was not their role to provide a façade to facilitate South Africa's re-entry into Test cricket.

The first to reject the 'Varachia league' were Azads in Lenasia, gathering support from a number of coloured as well as Indian clubs.[68] To provide an alternative home the TCB, with eight teams, was founded early in the 1977/78 season as an affiliate of Howa's SACB. The first TCB president was Percy Pfeffer, followed by Dr Abu-Baker 'Hurley' Asvat in 1979, and Ahmed Mangera in 1981. A major problem for the rival league was grounds: the TCC had negotiated a monopoly of the Lenasia grounds with the Johannesburg Cricket Council, a body the TCB refused to recognise. Through the influence of Pfeffer, whose brother was on the Coloured Management Council, grounds in the coloured townships of Johannesburg had provided the TCB with its main venues, until it began 'invading' Lenasia grounds. By the start of the 1980/81 season the TCB claimed some 30 teams, as players began leaving the TCC in numbers. Abdul Bhamjee taunted that 'most of these people are over the hill and simply can't make the grade in the Transvaal Cricket Council', but those who 'defected' claimed they had become disillusioned with 'normal' cricket, that it had turned out to be 'multi-national' cricket. For some, what 'broke the camel's back' was a 'racial incident' at the Old Parktonians Club in Johannesburg towards the end of the 1979/80 season.[69]

In the Transvaal, as elsewhere, potentially the most contentious issue confronting 'normal' cricket was the access of black players and their supporters to white clubhouses and licensed premises. Normally, under the Separate Amenities Act and the Liquor Act, both were off-limits to black custom, but this prohibition was not supposed to apply to 'normal' cricket, which was granted administrative exemption. To complicate matters, the new Liquor Act of 1977, in one of late apartheid's more bizarre concessions, made provision for hotels, restaurants and clubs to acquire 'international' licences entitling them to serve all races. To begin with, the award of such licences was strictly patrolled by the Minister of Justice, Jimmy Kruger, and clubs were generally only granted 'international' status on the condition that mixed dancing was not permitted. Most clubs did not apply, some set aside a separate room to entertain black players or arranged lunch under the trees, and all clubs with bars had stringent regulations for visitors to be signed on by members before they could be served. The potential for 'misunderstandings' and hurtful 'incidents' was immense and it was inevitable that there would be some major incident.

Which is what happened in March 1980 when the Old Parktonians Club refused the players and supporters of Kohinoor open access to its facilities on the grounds that it did not possess an international licence. Earlier in the season the same club had been reprimanded for refusing bar service to two Indian players, members of the Krugersdorp Old Boys team, and its chairman had given the 'assurance that the like of it would never happen again at his club'. When it did, on Saturday 29 March, the Kohinoor team refused to continue the match on the Sunday, accusing Old Parktonians of racial discrimination. Anger in Lenasia at the incident, which was widely reported, intensified when the subsequent TCC ban on Old Parktonians was soon lifted in the light of the club's assurance that it was committed to making 'normal' cricket work.[70]

Increasingly thereafter, Lenasia closed ranks behind the TCB in a process that underlined that cricket was not played in a political vacuum. The Lenasia schools boycott of 1980, which prompted school children to challenge their parents over playing 'normal' cricket while gross inequalities still existed in society, and the hugely successful boycott of the Indian Council elections in November 1981, heightened the mood of non-collaboration. For the 1981/82 season only eleven Lenasia teams entered the TCC's leagues, with Kohinoor and Crescents having merged, and by season's end a mere three were left.

To explain this 'dwindling' support for the TCC in Lenasia Colin Bryden of Robin Binckes Promotions, the TCC's public relations consultants, prepared a confidential memorandum in February 1982 which highlighted 'the political situation' in a 'disenfranchised community': 'This is undoubtedly the biggest factor and is largely beyond the control of the TCC.' A second major factor was that the TCB and its supporters, who had backed the election boycott campaign, exerted 'pressure on TCC players' which, in a 'close-knit' community, was difficult to resist: 'Those who support the TCC are placed in an invidious position. They are accused of supporting a "white" institution and the situation arises where members of the same family find themselves on opposite sides of the fence.' The divisions were bitter, with the participants in TCC cricket being labelled as 'sell-outs'. What particularly agitated the TCC was the 'intimidation' and 'victimisation' that allegedly took place in Lenasia, particularly in SACOS-aligned schools.[71] Countrywide, the enforcement of the SACOS 'double-standards' resolution was gaining new intensity in 'Operation Cleanup', targeting players and officials who watched white sport, and also the offspring of those who played with whites.[72] By the 1982/83 season Lenasia had completely withdrawn from the TCC leagues, as had the large majority of coloured and Malay teams.

The failure of 'normal' cricket in the Transvaal underscored the limitations of SACU. Essentially the body was led by men whose sense of the relationship between politics and sport ended with the realisation that it had become necessary for cricket both to liberate itself from government political interference and to arrange for the playing of 'multi-racial' club cricket. In their perception, that was the boundary, and 'normal' cricket, once the 'pinpricks' had been ironed out, reached the boundary. It was a formalistic perception that failed to come to terms with a new sort of politics in sport that saw the crumbling of sports apartheid as a staging post on the road to the collapse of apartheid itself, and that rapidly and radically required cricket to move beyond the boundary into the realms of political change.

On the international front, SACU's formalistic efforts and expectations failed to score a boundary, with the result that the Springboks, as such, were never able to make their return to Test cricket. When South Africa was finally readmitted to official international cricket in 1991, the Springbok name was dropped.

9

Innings Closed

TO THE HORROR of both the Nationalist Government and white sports administrators in the late 1970s, the boundary ropes for South Africa's return to international sport had shifted. At the very moment that they finally moved towards de-politicising and de-racialising sport the radical opponents of apartheid deepened the sports boycott and intensified the politicisation of sport by demanding the dismantling of apartheid as a pre-condition for the 'normalisation' of sport and the return of South Africa to official international competition. In a situation replete with irony, the new South African Cricket Union (SACU) represented itself as the standard bearer for cricket free of outside political intervention, and blamed its failure to get back into official international cricket on the craven capitulation of the member countries of the International Cricket Conference (ICC) to the political dictates of their governments.

Although SACU perceived itself to be in the forefront of the move towards the 'normalisation' of team sport in South Africa, it signally failed to dent the sports boycott in so far as a return to Test cricket was concerned. Its one triumph was to secure a visit in March 1979 by a 'fact-finding' delegation of the ICC to ascertain what developments had taken place in South African cricket. The delegation commended SACU on the 'great progress' it had made, and implicitly accepted that it had met the conditions previously laid down by the Cricket Council and the ICC, but concluded that 'sport can no longer be divorced from political considerations' and recommended against any attempt to promote SACU membership of the ICC for fear of provoking 'serious repercussions affecting the welfare of the game'. It likewise recommended that there be no resumption of representative cricket between ICC member countries and South Africa. The Springboks, who had not graced a cricket field since 1970, were destined to remain outside the magic circle of Test cricket.

The recommendations of the ICC delegation infuriated the SACU hierarchy, but did not take them entirely by surprise. Even before the delegation arrived in the country, David Lewis, the Rhodesian delegate to SACU, predicted an unfavourable outcome in a letter to Boon Wallace, the SACU vice-president, in which he surveyed several possible future scenarios for South African cricket. As he made clear to Wallace, in the unlikely event that the delegation gave South Africa a favourable report, he did not believe it would secure the country's return to the international scene because of the 'inevitable consequences for political reasons of breaking up the ICC Test scene'. The Gleneagles Agreement was another negative factor.

SACU had to plan for such an eventuality, and Lewis began to investigate various possibilities. The first was that SACU should make 'the maximum noise and apply the maximum pressure' on the white countries particularly, 'to point out to them the moralities of the situation and call upon them to defy their governments in the way in which they requested us to do this and the way in which we did this'. He positively exploded: 'They cannot be allowed to get away with this one.' A second possibility would be to press for the resumption of 'unofficial' Tests against those countries prepared to play South Africa, and a third that South Africa be given associate status within the ICC, which would enable it to play lesser countries, like Sri Lanka. If, as seemed likely, all these attempts to operate through the ICC failed, SACU would have to consider 'going into the commercial field of buying players to tour South Africa', using such tours to provide South African players with a chance to acquire Springbok colours. 'I know,' Lewis added, 'that diehards say that these should only be awarded for proper international cricket but I am afraid times have changed and their views must not prevail.'[1]

Lewis suggested the broad outlines of the strategy that SACU would pursue in the years ahead. SACU would place enormous moral pressure on the 'imperial old-boy network' to recognise that it had 'more than met' the conditions for South Africa's return to the ICC and Test cricket, and that they should at least secure South African membership of the ICC. Membership of the ICC was not something SACU could apply for; it would have to be proposed and seconded by two full members, who would be expected to come from the white trio of England, Australia and New Zealand. Should SACU's attempts to gain some sort of acceptance by the ICC be rebuffed at every point, it would have every political justification for resorting to other mechanisms to provide South African players with international competition and an opportunity to win Springbok colours.

SACU AND THE ICC

The trio who spearheaded SACU's campaign were Rashid Varachia, Boon Wallace and Joe Pamensky. Varachia's charm and wit, together with his colour, made him a major asset, but for much of his time as SACU president he was plagued by ill health, leaving Wallace and Pamensky effectively in control of SACU's affairs. Wallace was an experienced hand, having served three terms as SACA president, and having represented the old guard in white cricket administration. Pamensky, a Johannesburg businessman, was the dynamic force within the trio. Involved in cricket administration since his student days at the University of the Witwatersrand, he had become the youngest board member of the TCU when elected in 1955 at the age of 25, and had served on SACA from 1969. He represented the new found progressivism of the Transvaal.

From the standpoint of securing South Africa's admission to the ICC, SACU could hardly have been launched at a less promising moment, immediately after the Soweto uprising, the Gleneagles Agreement and the formal adoption by SACOS of its radical new policy that South African sport should remain isolated until apartheid had been eradicated. Undeterred, the body sent a series of representatives abroad, beginning with a delegation to Lord's in March 1978, to lobby for South Africa's admission to the ICC. The upshot was the ICC's contested decision in July to send a delegation to South Africa to assess, in effect, the country's progress towards meeting the previously prescribed conditions for membership and a return to Test cricket. SACU was outraged when the delegation's positive assessment was accompanied by the negative recommendation that it had become politically impossible to promote its membership of the ICC or to readmit South Africa to Test cricket. The body's angry response to the ICC, in a letter later withdrawn, was that the delegation's conclusions and recommendations 'represent a classic example of expediency and surrender of principle, avoidance of controversy and abdication of normal responsibility by appeasement by reference to purely political factors'.[2]

The recommendations of the ICC delegation were predetermined. The conference's 'imperial old-boy network' could operate, with some difficulty, to give SACU a hearing, but politically there was no prospect of South Africa getting back into Test cricket, and not only because of the obstacle posed by the Gleneagles Agreement. In the ICC the stalemate between white and black Test-playing countries over South Africa re-emerged, but, as in the 1960s, that helped ensure the maintenance of the status quo, which now excluded South Africa from Test cricket. After Soweto the black member countries of the ICC simply would not hear of the Springboks making a return to Test cricket, and the white countries were not prepared to risk splitting the ICC for the sake of South Africa.

In August 1976 the Cricket Council was informed by its representatives to the annual meeting of the ICC that: 'It was clear from the discussions that certain of the Member Countries would have no dealings with South Africa at all whilst apartheid policies existed in South Africa, which was a backward step since previously these Countries were only against the fact that multi-racial cricket was not played in South Africa.'[3] Even before Hassan Howa had formulated the policy of 'no normal sport in an abnormal society', the black Test-playing countries had made it clear that apartheid itself would have to go before South Africa might return to Test cricket. It was not a view that the Cricket Council subscribed to, but it was one that would hugely constrain it.

Clyde Walcott, the great West Indian batsman of the Fifties who later represented the West Indies on the ICC, suspected that 'some of the predominantly white countries' would have done a deal with South Africa, even at the risk of splitting the cricket world in two, 'if the politicians had allowed them'.[4] That was unlikely. In rugby, sports administrators showed themselves prepared to defy the politicians and Gleneagles in order to resume Test match encounters with South Africa, but, despite a decided sympathy for South Africa among white cricket administrators, there was no such inclination in the cricket world. The strong 'establishment' tradition among white cricket administrations probably helped make them disinclined to challenge their governments, but it was the prospect of splitting the cricket world that constrained them most.

For England's Cricket Council, South Africa's chief conduit to international cricket, the formation of SACU in September 1977, represented a major challenge. Ever since 1970 the Council had held up the prospect of a resumption of Test cricket against England as the reward for South Africa's attainment of genuinely 'multi-racial' cricket, with the possibility even of an England tour of South Africa in 1977/78. The formation of SACU came too late for that, but even so SACU saw the Cricket Council as its main route back into Test cricket. Both the ebullient F.R. 'Freddie' Brown, who had managed the MCC team in South Africa in 1956/ 57 and who was chairman of the Council from 1974–79, and his successor, the more cerebral Charles Palmer, a former captain of Leicestershire, were generally regarded as well-disposed to South Africa, and anxious to help.

In the light, however, of the Gleneagles Agreement and the opposition of the black cricket-playing countries to any sporting contact with apartheid South Africa, the Council found itself obliged to reconsider its formal position. Unwilling to challenge the British Government over Gleneagles, or to risk splitting the ICC along racial lines by championing SACU's cause, it none the less believed that SACU deserved a hearing as well as encouragement to continue along the path of 'multi-racialism'. The ICC delegation to South Africa, headed by Palmer, embodied the Council's approach of continuing to keep South Africa on the outside, so as not to disrupt world cricket, but without quite shutting the door on an old friend whose efforts warranted encouragement. In the assessment of Sam Ramsamy, neither the Cricket Council nor the ICC was 'forthright' enough to tell SACU that it would remain isolated until apartheid was abolished, with the result that they provided 'white South Africans with the false hope that further adjustments might just help SACU into international cricket'.[5]

Immediately after the formation of SACU the Cricket Council sought an 'informal' meeting between Freddie Brown and Dennis Howell, the Minister of Sport in the Labour Government of Jim Callaghan, to clarify the situation concerning the Gleneagles Agreement and to 'ascertain to what extent the Cricket Council could continue encouraging the South African authorities in their efforts to establish multi-racial cricket'. In the interim, the Council advised SACU against applying for admission to the ICC 'in the light of the present political situation'.[6]

Howell repeated the Labour Government's long-standing demand that the South African Government repudiate all forms of apartheid in sport. His position, as communicated by Brown to SACU in December, was that nothing could be initiated in Britain until 'your Prime Minister makes it absolutely clear world wide that the policies you are pursuing are both within the law of the country and conform to Government policy'. In response to pressures from abroad for change, SACA had always insisted that it dared not defy the law and government policy; now it was being told that defiance of government policy was, in itself, meaningless. What was required was the conversion of the government.

For their projected visit to Lord's in March 1978, the best the SACU delegation could extract from government by way of a statement was a New Year's message from Koornhof intimating that 'normal' cricket accorded with government policy, and that membership of a club was not determined by any law. An exasperated Minister of Sport and Recreation also stated that 'he was prepared to give the Cricket Council anything they might wish for within the context of cricket, provided they in turn gave him an assurance in writing that as a result therefrom, South Africa would be taken back into International Cricket'.[7]

At the meeting at Lord's on 22 March 1978 between the Cricket Council's Emergency Executive Committee and the SACU delegation of Varachia, Wallace and Pamensky, Brown accepted Varachia's point that South Africa had met all the requirements for a return to international cricket, but indicated there had since been changes in world opinion and warned the delegation of the need for 'tact' in pursuing their aim, 'especially in the light of the political situation'. To assist SACU Brown agreed to write personally to the chairmen of the full member countries of the ICC stating how impressed the Emergency Executive Committee was with the recent developments in South African cricket and requesting them to give Varachia the opportunity to meet their boards.[8]

Thus armed, Varachia travelled virtually around the world, visiting India, Pakistan, New Zealand – under the Liberal/National Party Government of Malcolm Fraser, Australia was still out of bounds – as well as Miami in the United States, where he discussed matters with Jeff Stollmeyer from the West Indies.[9] In Wellington, New Zealand, Varachia was joined by Wallace and Pamensky for a crucial two-day meeting with Walter Hadlee, chairman of the New Zealand Cricket Council (NZCC), and Bob Parish, chairman of the Australian Cricket Board (ACB). Parish appreciated that a 'great deal' had been accomplished in South African cricket, but also pointed out that the problem was 'no longer simply a sporting one but has become political', with both the New Zealand and Australian Governments adhering to 'the somewhat confusing Gleneagles agreement'. Caution continued thereafter to characterise the ACB's approach to the South African question, whereas the NZCC became a major advocate of SACU. Hadlee, a Christchurch accountant, said he was so impressed that the NZCC would review its ban on ties with South Africa, and recommended that SACU invite the ICC to send a delegation to South Africa with a view to providing 'an independent fully representative report of an international body' that could be held up to governments.[10]

South Africa was not on the formal agenda of the annual meeting of the ICC at Lord's on 25–26 July 1978, which took place in the midst of Kerry Packer's World Series challenge to established international cricket, but was raised under 'other business' by David Clark, the MCC president who served simultaneously as ICC chairman. In the first of a prolonged series of annual pilgrimages to London for the ICC meetings, Varachia, Wallace and Pamensky were present in London at the time to lobby ICC members. Also present was Sam Ramsamy, the executive chairman of SANROC and spokesman abroad for SACOS, to ensure that the ICC was not 'fooled' into believing that cricket in South Africa was now fully non-racial. To buttress Ramsamy's brief, the SACOS president, Hassan Howa, sent to the ICC an emotive memorandum denouncing SACU as 'one of the most fraudulent schemes relating to sports ever perpetrated upon the people of South Africa'.[11]

In raising the question of South Africa, Clark made it clear that there were no immediate prospects of establishing cricketing links between member countries and South Africa or of South Africa joining the ICC. However, SACU had done so much that 'some form of encouragement was required if there was not to be a danger of South African Cricket reacting against ICC and ICC cricket'. The suggestion was that an ICC delegation be sent to South Africa to examine first-hand the progress there towards 'multi-racial' cricket. Thirteen countries indicated their support for a purely 'fact-finding' delegation and seven their opposition, with the six full member countries dividing along traditional racial lines. The West Indies, Pakistan, India, Sri Lanka, Bangladesh, Malaysia and East Africa all disassociated themselves publicly from the delegation.[12] From their standpoint, the continuation of apartheid made any investigation a futile exercise.

In August, SACU duly invited the ICC to send a 'fact-finding' delegation to South Africa, with SACU meeting the delegation's expenses within the country. Acting on the assumption that those countries that had publicly disassociated themselves from the delegation would not be in a position to accept the invitation, Jack Bailey, now MCC and ICC secretary, sent invitations only to those countries that had signalled themselves in favour. The Indian delegate, M.A. Chidambaram, later advised that his Board would have welcomed an invitation and he believed the Indian Government would have allowed Indian representation as part of an ICC delegation.[13]

The nine-man delegation that visited South Africa in the first two weeks of March 1979, towards the end of the third season of 'normal' cricket, was drawn from five countries, included a black member in A. Hunt of Bermuda, and was led by Palmer in his capacity as ICC chairman. Five of its members met Hassan Howa after he had had initially declined to see them. The delegation's report, written by Jack Bailey, was generally favourable. It found that cricket was played multi-racially at provincial and club level; that teams were selected on merit; that an increase in the quantity and quality of black players was likely, that SACU fulfilled the role of a truly representative body and that as far as the ICC was concerned it should be recognised as the governing body for cricket in South Africa. The sting came in the report's recommendations. Political considerations, and the prospect of a split in the ranks of the ICC, dictated that the delegation recommend against SACU's membership of the ICC and South Africa's return to Test cricket. Its one positive recommendation was that a strong team, representative of as many ICC countries as possible, be sent to play a series of matches in South Africa as a means of encouraging 'normal' cricket there.[14]

The delegation's report was on the agenda of the ICC's annual meeting in June 1979, which was chaired by Palmer, but, at the insistence of 'certain member countries', it was only received and not discussed. The Pakistan delegate, Lieutenant General Azhar Khan, contended that the report was not an official ICC report as the visit to South Africa had never been formally approved by the ICC.[15] In response to persistent pressure from SACU – in November 1979 Varachia visited Lord's to underline 'that he hoped and expected UK to take the lead in helping SACU' – the Cricket Council, supported by the NZCC, ensured that 'South Africa's position in the cricket world' appeared as item 5 on the agenda for the next ICC meeting on 14–15 August 1980.[16] The two bodies were not, however, prepared to propose and second SACU for ICC membership.

In its drive to get back into the world fold SACU contended that it was somehow 'morally' entitled to ICC membership and a return to international cricket. As the ICC delegation report manifested, it had 'more than met' the requirements previously laid down by the Cricket Council and the ICC. In an emotive letter to the chairman of the Cricket Council, drafted in September 1979 and sent on 13 March 1980, Varachia urged the body to ensure that 'we are appropriately proposed and seconded for membership of the ICC', and further that, as an independent organisation, the Council should 'resume cricketing relations with my country immediately now that we have acceded to the requirements set out by your Council both in 1970 and 1975'. He added: 'This is a serious moral commitment which I feel certain you will be inclined to meet.' The same SACU Board meeting of 15 September 1979 that authorised this letter also resolved that a 'frank' letter, drafted by David Lewis and signed by Varachia, be sent to the ICC president, with 23 copies for distribution to the members and associate members of the Conference. The letter, which contained a vehement, if indirect, attack on the ICC for its implied double standards, moral cowardice and readiness to 'place politics above sport', went through several drafts thereafter, going off in its final form on 4 March 1980. No doubt it reflected accurately the sense of outrage felt in SACU about the way the boundary rope had shifted, and sought to put moral pressure on the white countries not to allow sport to be used as a political weapon against South Africa: 'If it becomes necessary for the cricketing world to divide itself into those who disavow and resist politics in sport and those who do not feel or feel disinclined so to do, then that is the consequence that men of principle and standing should be prepared to take.'

Billy Griffith, then ICC chairman, advised that the letter not be distributed. In his view the letter was 'not entirely truthful' and its 'unfortunate tone' would likely prove 'disastrous for the SACU'. The original was later reclaimed from Lord's on the assurance that the copies would be destroyed. Although formally withdrawn, the letter, in the opinion of Mark Henning of the SACU Board, had 'served a purpose in gingering up the Englishmen'.[17]

The letter made four demands of the ICC: that SACU representatives be permitted to appear before its August 1980 meeting 'in fulfilment of the principle of natural justice'; that it arrange for SACU to be 'proposed, seconded, recognised and admitted to full membership' at that meeting; that it allow with immediate effect for 'their cricketers to participate as individuals in a series of matches in South Africa at the highest representative level in consistency with the recommendations of its Delegation'; and, in respect of the Gleneagles Agreement, that all other countries be investigated for evidence of discrimination, with the assurance that those guilty would be 'dealt with in no way different from that meted out to the SACU'. Implicit in what was not demanded was the recognition by SACU that a return to Test cricket was not an immediate prospect.

Instead of the SACU letter, what went out to ICC member countries was a letter from the Cricket Council, written on 16 April, exploring the possibility of sending some sort of non-representative touring team to South Africa. In December 1979 the Council had sounded out the attitude of the new Conservative Government of Margaret Thatcher to sporting contacts with South Africa and was told very firmly that the government would do its best to discourage such contacts. Hector Munro, the Minister of Sport, told Palmer he 'apologised for the gloomy attitude, but the Prime Minister and the Foreign Secretary had clearly re-affirmed the Gleneagles Agreement'.[18] For the Cricket Council, that in itself ruled out any representative tours to South Africa, and it also appreciated that the ICC delegation's suggestion of a powerful touring team drawn from a range of ICC countries would probably be rejected by most countries. However, the Cricket Council, with its continuing sense of loyalty to South Africa's beleaguered cricket administrators, and also fearing that SACU might resort to 'unofficial' tours, was determined that 'some encouragement' had to be extended to SACU and 'South African cricketers of all races'. Hence the Council proposed that the ICC should raise no objection to any member country or countries sending a team of 'first class calibre' to South Africa, provided, among other things, that such teams did not play a 'representative' South African XI.

Wallace and Pamensky, despatched to England in late April 1980 to ascertain what was afoot in preparation for the next ICC meeting, were denied sight of the letter, but were given the gist of it by Palmer during a meeting in Leicester. Firstly, the letter advised that the United Kingdom and New Zealand requested the ICC to consider South Africa's position in the cricket world, taking into account the report of the 1979 delegation, and, more recently, the report of the British Sports Council delegation, headed by the former rugby international, Dickie Jeeps, which commented positively on the 'fundamental' changes made in South African cricket. Secondly, it requested ICC sanction for non-representative tours. The response of Wallace and Pamensky, who believed the Cricket Council to be 'pussy-footing', was that the letter 'really indicates nothing we presently do not enjoy', but they hoped it would occasion 'a full and comprehensive discussion on South Africa' at the next ICC meeting.[19]

To Palmer's chagrin, the letter of 16 April was only sent out by the ICC secretariat on 12 May, and then as a circular appendix, robbing it of much of its intended impact. He complained to Jack Bailey that he was 'disappointed, frustrated and annoyed' at what he could 'only interpret as cavalier disregard of our point of view'. Palmer's letter to Boon Wallace on 24 June caused its own disappointment. To obviate any misunderstanding, he made it clear that the United Kingdom would not press for the immediate reinstatement of South Africa to the ICC at the next ICC meeting or request South Africa's presence at the meeting. As he stressed, 'We have got to try to move forward without prejudicing good relations between ICC members.'[20]

On the eve of the August meeting of the ICC, the SACU delegation of Varachia, Wallace and Pamensky held discussions with representatives of all six full member countries. Both Walter Hadlee and R.A. Vance of New Zealand, and Bob Parish and Alan Barnes of Australia, made it clear that the support their respective governments gave to the Gleneagles Agreement ruled out any possibility of playing Test matches with South Africa, but they did not see why South Africa could not become a non-Test playing member of the ICC. The Cricket Council representatives, led by Palmer, intimated that their 'prime objective was to get member countries to talk about South Africa' and that while they would encourage and support South Africa's presence at the meeting, they would not actually propose it. For their part, the Indian and West Indies representatives indicated they would oppose South Africa's membership of the ICC, but Air Marshall Nur Khan, the new president of Pakistan cricket, intimated that he in no way wished to prevent the presence of the South African delegation when the South African issue came up for discussion.[21]

In the event, it was at the Air Marshall's suggestion that the ICC's meeting was adjourned to allow for 'an informal meeting between ICC representatives and representatives of SACU'. The opportunity given to Varachia to present SACU's case represented the high point for the South African delegation, as the ICC's deliberations thereafter generally went against them. No vote was taken, but Palmer indicated that he had received the meeting's clearly negative answer to his proposal that South Africa be given 'some encouragement' by way of non-representative tours. The delegates from the West Indies, Pakistan, India and East Africa made it clear that players who went to South Africa would not thereafter be allowed into their countries. Vance and Hadlee both urged strongly that South Africa be admitted as a member of the ICC, even if there was no question of playing cricket against the country. The New Zealanders contended that SACU deserved support for its achievements and that the ICC might assist in 'the break-down of apartheid' by granting membership.

The voting that followed was surrounded by controversy, with Mihr Bose later claiming in the London *Sunday Times* that the West Indies delegates voted in support of South Africa's re-admission. According to the clarification issued by the West Indies Cricket Board of Control (WICBC), a motion was proposed by New Zealand and seconded by the United Kingdom inviting SACU 'to make a written submission in support of their re-admission to ICC and that consideration should be given to the re-admission to the Conference in 1981'. At the behest, however, of the West Indies delegates the motion was divided in two. The first part, in favour of a written submission, was carried by 15 votes to 5, with India and Pakistan voting against but the West Indies supporting it. The second was defeated by the narrow margin of 11 to 10, with the West Indies voting against. According to a statement from the WICBC, 'It was our representatives' considered view that had the resolutions been taken together they would both have been passed with the probability of South Africa being re-elected to the Conference in 1981.' The WICBC added that 'voting for the SACU to make a written submission in support of their re-admission to ICC is a completely different matter to voting in favour of their re-admission'.[22] According to Bose in his *Sunday Times* revelations, South Africa lost the second vote because delegates from some 'obscure cricket playing nations' were absent, one of them attending a funeral.[23] The vote meant that South Africa's admission would not be on the agenda for the next ICC annual meeting.

That meeting, in July 1981, was effectively the funeral of SACU's ambitions of gaining ICC membership. As was rapidly made evident, the battle lines against South Africa had hardened considerably as a result of flanking advances by the sports boycott. In February 1981 the threat made at the previous ICC meeting was carried into effect when Guyana banned Robin Jackman, who had been flown in as a replacement by the England team touring the West Indies, because of his South African connections, thereby forcing the cancellation of the Georgetown Test. While the rest of the tour proceeded, Guyana's move prompted the United Nations Committee Against Apartheid Sport to introduce its 'blacklist' of sports people who visited South Africa.

Initially there were some promising portents for SACU at the 1981 ICC meeting with SACU believing that it could exploit the prospect of a white/black split in the ICC over the rights of individuals to play in South Africa that had been raised by the Jackman affair and the UN 'blacklist'. As Wallace underlined in notes for his colleagues, if South Africa remained excluded from the ICC it would mount a 'pirate operation' to bring an international team to the country, and that might rapidly lead to the disruption of world cricket, for which 'the ICC will have only themselves to blame'. 'To put it bluntly,' he advised, 'the ICC are going to find themselves destroyed by politics unless they take a strong stand NOW while they are on reasonably strong ground.'[24] The 'real danger' of South Africa embarking on a 'highly commercialised' international operation was one that particularly troubled the Cricket Council, given that England's players were likely to be targeted first. This concern helped to ensure that the Council again took the lead in assisting SACU's cause at the July meeting. Although it saw no immediate prospect of South Africa gaining membership of the ICC, it decided to propose, with New Zealand seconding, that SACU be officially recognised as the governing body for cricket in South Africa. The Council, furthermore, sent all member countries a memorandum which operated from the premise that from both a cricketing and a moral standpoint SACU deserved encouragement for fostering 'multi-racial' cricket, and proposed ways and means of assisting such cricket in South Africa, including approaches by ICC members to their governments to allow visits to and from South Africa by 'genuinely multi-racial teams'. On the eve of the ICC meeting, the Cricket Council formalised its own policy as one that 'would be to help and support multi-racial cricket throughout the world, including South Africa, but not to the detriment of International Cricket as a whole'.[25]

There were other positives for SACU at the meeting. Peter May, a known friend of the South African cricket establishment, was in the chair as MCC president; SACU had sent in its 'written submissions'; and its delegation, again headed by Varachia, was allowed another hearing on the grounds that it had new information in the form of a letter from the Prime Minister, P.W. Botha. The letter, addressed to Wallace as vice-president, promised that various discriminatory laws would be amended so that 'multi-racial cricket could be played generally and as of right'.

Despite these promising indications, the decisions reached were a disaster for SACU. The threatened racial split over the rights of individuals to play in South Africa did not materialise, with the meeting resolving that there would be no interference with team selections by member countries. Furthermore, another smouldering racial division was finally resolved with the award of full ICC membership and Test status to Sri Lanka. The country had been campaigning for

Test status for years, and at the 1980 ICC meeting the six full-member countries had divided 3-3 along racial lines, prompting Nur Khan to comment that this sort of racial division did not happen in other international sports. Walter Hadlee's hope of coupling full membership for both South Africa and Sri Lanka in a single motion was never feasible, and Sri Lanka's promotion was unanimously approved. The black full member countries of the ICC now outnumbered the white 4 to 3.

South Africa was next on the agenda, and SACU and its friends were generally given a pummelling. The resolution that SACU be recognised as the governing body for cricket in South Africa was defeated by 12 votes to 6, with Australia abstaining. Two written submissions, SACU's for membership and a South African Cricket Board (SACB) memorandum putting the case against SACU's admission, were considered. According to Palmer, in his report back to the Cricket Council, the latter 'received very little discussion, being seen merely as a weapon to discredit the SACU'. Palmer strongly urged the case for SACU's recognition as it was seeking to promote 'as much multi-racial cricket as possible', whilst the SACB 'specifically regarded cricket and other sports as a political tool'. In the end, Palmer conceded to his Council, the attempt to get SACU officially recognised 'backfired', and it was only with difficulty that the status quo was retained, with the ICC and member countries permitted to continue to communicate with SACU or any other body in South Africa.

The Cricket Council's own submission on 'ways and means of encouraging multi-racial cricket in South Africa' received, according to Palmer, no detailed consideration 'owing to the usual emotive and political arguments'. The best that SACU and it supporters got out of the meeting was a resolution that 'every encouragement should be given to the continued development of multi-racial cricket in South Africa', with members agreeing to discuss this matter with their governments.[26] The vague encouragement held out to SACU was that the Commonwealth prime ministers might reconsider the Gleneagles Agreement at their biannual meeting later in the year.

As a disheartened Varachia complained in his presidential address at the annual SACU meeting in Johannesburg on 19 September 1981, South Africa had been let down by its friends: 'Some who are our strongest allies are regretfully our weakest friends when it comes to decision making.' A frail man for some time, he died in December, his burning ambition of returning the Springboks to Test cricket having predeceased him.

CONCLUSION

By the end of the 1970s the Nationalist Government had become desperate to counter the sports boycott. In 1977 Koornhof even sought to engineer a meeting with Peter Hain to negotiate terms for South Africa's return to international sport. As Koornhof told a SACU delegation in December 1977, he saw himself as driving the movement towards 'normalising' sport, in so doing admitting 'that South Africa had learnt a lesson from allowing politics to interfere with sport'.[27] On another occasion Koornhof conceded to Joe Pamensky that the Vorster Government had made a 'grave mistake' when it had refused to allow D'Oliveira to tour with the MCC.

The efforts of the Nationalist Government in the late 1970s to distance itself from the 'errors' of the past, and enable sports bodies to break free of the isolation to which the government's previous sports policy had consigned them, were by no means entirely futile. In 1980 the Jeeps commission, which included Basil D'Oliveira as a member, praised the progress towards sports integration in South Africa and suggested lifting the sports boycott in those sports, like cricket, that had done everything they could to integrate. In rugby, the new 'multi-racial' South African Rugby Board (SARB), formed out of the old in 1977, moved aggressively to break the boycott, organising eight tours of various sorts between 1979 and 1981. In June 1980, in defiance of the Gleneagles Agreement, the British Lions toured South Africa, with the Thatcher Government declining to interfere with the freedom of the rugby union to make its own decisions. In the next year, in an effort to demonstrate that South African national teams could again tour abroad, the Springboks ventured to New Zealand, where the National Government of Robert Muldoon likewise refused to 'order the Rugby Union to abandon the tour'. With Halt all Racist Tours (HART) mounting a sustained campaign of civil disobedience, the tour tore New Zealand society apart, and in the process put into reverse South Africa's return to major international rugby. 'In 1981 we did not stop a tour,' HART's Trevor Richards recalled, 'we stopped all future tours.'[28] There was also a spill over into cricket, with the West Indies cancelling the tour by New Zealand scheduled for the following year.

Structurally, South African cricket was in a much weaker position than rugby to challenge its isolation from official international competition. The SARB was a member of the International Rugby Board, while SACU was outside the ICC. Furthermore, Varachia complained, SACU's friends on the ICC were 'weak'. All things being equal, administrators in the white cricket-playing countries would probably have welcomed South Africa's return to Test cricket, but all things were not equal. SACU's 'friends' were politically too constrained to secure South Africa's readmission. Evidently more deferential than their rugby counterparts to their own governments over the Gleneagles Agreement, the Cricket Council, the ACB and the NZCC were even more fundamentally constrained by the determined opposition of the governments and cricket boards of the major black cricket-playing countries to apartheid South Africa's return. Although the Cricket Council strongly objected to 'the growing tendency to use sport as a political weapon', outright opposition to its use, along the lines suggested by SACU, would have split world cricket. The considered policy of the Cricket Council was that it would do all it could to 'help the development of multi-racial cricket in South Africa, subject only to the constraint of the overall wish not to polarise international cricket on racial lines'. That approach, grumbled Richie Benaud, a former Australian captain, meant that the ICC members 'allowed the politicians of their countries to make the decisions for the future'.[29] But it was not only a matter of politics, it was also difficult for SACU's 'friends' to contemplate the hazards of a South African visit – underscored by the fate of the Springbok rugby tour of New Zealand – as against the profits of a West Indies tour.

With the ICC meeting of July 1981 again not finally closing the door but leaving little doubt that there was no prospect of South Africa's return to official international cricket under existing political circumstances, SACU turned to its alternative strategy to counter South Africa's cricketing isolation. On 12 March 1982, after an absence of twelve years, the Springboks went out to bat at the Wanderers in the first 'Test' against the South African Breweries English XI, with Jimmy Cook scoring his first 'Test' century. SACU, in its counterpart to SARB's offensive, had embarked on the era of 'unofficial' or 'rebel' tours.

SACU's justification for the 'rebel' tours was that they were necessary to maintain playing standards and public interest in cricket in South Africa, but they also represented a political ploy. By threatening, like the Packer World Series, to destabilise the world of Test cricket, SACU hoped the 'rebel' tours might force the ICC to reconsider its position. Instead, the 'cricket piracy' hardened attitudes. The requests made by SACU to be heard at the ICC meetings of July 1982 and July 1983 to report progress towards 'multi-racial' cricket, and to learn what else it had to do to obtain recognition, were both rejected. At the time of the first meeting the new SACU trio of Pamensky as president, Geoff Dakin as vice-president, and Ali Bacher dined with Cricket Council officials, and were bluntly told by Doug Insole: 'Until apartheid goes, you can forget about getting back into world cricket. England cannot support you. If we did, it would be the end of English cricket. The black nations would not play against us.'[30] Prior to the next meeting the SACU delegation again met with members of the Cricket Council to be informed, in an exchange that 'became a little heated at times', that the rebel tours had 'done us no good in that we have now alienated any vestige of friendship we had in World Cricket'. 'We knew this before we went to the meeting,' Dakin reported back, 'but we also felt that the hurt we had caused may have put us closer to acceptance because of their fear we could do much more damage.' They received instead an uncompromising message from ICC chairman Sir Anthony Tuke, who finally conveyed the ICC's position that there was no way back for South Africa until apartheid was abolished in its entirety, and not simply in sport.[31]

Epilogue

S OUTH AFRICA, in the form of the United Cricket Board of South Africa (UCBSA), was finally admitted to the International Cricket Conference (ICC) on 10 July 1991, thirty years after the South African Cricket Association had lost its membership of the old Imperial Cricket Conference. In November that year South Africa undertook its first ever tour of India – the brief 'Goodwill Tour' for three one day internationals – 21 years after its last official international game, and some sixty years after it had declined the opportunity to become the first Test team to tour India.

When the South Africans landed at Calcutta's Dum Dum airport, players, officials and supporters were garlanded, and vast crowds lined the pavements to greet the cavalcade that took them to their city hotel. In February and March 1992 South Africa participated in its first World Cup, held in Australia and New Zealand, reaching the semi-finals. This was followed in April by its first tour of the West Indies, its first Test since 1970 and its first Test ever against the West Indies at Bridgetown, Barbados, which it lost. At the end of the year India made its first tour of South Africa for the 'Friendship Series', and South Africa engaged in its first homes series since 1969/70, winning it 1-0. In the first Test, in Durban, the left-arm spinner, Omar Henry, became the first player of colour to represent South Africa in a Test since C.B. Llewellyn, another left-arm spinner, some eighty years previously. At forty Henry was the oldest South African player to make his Test debut, surpassing Geoff Chubb by several months.

Finally South Africa had returned to official international cricket, competing for the first time in the full Test arena, but not as the Springboks. In the negotiations leading to the formation of the UCBSA, SACU had reluctantly agreed to abandon the Springbok name and emblem, which Vorster had once insisted belonged only to whites. SACU officials held that black players would be 'thrilled' to wear the Springbok badge, but South African Cricket Board (SACB) officials rejected it outright as a symbol of white dominance. In 1992 the UCB adopted the King Protea as the emblem for its international teams, known henceforth as the Proteas.

The last Springboks in cricket had been those who represented South Africa in the 'Tests' against the 'rebel' teams that toured the country between 1981/82 and 1989/90.[1] In all, SACU mounted seven 'unofficial' or 'rebel' tours. The first, in early 1982, was by Graham Gooch's South African Breweries English XI, which included almost half the England team that had been touring India. The tour of India had only been rescued when Geoffrey Boycott and Geoff Cook, who had both played in South Africa, signed declarations confirming their opposition to apartheid, but Boycott promptly spent much of the tour recruiting his team-mates to go to South Africa. The English visit was followed in 1982/83 by the first black teams to tour South Africa, the rather weak Arosa Sri Lanka team, and Lawrence Rowe's powerful West Indies team, which toured again in 1983/84. In the second tour, the West Indies XI became the only rebel team to beat the Springboks in a series, winning both the 'Test' and one-day series. Kim Hughes led strong Australian combinations to South Africa in 1985/86 and 1986/87. In the third 'Test' of the second tour, in Durban in January 1987, Omar Henry joined Llewellyn as the only cricketers of colour to play as Springboks. The last of the rebel tours was that of Mike Gatting's English players in 1989/90, which was curtailed in the face of massive protest action. It also marked the end of the Springbok era in cricket.

One of the great ironies of the rebel tours was that the Nationalist Government, which had quite consciously helped to steer South African cricket into isolation through its rigid enforcement of sports apartheid, now took responsibility for subsidising tours by visiting black teams. The vast sums required to induce top players to rebel against their governments and boards, and jeopardise their careers were made possible by two things. One was the rapid commercialisation of sport in South Africa in the 1980s, and the eagerness of commercial sponsors to promote overseas sporting contacts. The other was the subsidy offered by the government in the form of tax rebates to sponsors and tax waivers to the rebel players. As Peter Cooke, the organiser of the first rebel tour, admitted: 'In actual fact the Government was actually financing it, if truth be known, through colossal tax breaks.'[2] An ingenious scheme ensured that the rebel players themselves were effectively exempted from tax in South Africa without incurring a liability in their home countries. Rebel tours were actively encouraged by the government as a mechanism for portraying internationally 'the new face of apartheid'. On one occasion, after an approach by Joe Pamensky and Geoff Dakin, the Minister of Foreign Affairs, R.F. 'Pik' Botha, offered to help SACU finance the West Indies tour with R4 million 'out of the foreign affairs budget'.[3] What the arrangements for financing the rebels underlined was that SACU, like its predecessor, the South African Cricket Association, basically worked with, rather than distancing itself from, the apartheid state.

The punishment meted out to rebel cricketers by their respective national boards varied considerably. The 'dirty dozen', as Graham Gooch's men were nicknamed by the press, were banned from Test cricket for three years; the Sri Lankans were suspended from any cricket in their own country for 25 years, and the West Indians for life, though several continued their careers thereafter in South Africa and England. The Australians were banned from domestic cricket for two years, and from Test cricket for three. In England and Australia, once the bans had been served rebels were quickly re-assimilated into the international arena. Gooch resumed his Test career in 1985 against Australia, and in 1988 was selected as captain of the England team to tour India, with John Emburey, another rebel, as vice-captain.

Rebel tours, together with the United Nations 'blacklist', helped ensure that the issue of South Africa continued to haunt the ICC, ultimately raising again the spectre of a fundamental split between black and white cricket countries. The problem for international cricket was the selection for tours to black countries of rebels who had served their bans or been 'blacklisted' by the United Nations for playing and coaching in South Africa. In 1986 Bangladesh and Zimbabwe cancelled tours by the England B cricket team as it included 'blacklisted' players who refused to sign declarations stating they would not continue their sporting contacts with South Africa. In 1988 the England tour of India was called off when the Indian Government objected to the inclusion in the touring team of eight players who had played and coached in South Africa. The threat of a black-white split in international cricket over the issue seemed to be becoming a reality.

Already in 1987, ahead of the Cricket World Cup due to be played in India and Pakistan, the Indian Government had threatened that it would enforce the United Nations 'blacklist' even if this resulted in the cancellation of the tournament. That threat was warded off by a promise from the ICC that it would take formal action on the matter of cricketers who played and coached in South Africa. In June 1987 a special ICC meeting was held to discuss the matter, with the West Indies proposing a ban from international cricket on all players who in future had 'sporting contact with South Africa'. As about twenty per cent of English county cricketers played or coached in South Africa during the English off-season, the Test and County Cricket Board (TCCB) not surprisingly voted unanimously not to support the West Indies resolution. In an effort to avert an immediate split, and rescue the World Cup, a select committee was set up under ICC chairman Colin Cowdrey to consider the matter further and report in time for the 1988 annual meeting. The decision was postponed until a special meeting of the ICC in January 1989, but in the interim the TCCB selectors chose eight 'blacklisted' players for the 1988 England tour of India. The chairman of selectors, the very same Peter May who had been part of the MCC selection committee that had initially omitted D'Oliveira from the team to tour South Africa in 1968/69, declared, 'We don't pick teams for political reasons.' The Indian Government, sensing deliberate provocation, particularly with the appointment of Gooch as captain, denied the blacklisted players visas, and the tour was cancelled.[4]

In an attempt to avert the 'ghastly break-up' of world cricket that was threatening, Raman Subba Row, the TCCB chairman, travelled in November to Jamaica to thrash out with Allan Rae, his West Indies counterpart, a formula to cover English players who went to South Africa. The compromise formula, adopted by the ICC at its special meeting in January 1989 and based on the Row/Rae draft, set up a penalty system. In future cricketers who played or coached in South Africa as individuals would automatically be banned from Test cricket for four years, and those who participated in organised tours for five years. Rae initially wanted to make the penalties retrospective, but Subba Row held that that was legally impossible.[5]

It was under the ICC's new penalty system that English players were recruited for the last rebel tour of South Africa, the ill-fated tour led by Mike Gatting, the former England captain. The tour was arranged in the context of a rapidly changing political situation in South Africa, and the emergence of a new national non-racial sports organisation, the National Sports Congress (NSC), formally launched at a meeting at the University of the Witwatersrand, Johannesburg, in July 1989 as 'an integral participant in the struggle to abolish apartheid'.

In August 1989 President Botha resigned, after a decade at the helm in which he had sought to ensure the preservation of apartheid in part by reforming and reformulating it, notably by incorporating coloureds and Indians in Parliament by way of the 'tricameral' Constitution of 1983 and by making a conscious effort to improve social conditions for urban Africans. By underlining the exclusion of Africans from central government the tricameral constitution served as the trigger for the creation of new extra-parliamentary opposition groups, most prominently the United Democratic Front (UDF), and a new wave of popular unrest. In 1989 the UDF and the powerful black trade union organisation, the Congress of South African Trade Unions (COSATU), came together to form the Mass Democratic Movement (MDM), organising a countrywide 'defiance campaign' to challenge apartheid institutions. By the end of Botha's tenure a stalemate had been reached in which, in Philip Frankel's assessment, 'the inability of dissidents to overthrow the hegemony of the state is countered by the incapability of the state to eliminate dissidence completely'.[6]

On 2 February 1990 Botha's successor, F.W. de Klerk, moved to break the stalemate by announcing in Parliament the unbanning of the ANC, the Pan Africanist Congress and the South African Communist Party, the impending release of Nelson Mandela and other political prisoners, and his readiness to begin all-party negotiations for a new constitution. After 27 years in prison Mandela walked free on 11 February. Three days later Dr Ali Bacher, managing director of SACU since 1986, announced the decision to curtail the Gatting tour to show 'support for the dramatic political changes' announced by De Klerk.

By then the tour had proved the most contentious and violent sporting tour in South African history. South African tours had previously generated militant mass protest action abroad; now for the first time a tour of South Africa elicited mass protest at home. From the moment the tourists landed in Johannesburg on 19 January they were beset by demonstrations mobilised by the NSC with a view to halting the tour's progress. By the time Mandela was due to be released the NSC had effectively succeeded in rendering the tour unworkable, as Bacher realised. He was given a way out when the ANC's Thabo Mbeki intervened to promote a meeting between Bacher and Krish Naidoo, the general secretary of the NSC, as the ANC was anxious to ensure that Mandela was not 'released into a climate of violence'. In the compromise negotiated between the two it was agreed to reduce the remainder of the tour to four limited-over games that would be free of demonstrations organised by the NSC, and to cancel the projected second leg of the tour.[7]

The Gatting fiasco was of prime significance for South African cricket. In much the way that the D'Oliveira Affair of 1968 had served as the catalyst for the process that resulted in South Africa's expulsion from Test match cricket, so the Gatting tour provided the catalyst for the process that resulted in unification and South Africa's return to Test cricket. For one thing, the tour catapulted the NSC into the forefront of the anti-apartheid sports movement at a critical moment. Politically aligned to the MDM, with strong roots in the townships, the NSC pro-actively sought to negotiate with white sports bodies for the formation of new unified, non-racial and democratic sports structures so as to prepare sport for a post-apartheid South Africa. The NSC simply outstripped the South African Council on Sport (SACOS), which was essentially Indian and coloured in its leadership and support and which remained attached to the politics of non-collaboration despite the rapid changes in the political environment. As Neville Alexander perceived, non-collaboration became sterile and ritualistic, and ultimately antagonistic to other anti-apartheid campaigns.[8] The NSC saw stopping the Gatting tour as a mechanism for forcing white cricket to the negotiating table, and so it proved to be. As Mike Brearley, a former England captain, commented in the *Observer*: 'The debacle was a watershed. The futility of cricket in such a setting proved to be Bacher's Road to Damascus. The white cricketing authorities determined on a radically different strategy; virtue was born of pain, if not necessity.' In April, Bacher, appointed by SACU as a one-man commission to investigate all aspects of cricket, formally announced an end to rebel tours, and wrote to the South African Cricket Board (SACB) suggesting talks between the two bodies.

Facilitated by the NSC and the ANC, negotiations for unity in cricket were initiated on 8 September 1990 when representatives of SACU, led by Geoff Dakin as president, and the SACB, led by its president, Krish Mackerdhuj, met in Durban, with the ANC's Steve Tshwete, 'Mr Fixit', serving as chairman. In 1984 Mackerdhuj had successfully challenged Hassan Howa for the presidency, and it was under his leadership that the SACB abandoned SACOS for the NSC and negotiations. Unity, and South Africa's admission to the ICC, were thereafter negotiated with remarkable speed, previous constraints and reservations simply being swept aside. At a final meeting of the two executives in Johannesburg on 20 April 1991 it was agreed to form one united non-racial body, the United Cricket Board of South Africa, to control all cricket in South Africa. On 29 June, after a gala banquet at the Sandton Sun hotel, the UCBSA was launched, and on 10 July it was admitted to the ICC. South Africa was now a fully-fledged participant in world cricket.

In the case of cricket, as in that of other sports, the ANC actively promoted South Africa's rapid incorporation in the international fold. As Douglas Booth has put it, in negotiating for a new South Africa the ANC effectively discarded sport as a bargaining chip, and instead 'identified international competition as a way to reassure whites about their future lifestyles under a black government'. The long-standing notion that there could be no return for South Africa to official international sport until apartheid was entirely abolished was set aside. As Mluleki George, the NSC president, expressed the new approach, 'We never demanded the eradication of apartheid as a precondition . . . When we perceive change towards a non-racial society in this country to be irreversible, we will gladly . . . reintroduce international contact.'[9] The government's repeal in June 1991 of the legislative pillars of apartheid, including the Group Areas Act and the Reservation of Separate Amenities Act, evidently allowed that perception.

During the negotiations for cricket unity it was initially agreed that there would be a moratorium on tours to and from South Africa, but this did not stop Mackerdhuj and Dakin from writing to the ICC on 24 December 1990 to report on the movement towards unity and to 'project our forward vision to the readmittance of our country to Test Match cricket'.[10] When Colin Cowdrey, the ICC chairman, phoned Bacher in March 1991 to advise that the best he could offer was that the ICC would meet the new unified board informally after its annual meeting in July, Bacher responded: 'No way. We are not coming for a cup of tea at Lord's. We are going for a full application.'[11] The problem was that South Africa was not on the ICC agenda, but at the urging of the ANC and John Major, the British Prime Minister, Cowdrey finally ruled that the annual meeting could accept a proposal for the country's admission. As the result of a major diplomatic offensive undertaken by both Bacher, the managing director of the new UCBSA, and Steve Tshwete on behalf of the ANC, the resolution for admission, proposed by India and seconded by Australia, was approved, with the West Indies abstaining. As Clyde Walcott explained, 'It is clear to us that the decision was taken from a political point of view as against any other reason.'[12]

Politics continued to govern the fortunes of South African cricket, but they were now the politics of inclusion rather than exclusion. Politically, the sports boycott had effectively run its course. Once described by Anthony Sampson as 'the most damaging blow against apartheid', the boycott had successfully challenged the legitimacy not simply of apartheid sports teams, but of apartheid itself, to the point where it had been able to establish as its goal the abolition not only of sports apartheid but of the overall apartheid system.[13] Of all forms of opposition to apartheid, the sports boycott was particularly sapping to white morale, and was the first to force major concessions out of the apartheid regime; in so doing it fatally compromised the very ideology of apartheid. Attempts to 'normalise' sport only served to underline the 'abnormality' of apartheid. 'Rhetorically and ideologically,' Grant Farred observed, 'the term *normal sport* incriminated the entire edifice of apartheid.'[14] As Adrian Guelke commented in 1986, the irony was that far from enhancing the legitimacy of the apartheid regime, reform served rather to deprive white power of its ideological justification and to stimulate challenge to white rule.[15]

But if the sports boycott succeeded in its wider political aim of undermining the apartheid regime, it was abandoned before it achieved its more specific goal of creating a truly 'non-racial' sporting environment in South Africa. In SACOS circles, certainly, the ANC was bitterly criticised for having prematurely jettisoned the sports boycott. The sense in SACOS was that in sports such as cricket and rugby the moratorium on international tours should have been maintained until the playing fields had been levelled for blacks and whites. As Ahmed Kharva, the former Natal Cricket Board president, complained in November 1991, 'It is disturbing that while the objectives of the sports moratorium to normalise South African society were far from achieved, there has been indecent haste to participate internationally.' These reservations were echoed by Hassan Howa, who said of the first South African cricket team to visit India: 'It represented only those who enjoyed the great benefits of racial discrimination. It was not a South African team but a White South African team.'[16]

At the heart of the sports boycott was the charge that Springbok teams were representative only of the white fraction of South African society. In the 'new' South Africa that emerged after the country's first democratic elections in April 1994 and the formation of the Mandela Government, the perpetuation of all-white teams representing South Africa at cricket and rugby, now on the basis of 'merit' selection, rapidly produced an untenable situation. In cricket, intense resentment among black players and administrators at their marginalisation in the board room as well as on the playing field, coupled with the government's drive to promote greater racial 'representivity' in the major institutions of society, including national sporting teams, forced a fundamental re-think about issues of transformation. The challenge, it was generally recognised by all sides, was to redress the imbalances of the past and to make teams, national and provincial, more representative of the population as a whole. The ways that challenge is being met, including a resort to racial quotas, continues to stir emotional and divisive debate, largely along racial lines, and to provide politicians with a ready agenda for intervention.

Notes

CHAPTER ONE

1. Kidson, Hayward. 1995. *The History of Transvaal Cricket*. Johannesburg, p. 3.
2. Basic sources on South African Test cricket history are: Brian Bassano. 1979. *South Africa in International Cricket, 1888–1970*. East London; and Jonty Winch. 1997. *Cricket in Southern Africa: Two Hundred Years of Achievement and Records*. Rosettenville.
3. Trevor Chesterfield and Jackie McGlew. 2003. *South Africa's Cricket Captains*. Cape Town, p. 6.
4. SACA minutes, 10 April 1903 and 4 January 1907.
5. Brian Crowley. 1994. 'A History of South African Cricket'. *Cricketer*, January.
6. *Wisden* 1910, p. 30 and 1913, p. 230. E.W. Swanton, G. Plumptre and J. Woodcock (eds). 1986. *Barclays World of Cricket: The Game from A to Z*. London, 3rd ed, p. 352; C. Merrett and J. Nauright. 1998. 'South Africa'. In B. Stoddart and K.A.P. Sandiford (eds), *The Imperial Game: Cricket Culture and Society*. Manchester, p. 64.
7. 'Sport as a Connecting Link'. 1894. *Cape Illustrated Magazine* 4(10), p. 370; Pelham Warner. 1906. *The MCC in South Africa*. London; Derek Birley. 1993. *Playing the Game: Sport and British Society, 1910–45*. Manchester, p. 25.
8. Jonty Winch. 2003. *England's Youngest Captain: The Life and Times of Monty Bowden and Two South African Journalists*. Windsor, pp. 63 and 79.
9. Historical Papers, University of the Witwatersrand, Johannesburg, A1586 (Reference kindly provided by Dr Simon Dagut).
10. Nigel Worden, Elizabeth van Heyningen and Vivian Bickford-Smith. 1998. *Cape Town: The Making of a City*. Cape Town, p. 241; S.E.L. West (comp) and W.J. Luker (ed). 1965. *Century at Newlands, 1864–1964: A History of the Western Province Cricket Club*. Cape Town, p. 21.
11. Information kindly provided by Jonty Winch.
12. André Odendaal. 1998. 'South Africa's Black Victorians: Sport and Society in South Africa in the Nineteenth Century'. In James A. Mangan (ed), *Pleasure, Profit, Proselytism: British Culture and Sport at Home and Abroad, 1700–1914*. London, p. 99; André Odendaal. 2003. *The Story of an African Game*. Cape Town, Part 1.
13. Odendaal, *African Game*, pp. 25–6.
14. Brian Willan. 1982. 'An African in Kimberley: Sol T. Plaatje, 1894–1898'. In Shula Marks and Richard Rathbone (eds). *Industrialisation and Social Change in South Africa: African Class Formation, Culture, and Consciousness, 1870–1930*. Harlow, p. 251.

15. Odendaal, *African Game*, pp. 51–2.
16. Ibid, pp. 79–80.
17. Abe Bailey. 1912. 'South Africa'. In Pelham Warner, *Imperial Cricket*. London, p. 315.
18. Birley, *Playing the Game*, p. 126; Eric Midwinter. 1986. *Fair Game: Myth and Reality in Sport*. London, p. 36.
19. J. Bradley. 1992. 'MCC, society and empire'. In James A. Mangan (ed), *The Cultural Bond: Sport, Empire and Society*. London, p. 2.
20. Vasili, P. 1998. *The First Black Footballer: Arthur Wharton 1865–1930: An Absence of Memory*. London, p. 78. This author's emphasis. Vasili writes about soccer but his insights are equally applicable to cricket.
21. W.R. Katz. 1984. *Rider Haggard and the Fiction of Empire: A Critical Study of British Imperial Fiction*. Manchester, p. 82; J.M. McKenzie. 1984. *Propaganda and Empire: The Manipulation of British Public Opinion*. Manchester, p. 258.
22. James A. Mangan. 1996. 'Muscular, Militaristic and Manly: The British Middle-Class Hero as Moral Messenger'. *International Journal of the History of Sport* 13(1), pp. 28–47; M.A. Tozer. 1992. 'A Sacred Trinity'. In Mangan (ed), *Cultural Bond*, p. 17.
23. P. Bailey. 1978. *Leisure and Class in Victorian England: Rational Recreation and the Context for Control, 1850–1885*. London, p. 127; Anthony Kirk-Greene. 1987. 'Imperial Administration and the Athletic Imperative: The Case of the District Officer in Africa'. In W.J. Baker and J.A. Mangan (eds), *Sport in Africa: Essays in Social History*. New York, p. 107.
24. J. Hargreaves. 1986. *Sport, Power and Culture: A Social and Historical Analysis of Popular Sports in Britain*. Cambridge, p. 34.
25. Eric Midwinter. *Fair Game*, p. 67.
26. David R. Black and John Nauright. 1998. *Rugby and the South African Nation: Sport, Culture and the New South Africa*. Manchester, p. 26.
27. Spufford, F. 1996. *I May Be Some Time: Ice and the English Imagination*. London, pp. 249–50; I. Baucom. 1999. *Out of Place: Englishness, Empire and the Location of Identity*. Princeton, NJ, pp. 17–18.
28. Marina Warner. 1993. 'Between the Colonist and the Creole: Family Bonds, Family Boundaries'. In S. Chew and A. Rutherford (eds). *Unbecoming Daughters of the Empire*. Sydney, p. 199.
29. Mihir Bose. 1990. *A History of Indian Cricket*. London, p. 19; Ramachandra Guha. 2002. *A Corner of a Foreign Field: The Indian History of a British Sport*. London, p. 50; James Morris. 1968. *Pax Britannica: The Climax of an Empire*. London, p. 146.
30. Brian Stoddart. 1988. 'Sport, cultural imperialism and the colonial response to the British Empire'. *Comparative Studies in Society and History* 30(4), p. 662; J. Morris. 1968. *Pax Britannica: The Climax of an Empire*. London, p. 132; D.A. Lorimer. 1978. *Colour, Class and the Victorians: English Attitudes to the Negro in the Mid-Nineteenth Century*. Leicester, p. 210; R.A. Huttenback. 1973. 'The British Empire as a White Man's Country'. *Journal of British Studies* 13(1), p. 109.
31. Odendaal. 'South Africa's Black Victorians', p. 204; R. Archer and A. Bouillon. 1982. *The South African Game: Sport and Racism*. London, pp. 28–9; Vivian Bickford-Smith. 1995. *Ethnic Pride and Racial Prejudice in Victorian Cape Town*. Johannesburg, p. 149.
32. Marsh was left out of the match between a New South Wales Country XI and the English tourists at Bathurst and subsequently out of the fourth Test of the 1901/02 series and

the tour to England. He was no-balled by one umpire in particular who may have been in collusion with M.A. Noble to stifle the development of Marsh's career. English batsmen who played him in 1903/04 argued that his action was legal and he was the best bowler in the world. His omission from the 1905 tour was widely seen as based on racism. See Colin Tatz. 1995. *Obstacle Race: Aborigines in Sport*. Sydney, pp. 72–5; Bernard Whimpress.1999. *Passport to Nowhere: Aborigines in Australian Cricket, 1850–1939*. Sydney, p. 171.

33. For Hendricks see Winch, *Cricket*, pp. 30–3 and *Youngest Captain*, pp. 259–68.
34. Ibid, p. 272.
35. *Star,* 10 February 1896; *Cape Times* (weekly edition), 26 February 1896.
36. Vivian Bickford-Smith, *Ethnic Pride*, pp. 149–50.
37. Winch, *Youngest Captain*, pp. 262 and 298.
38. J.M. Kilburn. 1975. *Overthrows: A Book of Cricket*. London, pp. 11 and 13; Brian Crowley. 1973. *Currie Cup Story*. Cape Town, p. 32.
39. Winch, *Cricket*, p. 41.
40. *Star*, 23 March 1899. Quoted in Jonty Winch. 2000. 'Playing the Games: The Unification of South African Sport'. Unpublished manuscript, chapter 3.
41. *South African Cricketers Annual* 1905–6, p. 89; *Wisden* 1909, p. 157.
42. SACA minutes, 19 August 1910.
43. A. Anderton. 1976. 'C.B. Llewellyn' [letter] *Cricketer* 57(3), March , p. 29.
44. Pelham F. Warner. 1951. *Long Innings: The Autobiography*. London, pp. 50–1; S.H.P. 'Charles Bennett Llewellyn'; *Wisden* 1911, p. 173; A.D. Nourse. 1927. 'A peep into the past'. In M.W. Luckin. *South African Cricket, 1919–1927*. Johannesburg, p. 48; H.S. Altham et al. 1957. *Hampshire County Cricket: The Official History*. London, p. 4; H.S. Altham 1962. *A History of Cricket*. London, vol. 1, p. 268; J. Arlott. 'C. B. Llewellyn'. In *Hampshire Handbook 1960*, p.35; Kilburn, *Overthrows*, p. 11. Christopher Merrett. 2002. 'Space and Race in Colonial Natal: C.B. Lewellyn, South Africa's First Black Test Cricketer', *Natalia* 32, pp. 19–35.
45. *Natal Almanac, Directory and Yearly Register*. 1896, p. 607.
46. *Cape Times*, 15 January 1972. Quoted in Winch, 'Playing the Games', chapter 3.
47. Crowley, *Currie Cup*, p. 33.
48. SACA minutes, 4 April 1903; *Rand Daily Mail*, 5 April 1903.
49. SACA minutes, 19 September 1910 and 5 March 1911.
50. Swanton, Plumptre and Woodcock (eds). *World of Cricket*, p. 118; Winch, *Cricket*, 66.
51. André Odendaal (ed). 1977. *Cricket in Isolation: The Politics of Race and Cricket in South Africa*. Cape Town, pp. 326–8; Brian Crowley. 1983. *Cricket's Exiles: The Saga of South African Cricket*. Cape Town, p. 113.
52. Odendaal, 'South Africa's Black Victorians', p. 211.
53. L.E. Neame. 1907. *The Asiatic Danger in the Colonies*. London, p. 29.
54. *Hiltonian* 9, 1906, p. 49.
55. B. Sacks. 1967. *South Africa: An Imperial Dilemma: Non-Europeans and the British Nation, 1902–1914*. Albuquerque, pp. 158 and 191.
56. Alan Cobley. 1997. *The Rules of the Game: Struggles in Black Recreation and Social Welfare Policy in South Africa*. Westport, p. 19; Archer and Bouillon, *The South African Game*, p. 86; R.H. McDonald. 1994. *The Language of Empire: Myths and Metaphors of*

Popular Imperialism, 1880–1918. Manchester, p. 22; M. Marqusee. 1994. *Anyone But England: Cricket and the National Malaise.* London, p. 185.

57. B. Wallach. 1928. 'The noble part played by cricket in our history'. *Outspan,* 24 February, p. 61.
58. Winch. *Cricket,* p. 44.
59. M.W. Luckin (ed). 1915. *The History of South African Cricket.* Johannesburg, pp. 803–6; Floris van der Merwe. 1992. 'Sport and Games in Boer Prisoner-of-War Camps during the Anglo-Boer War 1899–1902'. *The International Journal of the History of Sport* 9(3), pp. 439–54; Merrett and Nauright, 'South Africa', p. 59.
60. Warner, *MCC in South Africa,* pp. 219–20; Luckin, *South African Cricket,* foreword.

CHAPTER TWO

1. A.J. Christopher. 1976. *Southern Africa.* Folkestone, p. 190.
2. C.W. de Kiewiet. 1941. *A History of South Africa: Social and Economic.* London, p. 226; Saul Dubow. 1998. 'Placing Race in South African History'. In W. Lamont (ed). *Historical Controversies and Historians.* London, pp. 75 and 78.
3. André Odendaal. 1977. *Cricket in Isolation: The Politics of Race and Cricket in South Africa.* Cape Town, p. 23.
4. Ashwin Desai, Vishnu Padayachee, Krish Reddy and Goolam Vahed. 2002. *Blacks in Whites: A Century of Cricket Struggles in KwaZulu-Natal.* Pietermaritiburg, pp. 164–72.
5. M.W. Luckin. 1927. 'The Rise of South African Cricket'. In M.W. Luckin. *South African Cricket, 1919–1927: A Complete Record of all South African Cricket Since the War.* Johannesburg, p. 18.
6. M. Commaille. 1947. 'A Golden Opportunity for South African Cricketers'. *Outspan,* 1 August, p. 21.
7. W. Pollock. 1941. *Talking about Cricket.* London, p. 121.
8. Commaille. 1933. 'What is Wrong with South Africa's Cricket?'. *Outspan,* 24 November, p. 17.
9. Luckin, 'Rise of South African Cricket', p. 19.
10. A.C. Webber. 1927. 'The Control of Cricket in South Africa'. In Luckin, *South African Cricket, 1919–1927,* p. 21.
11. Alan Paton. 1964. *Hofmeyr.* London, p. 159.
12. Robert Blake.1977. *A History of Rhodesia.* London, p. 187.
13. Louis Duffus.1947. *South African Cricket 1927–1947.* Johannesburg, p. 343.
14. Commaille, 'Golden Opportunity', p. 21.
15. *South African Cricket Annual* 1 (1951/2), p. 208.
16. Gideon Haigh. 1997. *The Summer Game.* Melbourne, pp. 6–7.
17. Brian Bassano. 1979. *South Africa in International Cricket, 1888–1970.* East London, pp. 57–80.
18. Brian Crowley. 1973. *Currie Cup Story.* Cape Town, p. 76; Luckin, *South African Cricket, 1919–1927,* pp. 17–18; H.L. Crockett. 1927. 'Turf Wickets in South Africa'. In Ibid, p. 35; A.C. Webber, 'The Control of Cricket in South Africa'. In Ibid, pp. 23, 26 and 29.
19. Bassano, *South Africa,* pp. 81–110; Brian Crowley, *Currie Cup,* pp. 103 and 120; Duffus, *South African Cricket,* p. 11.

20. Duffus, *South African Cricket*, pp. 12, 338, 340, 343–4.
21. H.W. Taylor. 1927. 'How South African Cricket Should be Built Up'. In Luckin, *South African Cricket, 1919–1927*, p. 34.
22. S.E.L. West (comp.) and W.J. Luker (ed). 1965. *Century at Newlands, 1864–1964: A History of the Western Province Cricket Club*. Newlands, p. 114; C. Merrett and J. Nauright. 1998. 'South Africa'. In B. Stoddart and K.A.P. Sandiford (eds), *The Imperial Game: Cricket Culture and Society*. Manchester, p. 65.
23. Louis Duffus. 1947. *Cricketers of the Veld*. London, pp. 5–6, 11.
24. Maurice Turnbull and Maurice Allom. 1931. *The Two Maurices Again: Being Some Account of the Tour of the MCC Team Through South Africa in the Closing Months of 1930 and the Beginning of 1931*. London, p. 125.
25. Jack Fingleton. 1985. *Cricket Crisis: Bodyline and Other Lines*. London, p. 222.
26. W. Pollock, *Talking about Cricket*, pp. 116 and 152.
27. Douglas Alexander. 1999. 'The Most Remarkable Test Match Ever'. *Natal Witness*, 5 March.
28. Bruce Murray interview with Sir Donald Bradman, Adelaide, February 1998.
29. Alan Ross. 1983. *Ranji: Prince of Cricketers*. London, p. 205.
30. Learie Constantine. 1946. *Cricket in the Sun*. London, p. 90.
31. Rex Roberts and Simon Wilde. 1993. *Duleepsinhji*. Nottingham, p. 16.
32. MCC minutes, 15 July 1929; Cricket and Selection Sub-Committee minutes, 18 June 1929.
33. Faulkner to Duleepsinhji, 13 August 1929; Anonymous, 1932, West Sussex Record Office, Duleepsinhji Archive, Box 2.
34. Trevor Chesterfield and Jackie McGlew. 2003. *South Africa's Cricket Captains*. Cape Town, p. 141; Louis Duffus. 1969. *Play Abandoned: An Autobiography*. Cape Town, p. 172.
35. Ramachandra Guha. 2002. *A Corner of a Foreign Field: The Indian History of a British Sport*. London, pp. 305–18.
36. Mihir Bose. 1990. *A History of Indian Cricket*. London, p. 36; Ramachandra Guha, *A Corner of a Foreign Field*, pp. 305–18.
37. Brian Stoddart. 1988. 'Caribbean Cricket: the Role of Sport in Emerging Small-Nation Politics'. *International Journal* 43(4), p. 623.
38. Jack Williams. 1999. *Cricket and England: A Cultural and Social History of the Inter-War Years*. London.
39. Brian Crowley. 1983. *Cricket's Exiles: The Saga of South African Cricket*. Cape Town, pp. 113–16.
40. De Kiewiet, *South Africa*, p. 229.
41. M. Swanson. 1995. 'The Sanitation Syndrome'. In W. Beinart and S. Dubow (eds). *Segregation and Apartheid in Twentieth Century South Africa*. London, p. 38.
42. A.G. Cobley. 1997. *The Rules of the Game: Struggles in Black Recreation and Social Welfare Policy in South Africa*. Westport, p. 25; 'Report of the Tuberculosis Commission'. 1914. *Union Gazette* 34, para 251.
43. R.E. Phillips. 1930. *The Bantu are Coming: Phases of South Africa's Race Problems*. London, pp. 130–1.
44. Sarah G. Millin. 1934. *The South Africans*. London, p. 109.
45. Cobley, *Rules*, 31.
46. Philip K. Vundla. 1978. *PQ: The Story of Philip Vundla of South Africa*. Johannesburg, p. 17.

47. André Odendaal. 2003. *The Story of an African Game*. Cape Town, pp. 94–5.
48. Cobley, *Rules*, pp. 20–9; T. Couzens, 1983. 'An Introduction to the History of Football in South Africa'. In B. Bozzoli (ed), *Town and Countryside in the Transvaal*. Johannesburg, pp. 200, 204, 209.
49. Odendaal, *African Game*, pp. 84–99.
50. H.R. Burrows. 1943. *Indian Life and Labour in Natal*. Johannesburg, p. 32.
51. Desai et al, *Blacks in Whites*, pp. 51–3 and 91.
52. Robert Archer and Antoine Bouillon. 1982. *The South African Game: Sport and Racism*. London, p. 121.
53. *Rand Daily Mail*, 1 January 1944.
54. Jonty Winch. 1997. *Cricket in Southern Africa*. Rosettenville, p. 101; Tom Reddick. 1979. *Never a Cross Bat*. Cape Town, p. 94; Donald Woods 1981. *Black and White*. Dublin, p. 58; Archer and Bouillon, *South African Game*, p. 151.
55. SACA minutes 23 February 1931, 1 September 1935, 18 September 1937, 5 July 1946, 4–5 October 1947 and 3–4 April 1948.

CHAPTER THREE

1. Dan O'Meara. 1996. *Forty Lost Years: The Apartheid State and the Politics of the National Party 1948–1994*. Randburg, p. 56.
2. Denis Compton. 1958. *End of an Innings*. London, p. 177; Bobby Simpson. 1966. *Captain's Story*. London, pp. 19–20.
3. SACA minutes, 28 April 1956.
4. G. Haigh. 1997. *The Summer Game*. Melbourne, pp. 6–7.
5. M. Commaille. 1947. 'A Golden Opportunity for South African Cricketers'. *Outspan,* 1 August, p. 21.
6. C.J. Kaplan. 1946. 'Need for Bigger Cricket Nursery in the Free State'. *Outspan*, p. 33.
7. Luke Alfred. 2003. *Testing Times: The Story of the Men Who Made SA Cricket*. Cape Town.
8. A. Odendaal. 2003. *The Story of an African Game*. Cape Town, p. 105.
9. T. Reddick. 1979. *Never a Cross Bat*. Cape Town, p. 94; D. Woods. 1981. *Black and White*. Dublin, p. 58.
10. B. D'Oliveira. 1980. *Time to Declare: An Autobiography*. London, p. 5.
11. B. Crowley. 1983. *Cricket's Exiles: The Saga of South African Cricket*. Cape Town, p. 114.
12. *South African Cricketer: The National Cricket Journal of Southern Africa* 1(1) 1959.
13. 'D'Oliveira's Life Story', *Drum*, July 1960.
14. Crowley, *Cricket's Exiles*, p. 120.
15. Odendaal, *African Game*, p. 147.
16. M. Allie. 2000. *More Than A Game: History of the Western Province Cricket Board 1959–1991*. Cape Town, pp. 9–24; M. Wilson and A. Mafeje. 1963. *Langa: A Study of Social Groups in an African Township*. Cape Town, p. 125.
17. K. Kirkwood. 1951. *The Group Areas Act*. Johannesburg, p. 2.
18. D.S. van der Merwe (ed). *Extract from Joint Report of the Asiatic Land Tenure Laws Amendment Committee and the Land Tenure Act Amendments Committee* (UG 49–50), p. 5.

19. J. Western. 1981. *Outcast Cape Town*. Minneapolis, p. 80.
20. F.P. Rousseau. 1960. *Handbook on the Group Areas Act*. Cape Town, p. 17. The case in question was *R v Nicholas* 1958(3) SA 761 (T).
21. J.T. Schoombee. 1987. 'An Evaluation of Aspects of Group Areas Legislation in South Africa'. University of Cape Town, LLD thesis, p. 69.
22. Hogarth, 'It Just Wasn't Cricket'. *Sunday Times*, 8 November 1998, quoting from an address by Halton Cheadle at the memorial service for Justice John Didcott.
23. Ashwin Desai, Vishnu Padayachee, Krish Reddy and Goolam Vahed. 2002. *Blacks in Whites: A Century of Cricket Struggles in KwaZulu-Natal*. Pietermaritiburg, p. 236.
24. M. Horrell. 1956. *The Group Areas Act: Its Effect on Human Beings*. Johannesburg, p. 25.
25. Ibid, pp. 118–19.
26. University of Natal. Department of Economics. 1951. *Experiment at Edendale: A Study of Non-European Settlement with Special Reference to Food Expenditure and Nutrition*. Pietermaritzburg, p. 234.
27. C.A. Woods. 1954. *The Indian Community of Natal: Their Economic Position*. Cape Town, p. 102.
28. Odendaal, *African Game*, pp. 127–9, 139–43.
29. Quoted in B. D'Oliveira. 1969. *The D'Oliveira Affair*. London, p. 34.
30. A. Odendaal. 1976. *God's Forgotten Cricketers: Profiles of Leading South African Players*. Cape Town; D'Oliveira, *D'Oliveira Affair*, pp. 22–3.
31. Haigh, *Summer Game*, pp. 221–3.
32. A. Odendaal. 1997. *Cricket in Isolation: The Politics of Race and Cricket in South Africa*. Cape Town, pp. 337–8.
33. C. Cowdrey. 1976. *MCC: The Autobiography of a Cricketer*. London, pp. 113–14.
34. Undated (1959?) South African Sports Association document in the Brutus Papers, Borthwick Institute, University of York; D. Brutus. 1959. 'Sports Test for South Africa'. *Africa South* 3(4), p. 6; D. Brutus. 1968. 'Childhood Reminiscences'. In P. Wastberg (ed). *The Writer in Modern Africa*. Uppsala, p. 98.
35. A. La Guma, writing in *Fighting Talk* June 1957, quoted in A. Odendaal and R. Field (eds). 1993. *Liberation Chabalala: The World of Alex La Guma*. Bellville, p. 60.
36. Haigh, *Summer Game*, pp. 221–3.
37. A. La Guma, writing in *New Age* 20 April 1961, quoted in Odendaal and Field (eds), *Liberation Chabalala*, p. 178.
38. K.A. Yelvington. 1995. 'Ethnicity "not out"'. In H. Beckles and B. Stoddart. *Liberation Cricket: West Indian Cricket Culture*. Manchester, p. 220.
39. J. Slovo. 1995. *Slovo: The Unfinished Autobiography*. Johannesburg, pp. 142–3.

CHAPTER FOUR

1. Deborah Posel. 1991. *The Making of Apartheid, 1948–1961: Conflict and Compromise*. Oxford, chapter 9.
2. Robert Archer and Antoine Bouillon. 1982. *The South African Game: Sport and Racism*. London, pp. 189–91; Adrian Guelke. 1986. 'The Politicisation of South African Sport'. In Lincoln Allison (ed). *The Politics of Sport*. Manchester, chapter 6.

3. Anthony Steel. 1959. 'Sport Leads the Way'. *Africa South* 4(1), October–December, pp. 114–15.

4. Father Trevor Huddleston. 1956. *Naught For Your Comfort*. London, pp. 201–2.

5. Peter Hain. 1996. *Sing the Beloved Country*. London, pp. 45–6.

6. Verwoerd delivered his speech on 4 September 1965, and his statement on Maoris was ratified by the Cabinet three days later. The Cabinet minute of 7 September 1965 for Internal Affairs stated: '*Insluiting van Maoris in New Zealandse Span na SA – E[eerste] M[inister] se Optrede word Goedgekeur*' ('The Inclusion of Maoris in the New Zealand Team to SA – The PM's Action is Approved'). Notule Kabinet 14.9.64–1.12.65, National Archives, Pretoria, CAB1/1/3.

7. Peter Wynne-Thomas and Peter Arnold. 1984. *Cricket in Crisis: The Story of Major Crises That Have Rocked the Game*. Feltham, p. 114.

8. *Rand Daily Mail*, 21 September 1968.

9. Archer and Bouillon, *South African Game*, p. 195; Tim Couzens. 1983. 'An Introduction to the History of Football in South Africa'. In B. Bozzoli (ed). *Town and Countryside in the Transvaal*. Johannesburg, pp. 198–214.

10. Ashwin Desai, Vishnu Padayachee, Krish Reddy and Goolam Vahed. 2002. *Blacks in Whites: A Century of Cricket Struggles in KwaZulu-Natal*. Pietermaritzburg, p. 216.

11. *A Survey of Race Relations 1955–56*, p. 227.

12. Joan Brickhill. 1976. *Race Against Race: South Africa's 'Multinational' Sport Fraud*. London, p. 44.

13. B. Magubane. 1963. 'Sport and Politics in an Urban African Community: A Case Study of African Voluntary Organisations'. M Soc Sc thesis, University of Natal, Durban, p. 79.

14. For the affiliation policy see Brickhill, *Race Against Race*, pp. 56–7.

15. *A Survey of Race Relations 1958–59*, p. 297; Development Studies Group, University of the Witwatersrand. 1991. *Politics in Sport*. Johannesburg.

16. Interview with Dennis Brutus, Johannesburg, 21 January 2002.

17. Steel to SACA secretary, 23 July 1959, SACA correspondence, 'Non-White Cricket' files; Steel 1959. 'Sport Leads the Way'. *Africa South* 4(1), October–December, pp. 114–5; Robin Denniston. *Trevor Huddleston: A Life*. London, pp. 123–4.

18. Dennis Brutus. 1959. 'Sports Test For South Africa'. *Africa South* 3(4), July–September, pp. 35–9.

19. See Brian Stoddart and Keith A.P. Sandiford (eds). 1998. *The Imperial Game: Cricket, Culture and Society*. Manchester.

20. Christopher Merrett and John Nauright. 'South Africa'. In Stoddard and Sandiford, p. 70; Derek Birley. 1999. *A Social History of English Cricket*. London, p. 272.

21. Brutus to MCC Secretary, 29 August 1968, Anti-Apartheid Movement Papers (AAM), 1439.

22. C.L.R. James. 1963. *Beyond a Boundary*. London, pp. 228–9; Anna Grimshaw (ed). 1986. *Cricket*. London, pp. 88–90.

23. Brutus to Varachia, 28 February 1959; Brutus to WICBOC, 23 March and 3 June 1959, Brutus Papers.

24. SASA statement on tours to and from South Africa, 12 February 1959, SACA correspondence, 'Non-White Cricket' files; Brutus interview; Allie, *More Than a Game*, pp. 19–20; Desai et al, *Blacks in Whites*, pp. 220–1.

25. Campaign Against Race Discrimination in Sport to SACA, 23 July 1959, SACA correspondence, 'Non-White Cricket' files.

26. Aird to Frames, 19 April 1960, SACA correspondence; David Sheppard. 2002. *Steps Along Hope Street: My Life in Cricket, the Church and the Inner City*. London, pp. 84–5.
27. Frames to members of the Board of Control, 28 July 1960, SACA correspondence, 'Non-White Cricket' files.
28. Frames to members of the Board of Control, 29 March 1960; Private Secretary of the Minister of Interior to Frames, 16 June 1960, SACA correspondence, 'Non-White Cricket' files.
29. Frames to members of the Board of Control, 15 February 1961, SACA correspondence, 'Non-White Cricket' files.
30. ICC minutes, 19 July 1961.
31. ICC minutes, 18 July 1962; *The Times*, 19 July 1962.
32. ICC minutes, 17 July 1963.
33. ICC minutes, 17 July 1963 and 14 July 1966.
34. Jack Bailey. 1989. *Conflicts in Cricket*. London, p. 48.
35. Derek Birley. 1979 and 2000. *The Willow Wand*. London, p. 184.
36. Ronald Hyam and Peter Henshaw. 2003. *The Lion and the Springbok: Britain and South Africa Since the Boer War*. Cambridge, pp. 307–20.
37. Richard Thompson. 1964. *Race and Sport*. London, pp. 67–8.
38. Quoted in Jack Williams. 2001. *Cricket and Race*. Oxford, p. 54.
39. Donald Woods. 1980. *Asking For Trouble: Autobiography of a Banned Journalist*. London, pp. 194–5.
40. See John Waite. 1961. *Perchance to Bowl*. London, p. 47.
41. Bowley to members of the SACA Board of Control, 8 February 1962, SACA correspondence.
42. TCU minutes, 4 October, 6 December 1961 and 7 March 1962.
43. Letters circulated by Frames to members of the Board of Control on 'Affiliation of Non-European Cricketing Bodies', 26 April, 11, 16 and 25 May 1962, SACA correspondence, 'Non-White Cricket' files; SACA minutes, 20 May.
44. SACA minutes, 4 February and 15–16 September 1962.
45. SACA minutes, 31 March 1963.
46. TCU minutes, 4 September, 2 October 1963 and 15 January 1964; letters circulated by Frames to members of the Board of Control, 29 November 1963, SACA correspondence, 'Non-White Cricket' files.
47. NZCC Board of Control minutes, 28 October 1961.
48. Summary notes by D.A. Brutus of interview with Gordon Leggat, 15 February 1962, SACA correspondence, 'Non-White Cricket' files. Leggat accepted the accuracy of the minutes and a full report of the meeting was published in the *Evening Post* in Port Elizabeth. See also Richard Thompson. 1975. *Retreat from Apartheid: New Zealand's Sporting Contacts with South Africa*. Wellington, chapter 4; Trevor Richards 1999. *Dancing on Our Bones: New Zealand, South Africa, Rugby and Racism*. Wellington, pp. 29–30.
49. Telephone interview with Trevor Goddard, March 2003.
50. Luke Alfred. 2003. *Testing Times: The Story of the Men who made SA Cricket*. Claremont, p. 178.
51. Manager's Report, MCC Tour to South Africa 1964/65, MCC Archives, 'MCC Tour to South Africa 1968/69' file.
52. Anti-Apartheid Movement Annual Report, September 1965.

53. Gideon Haigh. 1997. *The Summer Game*. Melbourne, pp. 223–4.
54. SACA minutes, 18–19 September 1965.
55. Peter and Graeme Pollock. 1968. *Bouncers and Boundaries*. Johannesburg.
56. MCC Committee minutes, 8 March and 19 April 1967.
57. *Star*, 4 March 1967.
58. Richards, *Dancing on Our Bones*, pp. 33–4.
59. D.C. Bursnall, Hon Secretary of SACA, to the Australian Board of Control for International Cricket and the New Zealand Cricket Council, 16 September 1969, SACA correspondence, 'Non-White Cricket' files.
60. *House of Assembly Debates*, 26, 21 April 1969, 4404.
61. B. D'Oliveira. 1980. *Time to Declare: An Autobiography*. Johannesburg, p. 24; Peter Oborne. 2004. *Basil D'Oliveira – Cricket and Conspiracy: The Untold Story*. London, chapter 6.
62. MCC committee minutes, 18 January 1967; Minutes of MCC sub-committee to consider drafting of MCC statement for special general meeting, 18 September and 7 October 1968; Basil D'Oliveira. 1969. *The D'Oliveira Affair*. London, chapter 7.

CHAPTER FIVE

1. *Rand Daily Mail*, 18 September 1968.
2. The literature includes Basil D'Oliveira. 1969. *The D'Oliveira Affair*. London; Peter Hain. 1971. *Don't Play With Apartheid: The Background to the Stop The Seventy Tour Campaign*. London, chapter 5; R.E. Lapchick. 1975. *The Politics of Race and International Sport: The Case of South Africa*. Westport, Connecticut, chapter 4; André Odendaal (ed). 1977. *Cricket in Isolation: The Politics of Race and Cricket in South Africa*, Cape Town, chapter 1; Derek Birley. 1979. *The Willow Wand*. London, chapter 12; Tony Lewis. 1985. *Double Century: The Story of MCC and Cricket*. London, pp. 311–17; Jack Bailey. 1989. *Conflicts in Cricket*. London, chapter 3; Graeme Wright. 1993. *Betrayal: The Struggle for Cricket's Soul*. London, chapter 12; Mike Marqusee. 1994. *Anyone But England: Cricket and the National Malaise*. London, pp. 186–92; Jack Williams. 2001. *Cricket and Race*. Oxford, chapter 3; Peter Oborne. 2004. *Basil D'Oliveira – Cricket and Conspiracy: The Untold Story*. London, chapters 10–12.
3. Coy to Vorster, 4 September 1968, National Archives, Pretoria (NA), MEM 1/647, I38/2.
4. Wiley to Waring, nd, in Press Cuttings: D'Oliveira and the MCC Tour, NA MSO MS7/4/1.
5. 1968 Notuleboek, NA CAB 1/1/4.
6. Trevor Chesterfield and Jackie McGlew. 2003. *South Africa's Cricket Captains*. Cape Town, p. 138.
7. *House of Assemby Debates*, 19, 8 February 1967, cols 928–34.
8. *Parliamentary Debates* (*Hansard*), 5th Series, 740, 30 January 1967, cols 34–5.
9. Hermann Giliomee. 2003. *The Afrikaners: Biography of a People*. Cape Town, p. 551.
10. John D'Oliveira. 1996. *Vorster: The Man*. Johannesburg, pp. 215–20; Dan O'Meara. 1996. *Forty Lost Years* Randburg, pp. 150–9.
11. *House of Assemby Debates*, 20, 11 April 1967, cols 3952–96.
12. Sir John Nicholls to Foreign Office, Savingram No 14, 14 April 1967. The National Archives, London (TNA), FCO 25/709.

13. *Sunday Times*, 22 September 1968.
14. S.C. Griffith, MCC Secretary, to D.C. Bursnall, Honorary Secretary SACA, 5 January 1968, NA MEM 1/647, I38/2; MCC Committee minutes, 21 February and 21 March 1968; SACA minutes, 24 March 1968.
15. Coy to Vorster, 27 March 1968, NA MEM 1/647, I38/2.
16. Waring to Vorster, 7 March and 20 June 1968, NA MEM 1/647, I38/2.
17. D. Richard Thorpe. 1996. *Alec Douglas-Home*. London, p. 397; E.W. Swanton. 1985. *Gubby Allen – Man of Cricket*. London, p. 289; interview with Doug Insole, Cape Town, 4 January 2000.
18. Coy to Vorster, 27 March 1968, NA MEM 1/647, I38/2.
19. Itinerary for Douglas-Home visit to South Africa, February 1968, Lord Home of Hirsel Papers, Coldstream.
20. Basil D'Oliveira. 1980. *Time to Declare: An Autobiography*. Johannesburg, pp. 65–7.
21. Coy to Jack Cheetham, 4 March 1968, NA MEM 1/647, I38/2.
22. Rob Steen. 1999. *This Sporting Life: Cricket: Inside Tales from the Men Who Made the Game What it is Today*. Newton Abbot, p. 37.
23. Hain, *Don't Play*, p. 80.
24. Coy to Jack Cheetham, 4 March 1968, NA MEM 1/647, I38/2.
25. Proposed statement to be issued in the event of D'Oliveira being selected for MCC to tour South Africa, 28 August 1968, NA MEM 1/647, I38/2.
26. Sir John Nicholls to Commonwealth Office, 17 September 1968, TNA FCO 25/709.
27. C.M. Le Quesne, 13 February 1967, TNA FCO 25/709.
28. Dave Bursnall, Hon Secretary SACA, to S.C. Griffith, MCC Secretary, 1 March 1968, NA MEM 1/647, I38/2.
29. Coy to Vorster, 27 March 1968, Ibid.
30. D.B. Carr to South African Tour Committee, nd [March 1968], MCC Archives, MCC Tour to South Africa 1968/69 file.
31. Coy to Cheetham, 4 March 1968, and Coy to Vorster, 20 May 1968, Ibid.
32. Interview with the Rt. Rev. Lord Sheppard, West Kirby, 5 November 1999.
33. Steen, *Cricket*, p. 37.
34. Swanton, *Allen*, 289.
35. Secret. 'The Future of Anglo-South African Relations', 19 February 1968, TNA FCO 25/622.
36. Colin Cowdrey. 1976. *M.C.C. The Autobiography of a Cricketer*. London, pp. 195–6.
37. Lord Home. 1970. *The Way the Wind Blows*. London, p. 228.
38. Swanton, *Allen*, p. 289; Thorpe, *Home,* p. 397.
39. MCC Committee minutes, 21 March 1968; draft of the MCC Committee's statement for the special general meeting of 5 December 1968.
40. Swanton, *Allen*, p. 289.
41. When, in April 1969, it was revealed that Cobham had advised Griffith of Vorster's attitude, 'some criticism' was expressed within the MCC Committee that this had not been reported to them, but the secretary's offer to resign was rejected. MCC Committee minutes, 16 April 1969.
42. Lawrence Marks. 'Inside Story of the Dolly Row'. *Rand Daily Mail*, 26 September 1968.
43. Coy to Cheetham, 1 March 1968, and Coy to Vorster, 27 March 1968, NA MEM 1/647, I38/2.
44. SACA minutes, 24 March 1968.

45. Coy to Vorster, 20 May 1968, NA MEM 1/647, I38/2.
46. D'Oliveira. *Time to Declare*, p. 64; Oborne, *D'Oliveira,* pp. 157–60.
47. *Star*, 18 September 1968.
48. Bailey, *Conflicts*, p. 52.
49. Stephen Chalke. 2001. *At the Heart of English Cricket: The Life and Memories of Geoffrey Howard*. Bath, p. 206.
50. Interview with Jack Bailey, Southampton, 29 June 2000.
51. Interview with Doug Insole, Cape Town, 4 January 2000, and telephone conversation, 23 November 2001.
52. Marks, *Rand Daily Mail*, 26 September 1968. See also Swanton, *Allen*, p. 291.
53. Cowdrey, *MCC*, p. 201.
54. D'Oliveira, *Time to Declare*, pp. 65–6.
55. Peter May. 1985. *A Game Enjoyed*. London, p. 191.
56. Interview with the Rt. Rev. Lord David Sheppard, West Kirby, 5 November 1999.
57. Telephone interview with Lord Cowdrey, 9 November 1999; Cowdrey, *MCC*, p. 202; Chalke, *Howard*, p. 206; MCC Selection Sub-Committee minutes, 27 August 1968.
58. *Sunday Times*, 1 September 1968.
59. Tony Lewis, the official historian of the MCC, commented, 'Their every decision reeked of political expediency because the cricket argument for excluding D'Oliveira and then including him was tenuous.' Lewis, *Double Century*, p. 314.
60. Interview with Doug Insole, Cape Town, 4 January 2000.
61. Interview with Jack Bailey, Southampton, 29 June 2000; D'Oliveira, *Time to Declare*, chapter 5.
62. Interview with Jack Bailey, Southampton, 29 June 2000; interview with Raman Subba Row, Johannesburg, 19 January 2001.
63. Coy to Vorster, 4 September 1968, NA MEM 1/647, I38/2.
64. *Guardian,* 29 August 1968.
65. Steen, *Cricket*, p. 38; interview with the Rt. Rev. Lord Sheppard, West Kirby, 5 November 1999; David Sheppard. 2002. *Steps Along Hope Street: My Life in Cricket, the Church and the Inner City*. London, p. 87.
66. MCC Committee minutes, 12 September 1968.
67. Ibid.
68. D'Oliveira, *D'Oliveira Affair*, chapter 8.
69. *The Times*, 9 June 1969.
70. D'Oliveira, *D'Oliveira*, p. 99–100.
71. 'It Wan't Cricket'. Anti Apartheid Movement papers, Rhodes House Library, AAM MS 1441.
72. D'Oliveira, *Time to Declare*, p. 73; Oborne, *D'Oliveira*, p. 228; Cowdrey to Douglas-Home, 5 December 1969, Lord Home of Hersel Papers.
73. *House of Assembly Debates*, 26, 21 April, col 4405.
74. Ibid, col 4448.
75. Reprinted in the *Rand Daily Mail*, 4 September 1968.
76. *Guardian*, 18 September 1968.
77. Louis Duffus. 1969. *Play Abandoned*. Cape Town, chapter 29.
78. Mike Procter. 1994. *South Africa: The Years of Isolation and the Return to International Cricket*. Durban, p. 20.

CHAPTER SIX

1. For an earlier treatment of this theme see Jack Williams. 2000. *Cricket and Race*. Oxford, chapter 3.
2. Cricket Council statement, 19 May 1970, Cricket Council file, 1970 South African tour.
3. *The Times*, 2, 14 and 22 May 1970.
4. Minutes of special meeting of MCC Committee, 24 September 1968.
5. *The Times*, 6 December 1968; Interview with the Rt. Rev. Lord Sheppard, West Kirby, 5 November 1999; David Sheppard. 2002. *Steps Along Hope Street: My Life in Cricket, the Church and the Inner City*. London, p. 87.
6. Brutus to Cricket Council, 18 December 1968, Anti-Apartheid Movement papers, Rhodes House, AAM MS 1439; Wooller to Brutus, 31 December 1968 and Brutus to Wooller, 6 January 1969, Brutus papers.
7. Griffith to Brutus and the Anti-Apartheid Movement, 16 June 1969, AAM MS 1439.
8. Peter Hain. 1971. *Don't Play With Apartheid*. London, chapter 5 and *Sing The Beloved Country*. 1996. London, chapter 4.
9. See Kenneth O. Morgan. 1990. *The People's Peace: British History 1945–1989*. Oxford, pp. 292–8.
10. Interview with Peter Hain, London, 27 June 2001.
11. David Steel. 1989. *Against Goliath: David Steel's Story*. London, p. 63.
12. Richard Crossman. 1977. *The Diaries of a Cabinet Minister*, vol. 3. London, p. 846.
13. *Daily Telegraph*, 31 January 1970.
14. Resolutions adopted by AAM annual general meeting, 26 October 1969, AAM MS 14; National Committee meeting minutes, 28 February 1970, AAM MS 43; *Daily Express,* 22 January 1970.
15. Anti-Apartheid Movement Annual Report, September 1969 to August 1970, AAM MS13.
16. Jack Bailey. 1989. *Conflicts in Cricket*. London, p. 59.
17. TCCB minutes, 10 and 11 December 1969.
18. Hain, *Don't Play*, p. 163.
19. Hain, *Sing*, pp. 56–7.
20. 'South African Cricket Tour', minutes of Home Secretary meetings 27 and 29 January 1970, The National Archives (TNA) FCO 45/728; Bailey, *Conflicts*, pp. 61–2; telephone interview with Doug Insole, July 2001.
21. Report of the Emergency Executive Committee for TCCB meeting, 12 February 1970, Cricket Council file, 1970 South African tour.
22. Memorandum on 'South African Tour' sent to members of the Emergency Executive Committee, 4 February 1970; pamphlet 'Why the '70 Tour: The Cricket Council Answer', Lord's 1970, Cricket Council file, 1970 South African tour.
23. *The Times*, 13 February 1970.
24. Callaghan evidently raised this possibility with Michael Stewart, the Foreign and Commonwealth Secretary, but the Foreign and Commonwealth Office would have none of it. As the Home Office was advised on 16 February: '[T]he Government's policy of non-interference as it has so far been enunciated, most recently in particular by Mr Stewart to the South African Ambassador, prevents us from taking any action to influence other countries to exercise pressure for the tour to be cancelled'. TNA FCO 451/728.
25. Callaghan note to the Prime Minister, 'Proposed South African Cricket Tour', 30 April 1970, TNA PREM 13/3499.

26. Bailey, *Conflicts*, pp. 62–3.
27. 'South African Cricket Tour: Possible African Boycott of Commonwealth Games. Note by Foreign and Commonwealth Office', 28 April 1970, TNA CAB 164/674.
28. Richard Lapchick. 1975. *The Politics of Race and International Sport: The Case of South Africa*. Westport, Connecticut, p. 171.
29. Cabinet minutes, 30 April 1970, TNA CAB 128/45; Howell to Prime Minister, 24 April 1970, CAB 164/674; Howell to Prime Minister, 30 April 1970, PREM 13/3499.
30. Crossman, *Diaries*, vol. 3, p. 908.
31. Howell to Prime Minister, 6 May 1970, TNA PREM 13/3499.
32. Sheppard to S.C. Griffith, 13 May 1970, Cricket Council file, 1970 South African tour.
33. Williams, *Cricket and Race*, pp. 73–4.
34. Howell to Prime Minister, 24 April 1970, TNA CAB 164/674.
35. Minutes of emergency meeting of the Cricket Council, 18 May 1970.
36. Notes for the record: Telephone conversations between the Prime Minister and the Home Secretary, 22 May 1970, TNA PREM 13/3499.
37. Crossman, *Diaries*, vol. 3, pp. 846–7.
38. Notes for the Record: South African Tour, 21 and 29 May 1970, TNA PREM 13/3499. See also Kenneth O. Morgan 1999. *Callaghan: A Life*. Oxford, pp. 313–14.
39. Bailey, *Conflicts*, p. 66.
40. Foreign and Commonwealth Office Telegram No 403 to Pretoria, 21 May 1970, TNA FCO 45/729.
41. *Rand Daily Mail*, 25 May 1970; interview with Jack Bailey, Southampton, June 2000.
42. Hassan Howa. 1977. In André Odendaal (ed). *Cricket in Isolation: The Politics of Race and Cricket in South Africa*. Cape Town, pp. 272–3.
43. Subba Row to Griffith, 22 October 1969; minutes of Cricket Council sub-committee on 'non-cricketing matters connected with the South African tour', 5 September 1969, Cricket Council file, 1970 South African tour.
44. Coy to D.C. Bursnall, Hon Secretary of SACA, 28 October 1968, SACA correspondence, 'Non-White Cricket' files.
45. SACA minutes, 28–29 September and 22 December 1968.
46. Coy to Dyer and to Burnsnall, 3 January 1968, SACA correspondence, 'Non-White Cricket' files.
47. Jordaan to Hammond, 3 January 1969, and report from the Western Province Cricket Union, 22 January 1969, SACA correspondence, 'Non-White Cricket' files.
48. Hayward Kitson. 1995. *The History of Transvaal Cricket*. Johannesburg, p. 220; Ashwin Desai, Vishnu Padyachee, Krish Reddy and Goolam Vahed. 2002. *Blacks in Whites: A Century of Cricket Struggles in KwaZulu-Natal*. Pietermaritzburg, p. 272; SACA minutes, 18 February, 21 June and 9–10 August 1969.
49. SACA minutes, 9–10 August 1969; Deasai et al, *Blacks in Whites*, p. 272.
50. For the parlous condition of African cricket in the Western Province and Natal, see John Young (ed). 1997. *Langa Cricket Club – 21 Years 1976–1997*. Cape Town, p. 8; Desai et al, *Blacks in Whites*, chapter 3.
51. Secretary for Sport to the Minister, 5 December 1968, National Archives (NA), Department of Sport and Recreation MSO MS1/5/7 vol. 1.
52. SACA minutes, 18 February 1969, and verbatim minutes in SACA correspondence, 'Non-White Cricket' files.

53. 'Strictly Private and Confidential: Resumé of discussions with the Prime Minister on the 8th of August, 1969, when the South African Cricket Association was represented by Messrs E.R. Hammond, J.J. Cheetham, A.H. Coy and D.V. Dyer', SACA correspondence, 'Non-White Cricket' files.
54. Subba Row to Griffith, 22 October 1969, Cricket Council file, 1970 South African tour.
55. Paul Killick to John Macrae, Central and Southern African Department, Foreign and Commonwealth Office, 9 February 1970, TNA FCO 45/728.
56. Ibid.
57. SACA minutes, 22 February 1970.
58. Report of the Emergency Executive Committee for TCCB meeting, 12 February 1970, Cricket Council file, 1970 South African tour.
59. Waring to Secretary for Sport and Recreation, 24 July 1969, NA Department of Sport and Recreation MSO MS1/5/7 vol. 2.
60. Richard Holt and Tony Mason. 2000. *Sport in Britain 1945–2000*. Oxford, chapter 7.
61. Christopher Martin-Jenkins. 1984. *Twenty Years On: Cricket's Years of Change 1963 to 1983*. London, p. 96.
62. 'UK-South African Relations', Foreign and Commonwealth Office, 14 May 1970, TNA FCO 45/729.
63. David Butler. 1971. *The British General Election of 1970*. London, pp. 139–41.
64. Harold Wilson. 1971. *The Labour Government 1964–1970: A Personal Record*. London, p. 784.
65. Anti-Apartheid Movement annual report, 1970–71 and 1981–82, AAM MS13.
66. Coy to Carr, 24 June 1970, MCC Archives, South Africa Tour to UK 1970 (cancelled) box.
67. *Rand Daily Mail*, 25 May 1970.

CHAPTER SEVEN

1. SACA minutes, 25 September 1971.
2. Charles Williams. 1996. *Bradman: An Australian Hero*. London, pp. 268–9.
3. Irving Rosenwater. 1978. *Sir Donald Bradman: A Biography*. London, p. 372; Michael Page. 1983. *Bradman: The Illustrated Biography*. Melbourne, pp. 350–4; Roland Perry. 1995. *The Don*. London, p. 575; Brett Hutchins. 2002. *Don Bradman: Challenging the Myth*. Cambridge, pp. 122–7.
4. SACA minutes, 29 November 1970.
5. G. Bolton. 1996. *The Oxford History of Australia Volume 5: The Middle Way 1942–1995* (2nd ed). Melbourne, p. 197.
6. S. Harris. 1972. *Political Football: The Springbok Tour of Australia, 1971*. Melbourne.
7. Clem Jones to author, 11 November 2002.
8. For Menzies on politics and sport see Sir Robert Menzies. 1972. *The Measure of the Years*. London, chapter 24.
9. Item on 'Apartheid' prepared for Prime Minister, 12 April 1971, National Archives of Australia (NAA), A1838/264, 201/10/10/3 Part 1.
10. Keith Waller to Sir John Bunting, Secretary, Department of the Prime Minister and Cabinet, 5 April 1971, Ibid.
11. NAA A5909.

12. Department of Foreign Affairs Savingram No 19/71 from T.W. Cutts, 'South African Cricket Tour', 9 July 1971, NAA A41792/P 201/10/10/3.
13. South African ambassador's report on conversation with Sir Donald Bradman, June 1972, National Archives, Pretoria (NA), Department of Sport and Recreation, MSO MS6/5/9.
14. 'Secret. Cricket Tour of Australia by South African team. Discussion on 24 August', Cabinet paper, NAA A5882/2, CO1274.
15. *Star*, 9 September 1971; South African ambassador's report on conversation with Sir Donald Bradman, June 1972, NA MSO MS6/5/9.
16. South African ambassador to Secretary for Foreign Affairs, 9 September 1971, NA MSO MS6/5/9.
17. *Parliamentary Debates: House of Representatives* 73, col. 850.
18. ICC minutes, 19–20 July 1971; *Sydney Morning Herald*, 22 July 1971.
19. Bolton, *Oxford History of Australia Volume 5*, chapters 7 and 8.
20. Clem Jones to author, 11 November 2002.
21. Memorandum of Matters Relating to the Tour of Australia in the 1971/2 Season by a South African Cricket Team, March 1971, NA Department of Sport and Recreation MSO MS6/5/9.
22. SACA minutes, 27 September and 29 November 1970.
23. Cheetham advised his own board members of Bradman's attitude. Interview with Joe Pamensky, Johannesburg, October 2002.
24. Jack Pollard. 1992. *The Complete Illustrated History of Australian Cricket*. Melbourne, p. 446; Chris Harte. 1993. *A History of Australian Cricket*. London, p. 532.
25. SACA minutes, 15 August and 25 September 1971.
26. Interview with Sir Donald Bradman, Adelaide, 2 February 1998; manuscript prepared by Bob Parish, the ACB's honorary historian and a member of the the ad hoc committee; Harte, *Australian Cricket*, pp. 532–3; Page, *Bradman*, pp. 350–4; Perry, *The Don*, p. 575; Williams, *Bradman,* p. 268–9.
27. *Star*, 9 September and 14 October 1971.
28. *Rand Daily Mail*, 11 and 15 September 1971.
29. Rowan to Vorster, 7 August 1970, NA, Department of Sport and Recreation MEM 1/647 I 38/2; TCU minutes, 5 August 1970.
30. SACA minutes, 27 September 1970.
31. SACA minutes, 29 November 1970.
32. Department of Foreign Affairs Savingram No 19/71 from T.W. Cutts, 'South African Cricket Tour', 9 July 1971, NAA A41792/P 201/10/10/3.
33. SACA memorandum, 16 March 1970, NA Department of Sport and Recreation MS 6/5/9.
34. *The Times*, 21 May 1970.
35. Department of Foreign Affairs Savingram No 19/71 from T.W. Cutts, 'South African Cricket Tour', 9 July 1971, NAA A41792/P 201/10/10/3.
36. Mogamad Allie. 2000. *More Than A Game: History of the Western Province Cricket Board 1959–1991*. Cape Town, p. 93.
37. Waring to Hoek, 22 March 1971, and Hoek to Waring, 23 March 1971, NA MSO MS6/5/9.
38. 1971 Kabinets Notuleboek, NA CAB 1/1/4.
39. *Sunday Times*, 4 April 1971; *Rand Daily Mail*, 19 August 1971.

CHAPTER EIGHT

1. See James Barber and John Barratt. 1990. *South Africa's Foreign Policy: The Search for Status and Security 1945–1988*. Johannesburg, chapter 10.
2. Ibid, chapters 11–13; Dan O'Meara. 1996. *Forty Lost Years: The Apartheid State and the Politics of the National Party 1948–1994*. Randburg, Parts II and III; Hermann Giliomee. 2003. *The Afrikaners: Biography of a People*. Cape Town, chapters 15 and 16.
3. Jon Gemmell. 2004. *The Politics of South African Cricket*. London, p. 77.
4. See Adrian Guelke. 1986. 'The Politicisation of South African Sport'. In Lincoln Allison (ed). *The Politics of Sport*. Manchester, pp. 118–47.
5. SACU delegation meeting with Koornhof, 22 December 1977, SACU file, meetings with Minister of Sport.
6. Jonty Winch. 2000. 'Playing the Games: The Unification of South African Sport'. Unpublished manuscript, chapter 10.
7. Mike Procter. 1994. *South Africa: The Years of Isolation and the Return To International Cricket*. Durban, p. 62.
8. Joan Brickhill. 1976. *Race against Race: South Africa's 'Multinational' Sport Fraud*. London, pp. 35–6.
9. A.P.W. Northey to William Wilson, Central and Southern African Department, 10 April 1972, The National Archives, London (TNA), FCO 45/1026.
10. Ivor Wilkins and Hans Strydom. 1978. *The Super-Afrikaners*. Johannesburg, chaper 13.
11. *House of Assembly Debates* 33, 22 April 1971, cols 4994–5065.
12. Quoted in Christopher Merrett. 2001. 'Aurora: The Challenge of Non-Racial Cricket to the Apartheid State of the Mid-1970s'. *The International Journal of the History of Sport* 18(4), December, pp. 95–122.
13. Rodney Hartman. 2004. *Ali: The Life of Ali Bacher*. Johannesburg, p. 145.
14. Kabinet Notuleregister 1973. National Archives, Pretoria, (NA) CAB 1/1/5.
15. Wilkins and Strydom, *Super-Afrikaners*, pp. 250–1.
16. Donald Woods. 1980. *Asking For Trouble: Autobiography of a Banned Journalist*. London, p. 237.
17. *Sunday Tribune*, 21 August 1977.
18. Robert Archer and Antoine Bouillon. 1982. *The South African Game: Sport and Racism*. London, p. 220.
19. F.W. de Klerk. 1998. *The Last Trek – A New Beginning: The Autobiography*. London, p. 71.
20. Peter Hain. 1996. *Sing the Beloved Country: The Struggle for the New South Africa*. London, pp. 94–5.
21. For an overview of the sports boycott see Guelke, 'The Politicisation of South African Sport'; John Nauright. 1997. *Sport, Cultures and Identities in South Africa*. London, chapter 6; and Douglas Booth. 1998. *The Race Game: Sport and Politics in South Africa*. London, chapters 5 and 6.
22. *A Survey of Race Relations, 1977*, pp. 557–8.
23. *Rand Daily Mail*, 16 July 1977.
24. Douglas Booth. 1979. 'The South African Council on Sport and the Political Antimonies of the Sports Boycott'. *Journal of Southern African Studies* 23(1), March, p. 54.
25. Archer and Bouillon, *South African Game*, p. 332.
26. Interview with Sam Ramsamy, Johannesburg, 30 April 2003; Booth, *Race Game* pp. 110–

13; Trevor Richards. 1999. *Dancing on Our Bones: New Zealand, South Africa, Rugby and Racism*. Wellington, pp. 158–63.

27. For comprehensive overviews of the unity negotiations and the introduction of 'normal' cricket see André Odendaal. 1977. *Cricket in Isolation: The Politics of Race and Cricket in South Africa*. Cape Town, parts 1 and 2; and Guy Beresford. 1986. 'Playing Apartheid to Win or to Lose?'. *International Affairs Bulletin* 10(3), pp. 33–46.

28. SACA minutes, 25 September 1971 and 23 September 1972.

29. Ashwin Desai, Vishnu Padayachee, Krish Reddy and Goolam Vahed. 2002. *Blacks in Whites: A Century of Cricket Struggles in KwaZulu-Natal*. Pietermaritzburg, p. 275; *Rand Daily Mail*, 9 September 1971; *Star* 27 September 1971.

30. Odendaal, *Cricket in Isolation*, p. 273.

31. Cheetham to Griffith, 21 May 1971; Griffith to Cheetham, 14 July 1971, Cricket Council files.

32. J.P. Nason to M.E. Cook, Central and Southern African Department, 2 May 1972, TNA FCO 45/1206.

33. Minutes of meeting of national bodies controlling cricket in South Africa, held at Jan Smuts Holiday Inn, Johannesburg, on 30 April 1972, SACA files.

34. *Rand Daily Mail*, 28 May 1973.

35. Minutes of National Cricket Conference, Heerengracht Hotel, Cape Town, 25 March 1973, SACA files.

36. SACA minutes, 4 March 1973; Wallace report to the boards of the three national cricket bodies, 27 May 1973, Cricket Council file, Lord Caccia's visit to South Africa April 1974.

37. *Star*, 28 May 1973.

38. Foreign and Commonwealth Office note, January 1972, TNA FCO 45/1206.

39. Cricket Council minutes, 30 December 1971 and 6 January 1972.

40. K.J.A. Hunt. 14 January 1972. 'The Cowdrey Cricket Tour That Never Was'. TNA FCO 45/1206.

41. Wallace to Griffith, 27 June 1973; Griffith to Wallace, 18 July 1973, Cricket Council files.

42. Interview with Joe Pamensky, Johannesburg, 30 March 2003.

43. Merrett, 'Aurora'; SACA minutes, 22 September 1973.

44. *South African Cricket Annual 1974*, p. 7.

45. Pamensky report to TCU annual general meeting, TCU minutes 7 August 1975.

46. Odendaal, *Cricket in Isolation*, pp. 19–21.

47. Cricket Council minutes, 22 July 1975, Emergency Executive Committee minutes, 22 April and 22 August 1975.

48. Odendaal, *Cricket in Isolation*, p. 35.

49. Various addresses by Varachia, including his inaugural speech as SACU president, 18 September 1977, SACU minutes.

50. Visas were finally approved in principle on 20 November 1968 subject to the following conditions: '(a) All matches to be played only on fields at presently used by non-Europeans. (b) Only non-European spectators to be admitted to attend matches. (c) No social intermingling between members of the cricket teams and the European public, and (d) Accommodation must be so arranged to obviate any possibility of incidents which may embarrass either the players themselves and/or the South African authorities.' Secretary for the Interior to Secretary Transvaal Cricket Federation, National Archives, Pretoria, (NA) MSO 1/5/7 vol 1. For the Anti-Apartheid Movement (AAM) and the tour see AAM MS 1439.

51. Desai et al, *Blacks in Whites*, pp. 285–91; Richie Benaud, *On Reflection*. London, p .187.
52. *Sunday Express*, 17 October 1976.
53. Pamensky interview.
54. Notes of meeting held on the 10th floor Civitas Buildings, Pretoria, Monday, 1 July 1976, SACU file on meetings with Minister of Sport.
55. Cabinet Minute Book 1976, NA CAB 1/1/6.
56. *Rand Daily Mail*, 27 September 1976.
57. *Rand Daily Mail*, 8 October 1975.
58. SACU delegation meeting with Koornhof, 9–10 February 1977, SACU file, meetings with Minister of Sport.
59. Hassan Howa, 'First Abolish Apartheid Society'. In Odendaal, *Cricket in Isolation*, pp. 269–78; Desai et al, *Blacks in Whites*, pp. 287–8.
60. Mogamad Allie. 2000. *More Than A Game: History of the Western Province Cricket Board 1959–1991*. Cape Town, pp. 117–34.
61. Odendaal, *Cricket in Isolation*, pp. 76–85.
62. Interview with Krish Mackerdhuj, Johannesburg, 5 April 1998.
63. Odendaal, *Cricket in Isolation*, pp. 59–69; A.C. Parker. 1999. *Western Province Cricket: 100 Not Out*. Cape Town, p. 70; John Young (ed). 1997. *Langa Cricket Club – 21 Years 1976–1997*. Cape Town; 'Memorandum', 4 June 1980, SACU file on ICC 1979–80.
64. Desai et al, *Blacks in Whites*, pp. 309–16; Merrett, 'Aurora', p. 117.
65. André Odendaal. 2003. *The Story of an African Game*. Cape Town, chapter 27.
66. Ibid, chapter 26.
67. TCC minutes, 7 December 1977 and 1 February 1978.
68. Aslam Khota. 2003. *Across the Great Divide: Transvaal Cricket's Joys, Struggles and Triumphs*. Johannesburg, p. 31.
69. *Star*, 25 August 1980; *Rand Daily Mail*, 18 September 1980; *Voice Weekly*, 1–7 April 1981.
70. TCC minutes, 5 December 1979, 2 April, 28 May and 11 June 1980.
71. SACU file, 'Political'.
72. Desai et al, *Blacks in Whites*, pp. 321–2.

CHAPTER NINE

1. Lewis to Wallace, 3 November 1978, SACU file, ICC 1979–80.
2. Varachia to ICC President, 4 March 1980, SACU file, ICC 1979–80.
3. Cricket Council minutes, 24 August 1976.
4. Clyde Walcott and B. Scovell. 1999. *Sixty Years on the Back Foot*. London, p. 152.
5. *The Cricketer*, March 1983, pp. 26–7.
6. Cricket Council minutes, 24 August 1976 and 26 October 1977.
7. Brown to Pamensky, 2 December 1977; Boon Wallace, notes on meetings with Koornhof, 22 December 1977, 30 January, 16 February and 1 March 1978, SACU file, meetings with Minister of Sport.
8. Notes of meeting, 27 March 1978, Cricket Council file, South Africa 1978–80.
9. SACU minutes, 6–7 May 1978.

10. Parish to Brown, 13 June 1978; Hadlee to Brown, 16 June 1978; Varachia to Brown, 20 June 1978, Cricket Council file, South Africa 1978–80; *Daily Dispatch*, 30 May 1978; *Sunday Express*, 23 July 1978.
11. *Star,* 26 July 1978.
12. ICC minutes, 25–26 July 1978.
13. Bailey letter, 23 October 1978; Donald Carr, notes of phone call to Boon Wallace, 16 November 1979, Cricket Council file, South Africa 1978–80.
14. Report on their visit to South Africa in March 1979 by representatives of member countries of the International Cricket Conference, SACU file, ICC 1979–80.
15. ICC minutes, 28–29 June 1979.
16. Notes on informal discussion with Mr R. Varachia, South African Cricket Union, 5 November 1979, Cricket Council file, South Africa 1978–80; Cricket Council minutes, 9 October 1979 and 15 April 1980.
17. SACU minutes, 15 September 1979; correspondence in SACU file, ICC 1979-80, and Cricket Council file, South Africa 1978–80.
18. Report on visit to Minister of Sport, 5 December 1979; 'To consider South Africa's position in the cricket world: submission by the United Kingdom', Cricket Council file, South Africa 1978–80.
19. Boon Wallace report on visit to UK, 27 April to 3 May 1980, SACU file, ICC 1979–80.
20. Palmer to Bailey, 21 May 1980, and Palmer to Wallace, 24 June 1980, Cricket Council file, South Africa 1978–80.
21. Boon Wallace report on visit to UK, 3 to 16 August 1980, SACU file, ICC 1979–80.
22. Ibid; ICC minutes, 14–15 August 1980; WICBC media release, 2 December 1980, Cricket Council file, South Africa 1978–80.
23. *Sunday Tribune*, 26 October 1980.
24. Boon Wallace. 'An appraisal of South Africa's position vis-à-vis the ICC – July 1981', June 1981, Joe Pamensky Archive.
25. Cricket Council Emergency Executive Committee minutes, 14 January 1981; Cricket Council minutes, 27 January and 22 June 1981.
26. ICC minutes, 21–22 July 1981; Cricket Council minutes, 12 August 1981.
27. Peter Hain. 1996. *Sing the Beloved Country*. London, pp. 96–8; SACU delegation meeting with Koornhof, 22 December 1977, SACU file, meetings with Minister of Sport.
28. Trevor Richards. 1999. *Dancing on Our Bones: New Zealand, South Africa, Rugby and Racism*. Wellington, p. 234.
29. Cricket Council minutes, 12 August 1981 and 9 August 1982; Richie Benaud. 1984. *On Reflection*. London, chapter 9.
30. Rodney Hartman. 2003. *Ali: The Life of Ali Bacher*. Johannesburg, p. 175.
31. G.F. Dakin, report to SACU on visit to England, 17–30 June 1983, SACU files, ICC 1983–88.

EPILOGUE

1. For information about the organisation of the rebel tours see Rodney Hartman. 2004. *Ali: The Life of Ali Bacher*. Johannesburg, Part III.

2. Mihr Bose. 1994. *Sporting Colours: Sport and Politics in South Africa*. London, p. 133.
3. Grant Jarvie. 1985. *Class, Race and Sport in South Africa's Political Economy*. London, p. 78; Guy Beresford. 1986. 'Playing Apartheid to Win or to Lose?'. *International Affairs Bulletin* 10(3), pp. 33–46; Hartman, *Ali*, p. 185.
4. Mike Marqusee. 1994. *Anyone But England: Cricket and the National Malaise*. London, pp. 194–200; Jack Williams. 2001. *Cricket and Race*. Oxford, pp. 101–7.
5. Interview with Raman Subba Row, London, November 1999.
6. Nigel Worden. 1994. *The Making of Modern South Africa: Conquest, Segregation and Apartheid*. Oxford, chapter 6.
7. Hartman, *Ali*, chapter 20; Jonty Winch. 2000. 'Playing the Games: The Unification of South African Sport', unpublished manuscript, chapters 15 and 16.
8. Neville Alexander. 1992. 'Non-Collaboration in the Western Cape, 1943–1963'. In W.G. James and M. Simons. *Class, Caste and Color: A Social and Economic History of the South African Western Cape*. New Brunswick, pp. 180–90.
9. Douglas Booth. 1998. *The Race Game: Sport and Politics in South Africa*. London, pp. 184–5.
10. Ashwin Desai, Vishnu Padayachee, Krish Reddy and Goolam Vahed. 2002. *Blacks in Whites: A Century of Cricket Struggles in KwaZulu-Natal*, Pietermaritzburg, p. 366.
11. Bose, *Sporting Colours*, pp. 231–2.
12. Williams, *Cricket and Race*, pp. 107–8.
13. Anthony Sampson. 1987. *Black and Gold: Tycoons, Revolutionaries and Apartheid*. London, p. 117.
14. Grant Farred. 2000. *Midfielder's Moment: Coloured Literature and Culture in Contemporary South Africa*. Boulder, p. 134.
15. Adrian Guelke. 1986. 'The Politicisation of South African Sport'. In Lincoln Allison (ed). *The Politics of Sport*. Manchester, p. 145.
16. Ashwin Desai et al, *Blacks in Whites*, pp. 372 and 375.

Bibliography

ARCHIVAL COLLECTIONS

Anti-Apartheid Movement, Rhodes House, Oxford.

Australian Government, National Archives of Australia, Canberra.

British Government, The National Archives, Kew, London.

Brutus Papers, Borthwick Institute, University of York.

Cricket Council, England and Wales Cricket Board, Lord's, London.

Duleepsinhji Archive, West Sussex Record Office, Chichester.

Marylebone Cricket Club, MCC Library, Lord's, London.

New Zealand Cricket Board, Christchurch.

South African Cricket Association and South African Cricket Union, Historical Papers, Cullen Library, University of the Witwatersrand, Johannesburg.

South African Institute of Race Relations, Historical Papers, Cullen Library, University of the Witwatersrand, Johannesburg.

South African Government, South African National Archives, Pretoria.

Transvaal Cricket Union, Gauteng Cricket Board, Wanderers, Johannesburg.

NEWSPAPERS, PERIODICALS AND ANNUALS

Cape Times
Cricketer
Daily Dispatch
Daily Telegraph
Guardian
Hiltonian
Natal Almanac, Directory and Yearly Register
Outspan
Rand Daily Mail
South African Cricket Annual
South African Cricketer: the National Cricket Journal of Southern Africa
South African Cricketers Annual
Star
Sunday Express, Johannesburg
Sunday Times, Johannesburg

Sunday Times, London
Sunday Tribune
Survey of Race Relations
The Times
Wisden: Cricketers' Almanac

BOOKS, ARTICLES AND THESES

Alexander, N. 1992. 'Non-Collaboration in the Western Cape, 1943–1963'. In W.G. James and
    M. Simons. *Class, Caste and Colour: A Social and Economic History of the South African
    Western Cape*. New Brunswick: Transaction.
Alfred, L. 2003. *Testing Times: The Story of the Men Who Made SA Cricket*. Cape Town:
    Spearhead.
Allie, M. 2000. *More Than a Game: History of the Western Province Cricket Board*. Cape
    Town: Western Province Cricket Association.
Altham, H.S. 1962. *A History of Cricket: v.1. From the Beginnings to the First World War*.
    London: Allen and Unwin.
Altham, H.S. [et al]. 1957. *Hampshire County Cricket: The Official History*. London: Phoenix.
Archer, R. and A. Bouillon. 1982. *The South African Game: Sport and Racism*. London: Zed.
Arlott, J. 1960. 'C.B. Llewellyn'. In *Hampshire Handbook*.
Bailey, A. 1912. 'South Africa'. In P.F. Warner (ed). *Imperial Cricket*. London: London and
    Counties Press Association.
Bailey, J. 1989. *Conflicts in Cricket*. London: Kingswood.
Bailey, P. 1987. *Leisure and Class in Victorian England: Rational Recreation and the Contest
    for Control, 1830–1885*. London: Routledge and Kegan Paul.
Barber, J. and J. Barratt. 1990. *South Africa's Foreign Policy: The Search for Status and
    Security 1945–1988*. Cambridge: Cambridge University Press.
Bassano, B. 1979. *South Africa in International Cricket, 1888–1970*. East London:
    Chameleon.
Baucom, I. 1999. *Out of Place: Englishness, Empire, and the Location of Identity*. Princeton,
    NJ: Princeton University Press.
Benaud, R. 1984. *On Reflection*. London: Fontana.
Beresford, G. 1986. 'Playing Apartheid to Win or to Lose?'. *International Affairs Bulletin*
    10(3).
Bickford-Smith, V. 1985. *Ethnic Pride and Racial Prejudice in Victorian Cape Town*.
    Johannesburg: Witwatersrand University Press.
Birley, D. 1979. *The Willow Wand: Some Cricket Myths Explored*. London: Queen Anne Press.
———. 1993. *Playing the Game: Sport and British Society*. Manchester: Manchester University
    Press.
Black, D. and J. Nauright. 1998. *Rugby and the South African Nation: Sport, Cultures,
    Politics and Power in the Old and New South Africas*. Manchester: Manchester
    University Press.
Blake, R. 1977. *A History of Rhodesia*. London: Eyre Methuen.
Bolton, G. 1996. *The Oxford History of Australia: Volume 5, The Middle Way, 1942–1955*.
    Melbourne: Oxford University Press, 2nd ed.
Booth, D. 1997. 'The South African Council on Sport and the Political Antimonies of the
    Sports Boycott'. *Journal of Southern African Studies* 23(1).

——. 1998. *The Race Game: Sport and Politics in South Africa*. London: Cass.

Bose, M. 1990. *A History of Indian Cricket*. London: Deutsch.

——. 1994. *Sporting Colours: Sport and Politics in South Africa*. London: Robson.

Bowen, R. 1970. *Cricket: A History of its Growth and Development throughout the World*. London: Eyre and Spottiswoode.

Bradley, J. 1992. 'The MCC, Society and Empire: A Portrait of Cricket's Ruling Body, 1860–1914'. In J.A. Mangan (ed). *The Cultural Bond: Sport, Empire and Society*. London: Cass.

Brickhill, J. 1976. *Race Against Race: South Africa's 'Multi-National' Sport Fraud*. London: International Defence and Aid Fund.

Brutus, D. 1959. 'Sports Test for South Africa'. *Africa South* 3(4).

—— 1978. 'Childhood Reminiscences'. In P. Wastberg (ed). *The Writer in Modern Africa*. Uppsala: Scandinavian Institute of African Studies.

Butler, D. and M. Pinto-Duschinsky. 1971. *The British General Election of 1970*. London: Macmillan.

Chalke, S. 2001. *At the Heart of English Cricket: The Life and Memories of Geoffrey Howard*. Bath: Fairfield Books.

Chesterfield, T. and J. McGlew. 2003. *South Africa's Cricket Captains*. Cape Town: Zebra.

Christopher, A.J. 1976. *Southern Africa*. Folkestone: Dawson.

Cobley, A.G. 1997. *The Rules of the Game: Struggles in Black Recreation and Social Welfare Policy in South Africa*. Westport: Greenwood.

Compton, D. 1958. *End of an Innings*. London: Oldbourne.

Constantine, L. 1947. *Cricket in the Sun*. London: Stanley Paul.

Couzens, T. 1983. 'An Introduction to the History of Football in South Africa'. In B. Bozzoli (ed). *Town and Countryside in the Transvaal*. Johannesburg: Ravan.

Cowdrey, C. 1976. *MCC: The Autobiography of a Cricketer*. London: Hodder and Stoughton.

Crossman, R.H.S. 1977. *The Diaries of a Cabinet Minister*. v.3. London: Hamish Hamilton.

Crowley, B. 1973. *Currie Cup Story*. Cape Town: Nelson.

——. 1983. *Cricket's Exiles: The Saga of South African Cricket*. Cape Town: Nelson.

——. 1994. 'A History of South African Cricket'. *Cricketer*.

Davenport, T.R.H. 1991. *South Africa: A Modern History*. London: Macmillan, 4th ed.

De Broglio, C. 1970. *South Africa: Racism in Sport*. London: International Defence and Aid Fund.

De Kiewiet, C.W. 1941. *A History of South Africa: Social and Economic*. London: Oxford University Press.

De Klerk, F.W. 1998. *The Last Trek – A New Beginning: The Autobiography*. London: Macmillan.

Denniston, R. 1999. *Trevor Huddleston: A Life*. London: Macmillan.

Desai, A., V. Padayachee, K. Reddy and G. Vahed. 2002. *Blacks in Whites: A Century of Cricket Struggles in KwaZulu-Natal*. Pietermaritzburg: University of Natal Press.

D'Oliveira, B. 1969. *The D'Oliveira Affair*. London: Collins.

——. 1980. *Time to Declare: An Autobiography*. Johannesburg: Macmillan.

D'Oliveira, J. 1977. *Vorster: The Man*. Johannesburg: Stanton.

Douglas-Home, A. (Lord Home). 1976. *The Way the Wind Blows*. London: Collins.

Dubow, S. 1998. 'Placing Race in South African History'. In W. Lamont. *Historical Controversies and Historians*. London: UCL.

Duffus, L. 1947. *Cricketers of the Veld*. London: Sampson Low, Marston.

——. 1947. *South African Cricket 1927–1947*. Johannesburg: South African Cricket Association.

——. 1969. *Play Abandoned: An Autobiography*. Cape Town: Timmins.

Farred, G. 2000. *Midfielder's Moment: Coloured Literature and Culture in Contemporary South Africa*. Boulder: Westview.

Fingleton, J. *Cricket Crisis: Bodyline and Other Lines*. London: Pavilion, 1985.

Gemmell, J. 2004. *The Politics of South African Cricket*. London: Routledge.

Giliomee, H. 2003. *The Afrikaners: Biography of a People*. Cape Town: Tafelberg.

Guelke, A. 1986. 'The Politicisation of South African Sport'. In L. Allison (ed). *The Politics of Sport*. Manchester: Manchester University Press.

Guha, R. 2002. *A Corner of a Foreign Field: The Indian History of a British Sport*. London: Picador.

Haigh, G. 1997. *The Summer Game*. Melbourne: Text.

Hain, P. 1971. *Don't Play With Apartheid: The Background to the Stop The Seventy Tour Campaign*. London: Allen and Unwin.

——. 1996. *Sing the Beloved Country: The Struggle for the New South Africa*. London: Pluto.

Hargreaves, J. 1986. *Sport, Power and Culture: A Social and Historical Analysis of Popular Sports in Britain*. Cambridge: Polity.

Harris, S. 1972. *Political Football: The Springbok Tour of Australia 1971*. Melbourne.

Harte, C. 1993. *A History of Australian Cricket*. London: Deutsch.

Hartman, R. 2004. *Ali: The Life of Ali Bacher*. Johannesburg: Penguin.

Henry, O. 1994. *Omar Henry: The Man in the Middle*. Durban: Bok Books.

Holt, R. and T. Mason. 2000. *Sport in Britain 1945–2000*. Oxford: Blackwell.

Horrell, M. 1956. *The Group Areas Act: Its Effect on Human Beings*. Johannesburg: South African Institute of Race Relations.

Howat, G. 1975. *Learie Constantine*. London: Allen and Unwin.

Huddleston, T. 1956. *Naught For Your Comfort*. Johannesburg: Hardingham and Donaldson.

Hutchins, B. 2002. *Don Bradman: Challenging the Myth*. Cambridge: Cambridge University Press.

Huttenback, R.A. 1973. 'The British Empire as a White Man's Country: Racial Attitudes and Immigration Legislation in the Colonies of White Settlement'. *Journal of British Studies* 13(1).

Hyam, R. and P. Henshaw. 2003. *The Lion and the Springbok: Britain and South Africa Since the Boer War*. Cambridge: Cambridge University Press.

James, C.L.R. 1963. *Beyond a Boundary*. London: Stanley Paul.

James, C.L.R and A. Grimshaw (eds). 1986. *Cricket*. London: Allison and Busby.

Jarvie, G. 1985. *Class, Race and Sport in South Africa's Political Economy*. London: Routledge and Kegan Paul.

Katz, W.R. 1987. *Rider Haggard and the Fiction of Empire: A Critical Study of British Imperial Fiction*. Cambridge: Cambridge University Press.

Khota, A. 2003. *Across the Great Divide: Transvaal Cricket's Joys, Struggles and Triumphs*. Johannesburg: Gauteng Cricket Board.

Kidson, H. 1995. *The History of Transvaal Cricket*. Johannesburg: Transvaal Cricket Board.

Kilburn, J.M. 1975. *Overthrows: A Book of Cricket*. London: Stanley Paul.

Kirk-Greene, A.H.M. 1987. 'Imperial Administration and the Athletic Imperative: The Case of the District Officer in Africa'. In W.J. Baker and J.A. Mangan (eds). *Sport in Africa: Essays in Social History*. New York: Africana.

Kirkwood, K. 1951. *The Group Areas Act*. Johannesburg: South African Institute of Race Relations.

Lapchick, R.E. 1975. *The Politics of Race and International Sport: The Case of South Africa*. Westport: Greenwood.

Lewis, T. 1987. *Double Century: The Story of MCC and Cricket*. London: Hodder and Stoughton.

Lorimer, D.A. 1978. *Colour, Class and the Victorians: English Attitudes to the Negro in the Mid-Nineteenth Century*. Leicester: University of Leicester Press.

Luckin, M.W. (ed). 1915. *The History of South African Cricket*. Johannesburg: Hortor.

——. 1927. *South African Cricket, 1919–1927: A Complete Record of All South African Cricket Since the War*. Johannesburg: the Author.

Mackenzie, J.M. 1984. *Propaganda and Empire: The Manipulation of British Public Opinion, 1880–1960*. Manchester: Manchester University Press.

Magubane, B. 1963. 'Sport and Politics in an Urban African Community: A Case Study of African Voluntary Organizations'. MSocSc thesis, University of Natal, Durban.

Mangan, J.A. 1996. 'Muscular, Militaristic and Manly: The British Middle-Class Hero as Moral Messenger'. *International Journal of the History of Sport* 13(1).

Marqusee, M. 1994. *Anyone But England: Cricket and the National Malaise*. London: Verso.

Martin-Jenkins, C. 1984. *Twenty Years On: Cricket's Years of Change 1963 to 1983*. London: Willow.

May, P. 1985. *A Game Enjoyed*. London: Stanley Paul.

McDonald, R.H. 1994. *The Language of Empire: Myths and Metaphors of Popular Imperialism, 1880–1918*. Manchester: Manchester University Press.

Menzies, R. 1972. *The Measure of the Years*. London: Cassell.

Merrett, C. 2001. 'Aurora: The Challenge of Non-Racial Cricket to the Apartheid State of the Mid-1970s'. *International Journal of the History of Sport* 18(4).

——. 2002. 'Sport and Race in Colonial Natal: C.B. Llewellyn, South Africa's First Black Test Cricketer'. *Natalia* 32.

Merrett, C. and J. Nauright. 1998. 'South Africa'. In B. Stoddart and K.A.P. Sandiford (eds). *The Imperial Game: Cricket, Culture and Society*. Manchester: Manchester University Press.

Midwinter, E. 1986. *Fair Game: Myth and Reality in Sport*. London: Allen and Unwin.

Millin, S.G. 1934. *The South Africans*. London: Constable.

Morgan, K O. 1990. *The People's Peace: British History 1945–1989*. Oxford: Oxford University Press.

——. 1997. *Callaghan: A Life*. Oxford: Oxford University Press.

Morris, J. 1968. *Pax Britannica: The Climax of an Empire*. London: Faber.

Murray, B.K. 2001. 'Politics and Cricket: The D'Oliveira Affair of 1968'. *Journal of Southern African Studies* 27(4).

——. 2002. 'The Sports Boycott and Cricket: The Cancellation of the 1970 South African Tour of England'. *South African Historical Journal* 46.

Nauright, J. 1997. *Sport, Cultures and Identities in South Africa*. London: Philip.

Neame, L.E. 1907. *The Asiatic Danger in the Colonies*. London: Routledge.

Oborne, P. 2004. *Basil D'Oliveira – Cricket and Conspiracy: The Untold Story*. London: Little Brown.

Odendaal, A. 1976. *God's Forgotten Cricketers: Profiles of Leading South African Players*. Cape Town: South African Cricketer.

—— (ed). 1977. *Cricket in Isolation: The Politics of Race and Cricket in South Africa*. Stellenbosch: the Author.

——. 1988. 'South Africa's Black Victorians: Sport and Society in South Africa in the Nineteenth Century'. In J. Mangan (ed). *Pleasure, Profit, Proselytism: British Culture and Sport at Home and Abroad, 1700–1914*. London: Cass.

——. 2003. *The Story of an African Game*. Cape Town: David Philip.

Odendaal, A. and R. Field (eds). 1993. *Liberation Chabalala: The World of Alex La Guma*. Bellville: Mayibuye.

O'Meara, D. 1996. *Forty Lost Years: The Apartheid State and the Politics of the National Party 1948–1994*. Randburg: Ravan.

Page, M. 1983. *Bradman: The Illustrated Biography*. London: Macmillan.

Parker, A.C. 1990. *Western Province Cricket: 100 Not Out*. Cape Town: Western Province Cricket Union.

Paton, A. 1964. *Hofmeyr*. London: Oxford University Press.

Perry, R. 1995. *The Don*. London: Sidgwick and Jackson.

Phillips, R.E. 1930. *The Bantu are Coming: Phases of South Africa's Race Problems*. London: SCM Press, 2nd ed.

Pollard, J. 1992. *The Complete Illustrated History of Australian Cricket*. Melbourne.

Pollock, P. and G. 1968. *Bouncers and Boundaries*. Johannesburg: Sportsman.

Pollock, W. 1941. *Talking About Cricket*. London: Gollancz.

Posel, D. 1991. *The Making of Apartheid, 1948–1961: Conflict and Compromise*. Oxford: Oxford University Press.

Procter, M. 1994. *South Africa: The Years of Isolation and the Return to International Cricket*. Durban: Bok Books.

Reddick, T. 1979. *Never a Cross Bat*. Cape Town: Nelson.

Richards, T. 1999. *Dancing on Our Bones: New Zealand, South Africa, Rugby and Racism*. Wellington: Williams.

Roberts, R. and S. Wilde. 1993. *Duleepsinhji*. Nottingham: Association of Cricket Statisticians and Historians.

Rosenwater, I. 1978. *Sir Donald Bradman: A Biography*. London: Batsford.

Ross, A. 1983. *Ranji: Prince of Cricketers*. London: Collins.

Rousseau, F.P. 1960. *Handbook on the Group Areas Act*. Cape Town: Juta.

Sacks, B. 1967. *South Africa: An Imperial Dilemma: Non-Europeans and the British Nation, 1902–1914*. Albuquerque: University of New Mexico Press.

Sampson, A. 1987. *Black and Gold: Tycoons, Revolutionaries and Apartheid*. London: Hodder and Stoughton.

Schoombee, J.T. 1987. 'An Evaluation of Aspects of Group Areas Legislation in South Africa'. LLD thesis, University of Cape Town.

Searle, C. 1990. 'Race Before Wicket: Cricket, Empire and the White Rose'. *Race and Class* 31(3).

Sheppard, D. 2002. *Steps Along Hope Street: My Life in Cricket, the Church and Inner City*. London: Hodder and Stoughton.

Simpson, B. 1996. *Captain's Story*. London.

Slovo, J. 1995. *Slovo: The Unfinished Autobiography*. Johannesburg: Ravan.

Spufford, F. 1996. *I May Be Some Time: Ice and the English Imagination*. London: Faber.

Steel, A. 1959. 'Sport Leads the Way'. *Africa South* 4(1).

Steel, D. 1989. *Against Goliath: David Steel's Story*. London: Pan.

Steen, R. 1999. *This Sporting Life: Cricket: Inside Tales from the Men Who Made the Game What it is Today*. Newton Abbot: David and Charles.

Stoddart, B. 1988. 'Caribbean Cricket: The Role of Sport in Emerging Small-Nation Politics'. *International Journal* 43(4).

——. 1988. 'Sport, Cultural Imperialism, and Colonial Response in the British Empire'. *Comparative Studies in Society and History* 30(4).

Stoddart, B. and K.A.P. Sandiford (eds). 1998. *The Imperial Game: Cricket, Culture and Society*. Manchester: Manchester University Press.

Swanson, M. 1995. 'The Sanitation Syndrome'. In W. Beinart and S. Dubow (eds). *Segregation and Apartheid in Twentieth Century South Africa*. London: Routledge.

Swanton, E.W. 1985. *Gubby Allen: Man of Cricket*. London: Hutchinson.

Swanton, E.W., G. Plumptre and J. Woodcock (eds). 1986. *Barclays World of Cricket: The Game from A to Z*. London: Willow Books, 3rd ed.

Tatz, C. 1985. *Obstacle Race: Aborigines in Sport*. Sydney: University of New South Wales Press.

Thompson, R. 1964. *Race and Sport*. London: Oxford University Press.

——. 1975. *Retreat from Apartheid: New Zealand's Sporting Contacts with South Africa*. Wellington: Oxford University Press.

Thorpe, D.R. 1996. *Alec Douglas-Home*. London: Sinclair-Stevenson.

Tozer, M. 1992. 'A Sacred Trinity: Cricket, School, Empire: E.W. Hornung and his Young Guard'. In J.A. Mangan (ed). *The Cultural Bond: Sport, Empire and Society*. London: Cass.

Turnbull, M. and M. Allom. 1931. *The Two Maurices Again: Being Some Account of the Tour of the MCC Team Through South Africa in the Closing Months of 1930 and the Beginning of 1931*. London: Allom.

University of Natal. Department of Economics. 1951. *Experiment at Edendale: A Study of Non-European Settlement with Special Reference to Food Expenditure and Nutrition*. Pietermaritzburg: University of Natal Press.

University of the Witwatersrand. Development Studies Group. 1981. *Politics in Sport*. Johannesburg: Development Studies Group.

Van der Merwe, F. 1992. 'Sport and Games in Boer Prisoner-of-War Camps during the Anglo-Boer War 1899–1902'. *The International Journal of the History of Sport* 9(3).

Vasili, P. 1998. *The First Black Footballer: Arthur Wharton 1865–1930: An Absence of Memory*. London: Cass.

Vundla, K. 1978. *PQ: The Story of Philip Vundla of South Africa*. Johannesburg: Moral Re-Armament.

Waite, J. 1961. *Perchance to Bowl*. London: Kaye.

Walcott, C. and B. Scovell. 1999. *Sixty Years on the Back Foot*. London.

Warner, M. 1993. 'Between the Colonist and the Creole: Family Bonds, Family Boundaries'. In S. Chew and A. Rutherford (eds). *Unbecoming Daughters of the Empire*. Sydney: Dangaroo.

Warner, P.F. 1906. *The MCC in South Africa*. London: Chapman and Hall.

——. 1951. *Long Innings: The Autobiography*. London: Harrap.

West, S.E.L . (comp) and W.J. Luker (ed). 1965. *Century at Newlands, 1864–1964: A History of the Western Province Cricket Club*. Newlands: Western Province Cricket Club.

Western, J. 1981. *Outcast Cape Town*. Minneapolis: University of Minnesota Press.

Whimpress, B. 1999. *Passport to Nowhere: Aborigines in Australian Cricket, 1850–1939*. Sydney: Walla Walla.

Wilkins, I. and H. Strydom. 1978. *The Super-Afrikaners*. Johannesburg: Jonathan Ball.

Willen, B. 1982. 'An African in Kimberley: Sol T. Plaatje, 1894–1898'. In Shula Marks and Richard Rathbone (eds). *Industrialisation and Social Change in South Africa: African Class Formation, Culture and Consciousness, 1870–1930*. Harlow: Longman.

Williams, C. 1996. *Bradman: An Australian Hero*. London: Little, Brown.

Williams, J. 1999. *Cricket and England: A Cultural and Social History of the Inter-War Years*. London: Cass.

——. 2001. *Cricket and Race*. Oxford: Berg.

Wilson, H. 1971. *The Labour Government 1964–1970: A Personal Record*. London: Penguin.

Wilson, M. and A. Mafeje. 1963. *Langa: A Study of Social Groups in an African Township*. Cape Town: Oxford University Press.

Winch, J. 1997. *Cricket in Southern Africa: Two Hundred Years of Achievement and Records*. Rosettenville: Windsor.

——. 2000. 'Playing the Games: The Unification of South African Sport' (unpublished manuscript).

——. 2003. *England's Youngest Captain: The Life and Times of Monty Bowden and Two South Africa Journalists*. Windsor: Windsor Publications.

Woods, C.A. 1954. *The Indian Community of Natal: Their Economic Position*. Cape Town: Oxford University Press.

Woods, D. 1980. *Asking for Trouble: Autobiography of a Banned Journalist*. London: Gollancz.

——. 1981. *Black and White*. Dublin: Ward River Press.

Worden, N. 1994. *The Making of Modern South Africa: Conquest, Segregation and Apartheid*. Oxford: Blackwell.

Worden, N., E. van Heyningen and V. Bickford-Smith. 1998. *Cape Town: The Making of a City: An Illustrated Social History*. Cape Town: David Philip.

Wright, G. 1993. *Betrayal: The Struggle for Cricket's Soul*. London: Witherby.

Wynne-Thomas, P. and P. Arnold. 1984. *Cricket in Crisis: The Story of Major Crises That Have Rocked the Game*. Feltham: Newnes.

Yelvington, K.A. 1995. 'Ethnicity not out'. In H. Beckles and B. Stoddart. *Liberation Cricket: West Indian Cricket Culture*. Manchester: Manchester University Press.

Young, J. (ed). 1997. *Langa Cricket Club – 21 Years 1976–1997*. Cape Town: Langa Cricket Club.

Index

racial
  discrimination 71
  exclusivity 3, 14, 65
  grouping 49
  incident at Old Parktonians Club 187–8
racism ix, 24, 31, 50, 120, 136
Rae, Allan 210
Ramadhin, Sonny 73
Ramsamy, Sam 169, 194, 196
Rand Daily Mail 47, 66, 70, 136, 143, 170, 181
Ranji Trophy 40, 54
Ranjitsinhji, K.S. (Jam Saheb of Nawanaga) 26, 36, 37, 87
Raziet, Salmoodien 54, 58
Read, W.W. 6, 10, 15
rebel
  cricketers, punishment of 209, 210
  tours 205–6, 208–12
Reddick, Tom 47
Reeves, Bishop Ambrose 89
Rembrandt Tobacco Company 96
Representation of Natives Act (1936) 29
Reservation of Separate Amenities Act (1953) 49, 57, 166, 213
restricted franchise 29
Rhodes, Cecil John viii, 3–4, 16
Rhodes University College 46
Rhodes, Wilfred 19
Rhodesia, UDI regime in 96, 102–3, 128, 143
Rhodesians in South African cricket 32, 143
Richards, Trevor 204
Roberts, Rex 37
Robin Binckes Promotions 176, 188
Robins, Derrick 176, 181
Robinson, Jackie 50
Robinson, Ray 59
Rondebosch Camp Ground 4
Roro, Frank 40–1, 53
Ross, Alan 36, 115
Roux, Eddie 44
Rowan, Eric 81, 83, 155
Rowe, Lawrence 208
Rugby tours 204
  of Australia (1971) 153
  of Britain (1969/70) 123, 147, 153
  of New Zealand (1973), cancelled 164
Rupert, Anton 86, 96

Salie, Taliep 41, 47
Saloojee, Essop 47
Samoodien, L. 10
Sampson, Anthony 213–14
Schoeman, Ben 91, 135
school cricket encouraged by Lord Nuffield 32
Schoolboys tour postponed (1969) 139–40
Schwarz, Reggie 7, 22
segregation ix, 3, 26, 39, 47
  era 29–30
  social 56
  of sporting activities 49–50, 64
  and unequal facilities 41–6
selection
  of mixed representative teams 93
  on merit 141–2, 155, 164, 172–3, 177
Seventy Tour called off (May 1970) 118, 144–6
Sewgolum, Sewsunker ('Papwa') 93
Sharpeville massacre (1960) 63
Shepherd, John 176
Sheppard, Reverend (later Rt. Rev. Lord) David 75, 97, 102, 120, 129, 130
  and MCC 100, 108, 110
Sigamoney, Reverend B.L.E. 48, 55
Simpson, Bobby 50
Sinclair, J.H. 20
Sir David Harris Trophy 39
Sisulu, Walter 74
Slovo, Joe 60
Smith, Aubrey 6, 9
Smith, Ian 128
Smuts, General Jan 49
Snelling, Sir Arthur 144
Soames, A. 19
Sobantu (township) 43
Sobers, Gary 73, 142
soccer 45
social
  integration 155
  segregation 56
South African African Cricket Board of Control (SAACBC) 55, 137, 139, 171